LEADERS IN THE CRUCIBLE

LEADERS IN THE CRUCIBLE

The Moral Voice of College Presidents

Stephen James Nelson

BERGIN & GARVEY
Westport, Connecticut • London

Library of Congress Cataloging-in-Publication Data

Nelson, Stephen James, 1947–
    Leaders in the crucible : the moral voice of college presidents / Stephen James Nelson.
      p.   cm.
    Includes bibliographical references (p.   ) and index.
    ISBN 0–89789–742–0 (alk. paper)
    1. Educational leadership—Moral and ethical aspects—United States.   2. College
presidents—Professional ethics—United States.   I. Title.
    LB2341.N386   2000
    378.1'11—dc21   00–020485

British Library Cataloguing in Publication Data is available.

Library of Congress Catalog Card Number: 00–020485
ISBN: 0–89789–742–0

First published in 2000

Bergin & Garvey, 88 Post Road West, Westport, CT 06881
An imprint of Greenwood Publishing Group, Inc.
www.greenwood.com

Printed in the United States of America

The paper used in this book complies with the
Permanent Paper Standard issued by the National
Information Standards Organization (Z39.48–1984).

10 9 8 7 6 5 4 3 2 1

To Janet and Geoffrey

Contents

Acknowledgments

My ideas about the college presidency and the academy, pieces of which have found their way into this book, have become my "life work." Throughout my life's journey, I have been supported and guided by many people.

I am most indebted to my Ph.D. adviser, Professor William Jellema, now professor emeritus at the University of Connecticut. He has been a profound source of wisdom and encouragement. Professor Jellema's experience as a college president and extraordinary knowledge of higher education are invaluable. Early on, he embraced my dream of writing a book about the moral voice of the college president.

Much of the research for this book depended on the cooperation and assistance of archival librarians and presidential staff. At Amherst College they were Daria D' Arienzo, college archivist, Emily Silverman, archives staff, and Emily de Rotstein, assistant to the president; at Clark Atlanta University, Minnie Clayton, interim director of archives, Wilson Flemister, former director, and Hattie Bell, executive assistant to the president; at Columbia University, Bernard Kristol, archivist, Kathy Anderson, executive secretary to the president, and Fred Knubel, director of public information; at Notre Dame University, Matthew Cullinane, assistant to the president, Dennis Moore, public relations director, and William Kevin Cawley, associate archivist; at the University of Michigan, Margaret Mustard, assistant to the president, Wilbert Mckeachie, professor of psychology, Marjorie Barritt, university records archivist, and Anne Frantilla, archives staff; at Wellesley College, Wilma Slaight, archivist, Jean Berry, archives staff, and Jane Bachman, assistant to the president.

I am greatly indebted to Presidents Thomas Cole, James Duderstadt, Thomas

Gerety, Edward Malloy, George Rupp, and Diana Chapman Walsh for their willingness to be interviewed and to share ideas about the state of the college presidency. I have also been assisted and encouraged in my work by two former presidents of Brown University, E. Gordon Gee, and Vartan Gregorian.

Many teachers and professors have taught me throughout my life. Though not fair to single out one, I specially note Professor Louis Hammann, now retired (but still teaching) from the religion faculty of Gettysburg College after a forty-year teaching career. Professor Hammann is one of the finest teachers I have known. I owe much to his probing, challenging, and engaging commitment to teaching and learning.

My wife of thirty years, Janet Cooper Nelson, has provided counsel, encouragement, and intellectual gifts. Her presence and understanding have supported my work, especially the writing of this book. My son, Geoffrey, has also been a support even when writing displaced other, more inviting activities.

My deceased parents, James W. Nelson and Elinor S. Nelson, would take great pride in the publication of this book. Though neither went beyond high school, education was of great importance to them. They provided an upbringing that valued thinking and learning and nurtured concern about moral issues. Their voices are heard in these pages.

I tell the college students in my classes that writing takes great work and that I learned truly how to write as a doctoral student. That learning came in part from Susan Dearing, who directs the writing center and teaches at Wheaton College in Massachusetts. Susan's critical guidance transformed early "best" drafts of the dissertation to markedly improved versions.

Finally I wish to thank Jane Garry, Editor, and Andrew Hudak, Assistant Production Editor, and other colleagues at Greenwood Publishing Group for their investment and commitment to this work.

I assume full and complete responsibility for the research, interpretations of material, and point of view expressed in this book. This work is offered in the hope that it advances our understanding of the college presidency in America. My modest goal is to contribute to the discussion about the heritage of the moral voice of presidents in the academy, and to offer my hope for its future health.

Introduction

In 1978 I joined to Dartmouth College as a member of their administration. Though I did not realize it then, this was the beginning of a journey of interest in the college presidency.

The inspiration for my interest was Dartmouth's president, John G. Kemeny. When I arrived on campus, Kemeny had been president for eight years. He was to serve another three, leaving the presidency in 1981, a year longer than the ten years he had from the outset claimed would be the duration of his tenure. What Kemeny had planned, and was successful in doing after departing the presidency until his untimely death in 1992, was to return to the faculty as simply a professor of math. He had taught two courses every year during his presidency. But he yearned once again to focus his intellectual gifts and energies on the teaching of undergraduates and to catch up on more than ten years of scholarship in his field.

Kemeny's interests were broad and his abilities extraordinary. He was an esteemed mathematician, a genius in the minds of many. As a young graduate student he was involved in the Manhattan Project. As a professor and later as president, Kemeny led the nation in introducing computers to college campuses, and he was continually eager to learn how these new tools could and should be used. He argued strenuously for better preparation of students planning careers as elementary and secondary mathematics teachers. In addition to all these and many other traits, Kemeny was a consummate and wise educator and philosopher with a wide range of ideas about education, public policy, public decision making, and democracy.

But most profoundly, Kemeny was a superb leader. During his presidency, his moral voice led Dartmouth. He exercised moral leadership within and beyond the gates of the college. For example, it was John's voice on the college radio, not that of student protesters, that the Dartmouth community remembers leading the institution's response to the murders of four students at Kent State in May 1970. This remarkable moment is discussed in detail later in these pages. In the early years of his presidency, Kemeny led Dartmouth through difficult debate about whether to accept women students, was the primary architect of the decision to do so, and skillfully engineered the transition to coeducation of an institution that was exclusively male for more than two hundred years.

Although I would not have known to label it so then, what I now label the moral voice of the college president was heard during each opening convocation in Kemeny's presidency. After coeducation, these addresses to students, faculty, administrators, and other interested members of the community began with what became his signature greeting: "Men and Women of Dartmouth," always followed by rousing applause.

Moral leadership can be as powerful as spoken word. Intentionally using these public occasions, he always had something of significance to say. Public addresses were opportunities to test ideas and press issues. When Kemeny spoke, audiences were pushed to think critically about the importance of education, the responsibilities of educated people in the world, and the issues in society demanding attention. He spoke about how easy it was to be only critical rather than engaging the difficult intellectual work of analysis and synthesis as well as criticism. He spoke about the issues and problems faced by Dartmouth and by all colleges and universities. And he spoke about the great challenges facing democracy, especially in America, and most dramatically in an advanced scientific and technological age.

While many other examples of his leadership could be mentioned, in the latter years of his presidency Kemeny responded to a call to lead and serve beyond the gates when asked by the nation's president to chair an investigation of the accident at Three Mile Island, which came to be known as the Kemeny Commission. In order to undertake this responsibility, Kemeny concluded that the only right course for the college was for him to take leave of his presidential duties for the six months of the commission's work.

On the morning of the day of his return, Kemeny learned that he was to speak to an alumni group on campus that evening. Events seemed to dictate that he speak about the commission and the findings of the report. Within hours, the small alumni speech had turned into a major campus address. Following a day-long briefing with congressional leaders in Washington about the commission's conclusions, Kemeny arrived on campus early in the evening. Though physically and mentally exhausted from months of work and from the final stages of producing the report, he felt obligated to give the speech. He knew how important it was for him to share what was learned and what it meant for the nation.

Using no notes, as was his custom, Kemeny gave an engaging, at times entertaining, professorial "lecture" to nearly a thousand gathered people from the college and the local community. I recall that moment, so characteristic of who he was as a leader and an educator, as vividly as if it happened yesterday. Here was an educator delighting in educating his audience. As the hour drew late and after nearly two hours of talk, including numerous questions from the audience, Kemeny requested politely that the session conclude so he might get home to some much-needed rest.[1]

On so many occasions, Kemeny's leadership and public words provoked my curiosity about what college presidents had said and written and about the relationship of presidential leadership and rhetoric to the history of America's colleges and universities. What traditions were embedded in the college presidency? What did presidents discuss publicly? How had they shaped the traditions and values of higher education and of the nation?

Next on the itinerary of this journey was Harold Shapiro. In 1987 Shapiro left the presidency of the University of Michigan to become president at Princeton University. Shapiro is a probing thinker and philosopher. His Princeton inaugural address, "Tradition, Continuity, Discovery, and Change: A Conversation with Princeton's Past," deepened my interest in college and university presidents and fed the inquiry I would undertake as a doctoral student. Shapiro crafted the address as an incoming president's conversation with some of his Princeton predecessors about timeless and fundamental concerns of the academy. Shapiro provided a model for what became a quest in my research and scholarship: allowing college presidents to speak to us in the present and for the future.

However, beyond the inspiration of academic leaders such as Kemeny and Shapiro, particularly as the twentieth century draws to a close and the twenty-first begins, I believe there to be crucial, pressing, and unavoidable questions about the college presidency, about the state of higher education, and about their significantly intertwined fortunes. In many respects the shape of the college and university presidency—whether characterized as an office of moral, philosophical, and educational leadership or as one of merely bureaucratic management, financial, and political duties—is a bellwether for the future of the academy, including its role as the place of learning and considered thought in the life of a democracy. The heritage, traditions, and moral expectations of the college presidency, and the parallel and closely connected fundamental principles and values of the academy in America, thereby create a framework for this book.

In recent years we have witnessed a renewal of attention to traditions long embedded in the college presidency. These traditions are worthy of emphasis as we consider the present and future leadership of colleges and universities. Public commentary has included Rita Bornstein's contention that the president should be a "public intellectual" and James Freedman's idea that presidents should not allow the burdens and distractions of the office to "silence their wisdom." These urgings direct our focus to the personal characteristics of college and university presidents and to the importance of their public leadership.

This increased attention to the fundamental personal characteristics and leadership expectations of presidents is a positive change. It recalls a time when presidents were assumed to inspire institutions, to shape people of character, and to make proclamations about national and world issues. It heralds a shift in the emphasis begun in the late 1970s, continuing into the 1990s, and still very much with us: the president as "CEO," fundraising genius, mediator, and public-relations expert. This trend has led many to the conclusion that the business of education was business rather than education.

This recent era has been characterized by presidential searches that routinely focused on the ability of candidates to administer ever more complex bureaucracies, develop ever scarcer financial resources, and negotiate ever more politicized environments. Many of those in positions to select presidents increasingly viewed successful appointments as those that fit, not surprisingly, the mold of the president as manager, fundraiser, politician, mediator, and public-relations expert.

On one level this is a caricature of the contemporary presidency. But like any caricature it contains significant, even if only partial, truths. The intention of Presidents Bornstein and Freedman and others is to counter the caricature and refocus the image of the college presidency. They draw attention to presidential qualities of public vision, social concern, and civic duty, qualities for which both campus and society yearn. They believe that college and university presidents should lead in the public square, comment on matters of social consequence, encourage debate about critical cultural and political issues, and be public intellectuals. And they remind us of the character and influence historically associated with presidents of what many think is a long bygone era.

Such qualities of presidents must not be overlooked or taken for granted. Indeed, as in so many of life's endeavors, what we seek in presidents is what we will get. Today's presidential appointments will shape the future of an office traditionally esteemed for its service to campus and society.

However, advocacy for presidents to use their "pulpits" with greater frequency and to be public intellectuals rediscovers only part of the heritage of the office and its role. It is good to think of college and university presidents as leaders who contribute to intellectual debate, who are teachers and educators, and who exert wisdom in public pronouncements on issues of the day. But these qualities tell only a portion of the story. They capture only a piece of the historical picture of what has made college presidents such captivating figures and why some commentators believe that the titans and Olympian presidents of old simply no longer exist. More pointedly, the legacy that today's presidents should embrace is the one that some fear has diminished to insignificance—*the moral voice of the president.*

Our day and age shows a great reluctance to use terms like *moral voice* and *leadership.* Some of this reluctance is understandable. Dangers lurk in the values debate (read: the dreaded discussion about whose values). Those who advocate values frequently risk justified accusations of moralizing. However, the language used to describe the presidency is an important indicator of the public's thoughts and expectations about the office. And to avoid associating moral leadership with the college and university presidency is itself symptomatic of higher education's difficulties and dilemmas.

The moral voice of the college and university presidency has a rich history, including very strong and embarrassingly weak examples. But this voice is not merely a relic. Reclaiming and reaffirming moral leadership in the presidency requires overcoming resistance to the assertion that moral language is essential to the office and its responsibilities. The extent to which presidents are expected to be moral leaders is positively and directly correlated with the future shape and significance of the presidency in the academy.

Presidents are chosen to lead colleges and universities for a variety of reasons. The best of intentions do not protect these choices from being fraught with confusing and even conflicting expectations. Presidential searches confirm the adage that you reap what you sow. Put another way: "Be careful about what you pray for, you just might get it." The qualities of intellect, public presence, and insight about education, including expressed commitment to ethical and moral issues, may make a candidate attractive during the search process. But once in office, these same qualities may be difficult to employ without controversy. Certainly presidents will experience pressure to avoid the unpopular in their public positions. But despite these pressures, the tradition of moral leadership in the presidency is not to be equated with mere expression of the unpopular or controversial. This tradition is one of substance and engagement, and if today's academic presidents do not embrace and exercise it, the tradition could easily fade into a dim memory.

My hope is that the stories about presidents past and present that follow will instruct, inspire, and encourage a return to the presumption that moral leadership is a fundamental criterion and expectation of those who serve as college presidents. Historically, the moral authority of the college president is well attested. And though sometimes threatened and facing a less than certain future, the moral presidency lives, and its manifestation contradicts those who contend that the days of presidential giants are gone.

The founders and early leaders of many of the nation's colleges and universities were exemplary moral leaders of campus communities and society. Contemporary presidents inherit this legacy, and their stories continue to tell of a tradition of moral courage in the ivory tower. The college presidency has indeed been a crucible of moral leadership, but today the competing expectations imposed on the presidency are heightened, often unrealistically. Though presidential responsibilities have not changed, the dynamics of the environment in which they lead has. Justifiably or not, these forces have led many to conclude that the tradition of moral leadership is no longer at the core, maybe even barely at the margins, of the presidency.

Presidents must indeed confront numerous and rapid changes in society. Their task is complicated by an increasingly secular and visibly more diverse culture. Moral beliefs and values are more intensely debated. The political climate is more polarized, argument less civil, than in bygone eras. Presidents face numerous distractions created by the demands of complex bureaucracies, competition for fiscal resources, and the need to appeal to constituencies increasingly less attentive. Yet moral leadership becomes even more critical in an environment charged with emotions and political agendas—race relations, sexual mores, gender confrontations, often controversial scientific research, and free speech. As James Freedman has warned, the temptations of silence are great.

"Moral leadership," especially when exercised as a moral voice in the college presidency, is thought simply to no longer exist in some quarters. There was once a tradition of expecting college presidents to be moral leaders, while the primary selection criteria for presidents seem now to be (and may for sometime have been) their capacity as fundraisers, managers of large and complex academic bureaucracies, public-relations magicians, and astute politicians. They work "strategically" with constituents on campus—faculty, students, administrators, parents, alumni, and trustees—and foster external relationships with corporations, government, foundations, and friends in order to meet diverse and competing (frequently mutually exclusive) wants and needs.

Cynics argue that presidents are no longer appointed for their intellectual gifts, for their educational vision, for their ability to address the educational issues of the academy. Presidents no longer embody the bygone tradition of preacher- or even scholar-presidents. The era of moral giants in the presidency was probably over even before the beginning of this century. In this view, the moral "bully pulpit" of the college presidency is an artifact of the past, something neither desirable nor valued in today's higher education world.

It is to this point and problem that this book is addressed. My premise is that the tradition of moral leadership by college presidents is at the core not only of the office of the presidency, but of the fundamental articulation and defense of principles, values, hopes, and aspirations of what we mean when we claim a higher education. I find significant evidence that this tradition of moral leadership persists into present times, but cultural, religious, and societal changes have altered it substantially and the tradition is far from secure. It will not continue absent intentions and expectations that presidents can and should be moral leaders. This means attentive interest by everyone from observers concerned about college and university life to the people who make the decisions today about who the presidents of tomorrow will be.

College presidents and aspirants must acquire and exercise these skills of moral leadership and oration. Failure to do so compromises the fundamental purposes of the university and the inherent values of the academy, specifically, learning, freedom of expression and inquiry, analysis, knowledge, and wisdom. Proceeding naturally from these foundations is the obligation to address the development of institutions, form people of character, and establish the balance between competence and compassion (as John Sloan Dickey observes), which finally makes possible the nurturing of civic values and democratic responsibility.

The tradition of presidential moral leadership embraces these values. Contemporary presidents can aspire to leadership, which is at its foundation moral. They should be expected and supported to be and to do nothing less. It is my hope in writing this book that the reader will gain a greater appreciation for the roots of the tradition of the moral voice in the college presidency, an awareness that this tradition has indeed continued into the present day, and an understanding of its crucial role in the future.

This is a story about what college presidents have to say and how they say it. It is about rhetoric in the public square. It is about the development of philosophies—of education, of institutional mission and purpose, and of politics and social affairs—by men and women who have led within the gates of the academy and beyond. In many cases we see how deeds are closely connected to words. The critical question is what will be the future of the heritage and expectation that presidents of colleges and universities should be public leaders addressing moral questions, issues, and dilemmas both within and beyond the gates. I invite you, then, to hear the voices of presidents come alive, testifying to this heritage and leading as examples of what can and ought to be expected of presidents now and in the future.

NOTE

1. For a delightful account of this event and other aspects of the Kemeny presidency, see Tim Clark, "All Things We Do, He Does Better," *Yankee Magazine*, March 1980, pp. 67–71, 120–36.

PART ONE

PROLOGUE

1

The Moral Leadership of College Presidents

The founders and leaders of America's colonial colleges were almost always minister-presidents. Moral and religious leadership was expected and was viewed as essential to the office. In what came to be known as the ivory tower, presidents made moral judgments and provided moral insights within and beyond the gates. Their voices enhanced the reputations of campuses and inspired the development of character and education for generations of students. Their invaluable leadership and critical ideas contributed immeasurably to public discourse, to the public square, and to the life of the nation.

For more than two hundred fifty years from the founding of Harvard to the beginning of the twentieth century, the image of the college president as moral leader persisted and predominated. During the last hundred years major changes in higher education have occurred as the character of American society and culture has become increasingly pluralistic and secular. The religious foundations of American colleges have not disappeared. But they are noticeably less often conspicuous and frequently viewed as quaint, even archaic. For the most part the era of "preaching" presidents is over.[1] The status of the contemporary heir of the scholar president is at best fragile and threatened.

This is where our story begins. Presidential profiles of moral courage and leadership are not merely relics of the past but indeed endure in the present. Even the most casual observer would agree with the characterization of the historical presidency as a celebrated position of moral influence. However, when contemporary presidents act out this heritage, their words and deeds of moral leadership are frequently unnoticed. The moral voice of today's presidents is unappreciated and at times dismissed by even seasoned observers.

The challenge that today's presidents face in choosing to be moral leaders is extraordinarily complicated. The difficulty of this challenge for presidents is greatly complicated by critics both inside and outside the gates about the moral life in the academy. What picture emerges of the colleges and universities within which presidents assert leadership?

Simply put, the academy has become an ideological battleground rather than a place of rational discourse. Characterized by high emotion and exclusive moral certitude, it is a battleground that ironically impinges on presidents while creating ever greater demand for their moral leadership. This battleground mirrors that in society, but ideological conflict is more intense on campuses because of the value the academy places on the principles of discourse. Ideas are (in theory) openly discussed, differences of opinion a way of life, and disagreement *de rigueur*. On one side are advocates of what is called "political correctness." On the other side are upholders of the traditional purposes of the university. The shape of the contemporary debate was established in the social and political movements on campuses such as Berkeley in the 1960s. Allan Bloom, William Bennett, and fellow commentators react to that era and declare that its reforms have caused the failings of the modern university. And who is viewed as more responsible for these failures than its leaders: college and university presidents?

Joining Bennett and Bloom, diverse critics such as Pat Robertson, Stephen Carter, Robert Bellah, Arthur Schlesinger, and others characterize the contemporary cultural crisis as a search for values in a society perceived to lack core mores and principles. An aspect of this crisis in the university is the age-old debate about whether values have any place in the academy. Purists argue no, but their contention is more rhetoric than practice. Claims that the academy can or should be value-neutral are unsustainable. However, advocates of this position succeed on one or both of two fronts. Values are pushed to the periphery and their importance is diminished to a level of inconsequence. Or all values are given equal weight, but have no effect in shaping society. On the other side are those who believe that values must be embedded in the university and that they will dictate the codes of meaning and action for the academy. In either case, when values are at stake the question becomes a debate about "whose values"?

The difficulties and dangers for presidents become particularly pronounced when the subject of values enters the equation. Battles about values inevitably lead to questions and contests of whose values will prevail. At their core these arguments are ideological. This situation, increasingly prevalent in the academy, has led Stephen Trachtenberg, president of George Washington University, to warn that

presidents need to keep their eyes and the eyes of their audiences fixed on the dangerous potential of a movement of this land some of whose caricatures are not altogether different from the scapegoating of the 1920s and '30s. . . . In short, today's president must be prepared to deal with a new ideological edge that has entered American discourse and may well intensify in the 1990s. In its beneficent guise, it is often called a "search for values." In its more ambivalent guise, it seems also to be a longing for authority and discipline.[2]

In the contemporary climate the challenge of this debate creates an imperative for presidents. They must battle ideologies on both the left and right of the political divide. Both sides use political ideologies and agendas to argue, often ironically and disingenuously, that the opposition controls the agenda on campuses. Both sides want their values to determine the future course of the academy.

This antagonistic ethos creates continual and pressing demands on day-to-day presidential leadership. Presidents cannot escape the temptation to be morally silent. However, competing ideological constituencies impatiently and irrepressibly demand definitive moral sanction for distinct and incompatible moral positions. Beyond all the rhetoric lies the true issue: a battle for the soul of the university.

Presidential choices and decisions on issues of moral and ethical consequence are nearly always ones between and among opposing goods. Thus, presidents continually confront impossible choices of moral calculus. But the golden mean is a variable measure. It is situationally determined by disparate constituencies whose actions, regardless of protests to the contrary, are frequently based on the ends justifying the means. Presidential moral leadership requires opposing these forces. It includes pleasing some constituency on one occasion and on another incurring heated resistance and outrage from the same group.

Colleges and universities are expected simultaneously to engage in both the pursuit of truth and the pursuit of knowledge, to provide a superior education while ensuring the development of moral principles and character. The fundamental task is twofold: to maintain enduring values and principles *and* to search for new knowledge. The public expects that modern colleges and universities can simultaneously preserve proven values and unearth new knowledge to produce change. For the better part of the last century emphasizing these twin aspirations has been the assumed mission of colleges and universities.

The advocates of these distinct goals form opposing camps. At best, they coexist uneasily, if not unwillingly. Freedom of thought and rational discourse in the academy should encourage challenges to orthodoxies of whatever stripe. However, in recent years competing ideologies and values have produced strident and contentious debates about what will and what will not be preserved in the academy. The resulting competition for superiority and inherent conflict between values and knowledge pose dilemmas for the moral voice of presidents.

Interestingly, the tradition of presidential moral leadership parallels an equally important tradition, also often overlooked today: that education is at its core a moral quest. No less an authority than the Harvard "Redbook" claims that "[M]oral character arises from the molding of the native powers to ideal aims. The final secular good is the dedication of the self to an ideal higher than self— the devotion to truth and to one's neighbor."[3] In the academy there is no catechism for teaching moral values. But they are not to be divorced from the pursuit of learning and knowledge.

Similar expectations of the purpose of education led Robert Hutchins to coin the term Great Conversation "to convey[s] what human beings have carried on in dealing with the basic questions of humanity."[4] A major feature of the moral voice of college presidents is its relationship to the issues embodied in this "Great Conversation," the fundamental notion that there are basic questions faced by humanity throughout the ages that education can and must address.

Our concern here is to use the tradition of moral leadership in the college presidency to guide its future. But what about that future? To what extent has the state of American college and university leadership changed? Does a profile of leaders in the ivory tower suggest more optimism or more pessimism about the future of presidential moral vision? Are presidents capable of influencing the mores of the campus and society? Does the historical foundation of the moral voice still exist? If not, what may be required of us to rebuild that foundation? Finally, are changes that have occurred in the presidency so consequential that the moral voice of presidents has already become, as some suggest, an oxymoron?

The moral leadership of college presidents undergirds the fundamental principles of college and university campuses. Presidents can answer the yearning in many corners of American society for meaning, values, ethics, and civic virtue in the commonweal. Rhetoric and action are fundamentally joined in the presidential pulpit. Presidential leaders inspire the highest ideals of education, especially its relationship to society and the world. Robert Birnbaum has aptly noted: "As symbolic leaders, presidents who consistently articulate the core values of the institution and relate them to all aspects of institutional life reinvigorate the myths that lead people to create a common reality."[5]

Presidents face the challenges of office in a dynamic context influenced by the beliefs, mores, and politics of the campus and society. Political, ideological, and philosophical forces have always affected presidential leadership. The colonial colleges were founded and their first presidents served to ensure that an educated elite, primarily clergy, would be prepared to lead a society independent of British power and influence. But in the contemporary climate political and philosophical ideologies are magnified and they complicate the college presidency.

Contemporary presidents wrestle with the effects of the complex demands of the office on moral vision and action. On one hand, presidents profess a certain reluctance to speak on public issues. On the other hand, they claim to "have an important role to play in public debate on policy issues."[6] There is an ever-present fear of offending increasingly diverse constituencies. This difficulty is coupled with the near-impossibility of divorcing personal beliefs from institutional identity as presidents. Facing these realities, James Freedman, president of Dartmouth, counsels colleagues that exigencies of the presidency "should not silence our wisdom."[7]

Even as ideological forces work together to make the exercise of moral authority less straightforward than in the past, society more than ever needs moral vision and leadership. Thus, while the presidential task may have become increasingly difficult on one hand, there is greater public receptivity of moral leadership on the other. Conventional assumptions that the moral voice has been reduced to silence are simply unfounded.[8] And contemporary moral leadership is not merely voiced in the ivory tower, but indeed has influence and consequences in society as well.

The stories of the presidents in this book form a conversation between the dead and the living. Their stories invite us to converse with presidents, past and present, to hear expressions of ethics and values and to glimpse the courage demanded of leadership. These profiles reflect the character required of the men and women who fulfill the responsibilities of the presidential office.

The tradition of moral leadership must be fully appreciated in order for it to be sustained. This is important for one very obvious reason: tomorrow's college presidents surely stand on the shoulders of their predecessors.

The college presidency has been and remains enormously complex and complicated. Historically, presidents have raised concerns about the nature of the job—the difficulties of doing the job well and satisfying competing constituents. Eliot of Harvard claimed that there is "no equal in the world" to the college president.

Great demands are a primary feature of today's college presidency. Presidents must manage politically charged academic bureaucracies. They have little choice but to raise the enormous resources required to keep their campuses operating. They must be concerned about maintaining educational quality. And they continually confront vocal, at times increasingly less civil, critics inside and outside the academy.

The perspective of history is informative. It must be remembered that presidents of old, the founders and their successors, individuals such as Eleazor Wheelock at Dartmouth beginning in 1769, performed all these tasks and more. They led, administered, taught, preached on and off campus, hired faculty and staff, counseled and disciplined students, raised funds, built buildings, established and maintained mission and purpose, and secured the resources to ensure the future of their institutions. Presidents integrated all these responsibilities in a fashion that still enabled them to be moral leaders. This heritage was then and continues to be critical and fundamental to the presidency and to the experience we call higher education.

Though there have been changes in the presidency, the office has not changed as dramatically as may appear at first glance. If presidents such as Wheelock bore burdens equal to, if not greater than, those of presidents today, what is different?

Certainly, there have been changes in the dynamics and complexities of the office. But many of these changes in complexity and expectation are counterbalanced by greater support from larger staffs and broader delegation of responsibilities. A knowledge of the business of education answers some of the questions about what has changed for presidents. Today's presidents are more distracted than their predecessors by the complications and demands of the office, by the expectations of key constituencies, especially those—trustees, governing boards, influential alumni, and even donors—responsible for placing presidents in office in the first place.[9]

If presidents have become increasingly distracted from their roles as moral leaders and teachers, one may only speculate about the causes. Possibly, the primacy of interest in the financial bottom line (and its close connection to the perception of job effectiveness) may be a source of greater anxiety and insecurity for presidents in the latter twentieth than predecessors earlier this century and before. It is possible, though more speculative, that at least for some presidents the tendency to be distracted results from being less integrated as persons.

Presidents confront intense pressure from areas such as enrollment, resource development, and public relations. In this climate, several important questions about the nature of the presidency must be contemplated. First, are presidents likely to become even further distracted by the pressures of the office from attention to moral issues, from a free exercise of moral voice? Second, will the path to the presidency and judgments about job effectiveness rest solely on the ability to manage bureaucracies, raise funds, and negotiate political problems?

These issues lead to important questions about who will be the presidents of the future. Who will they be as people and as presidents? Michael Katz claims that the next crisis of the university will be moral.[10] If true, college and university leaders will be required to possess the personal compass necessary to face the moral challenges of leadership.

And yet in a recent publication about the presidency the Association of Governing Boards—an extremely influential force in higher education—does not even mention the value or role of religious, moral, or philosophical beliefs in undergirding presidential character and leadership.[11] They believe presidential leadership is defined and guided by institutional mission. This position ignores the prospect that mission statements, especially as frequently refashioned by institutional predilections for strategic planning, may often be little more than expedient attempts designed to survive a highly competitive marketplace. Even if mission remains true to institutional history and educational principles, presidents should be its interpreters and stewards, not its slaves.

Also, changes in the role of collegiality on campus have complicated the prospects for moral discourse. In the late 1970s, A. Bartlett Giamatti decried a subtle but significant shift in the ethos of the campus. Though deliberate and slow, rational dialogue and reasoned understanding, if not always reaching consensus, has historically served campuses well. Giamatti warned that this traditional and primary way for addressing problems was rapidly eroding. In its place colleges and universities were increasingly resolving conflicts by the seductive use of "codification."[12]

As it turns out, Giamatti was prescient about developments in the decades ahead. Today, an ever-expanding ethos that relies on codification instead of consensus can reduce the ability of presidents to be moral leaders. In the twenty years since he voiced this concern, Giamatti's prophetic warning has not been seriously, if at all, heeded. It has fallen victim to the forces of oblivion that characterize modern society. A symptom of this oblivion is a reliance on "values" in place of the thoughtfulness of reason. This is where the forces of "political correctness" on both the right and left of the political spectrum erode the fundamental foundation of the university and significantly complicate the moral voice of presidents.

Despite these difficulties and complications, there are college presidents who assume the mantle and sustain the tradition of moral leadership. They possess qualities enabling them to succeed as moral leaders in higher education and to influence the course of American colleges and universities and society.

Dartmouth College's John Sloan Dickey is a noted president who viewed morals and ethics as crucial ingredients of education. His classic comment is that "the American liberal arts college, whether church-related or not, has a had a 'unique' mission in the duality of its historic purpose: to see men made whole in both *competence* and *conscience*."[13] Either characteristic without the other produced, in Dickey's view, an education lacking fullness and coherence. Dickey led the college to educate students both in knowledge, basic learning, and essential skills *and* in wisdom, ethics, and values. In slightly different language a few decades later, Henry Rosovsky claimed that education produces in individuals "the informed judgment that enables them to make discriminating moral choices."[14]

There are several threats to the capacity of colleges and universities to seek and support leaders who understand the place of moral issues in education and who will speak publicly about morals and ethics. One critical concern for the future of the presidency is the degree to which apparent, and to some increasingly excessive, administrative burdens will continue to define the nature of the office and to dictate presidential priorities. These pressures create a risk to the presidency from the gravitational pull (and relative safety) of the routines of organization and administration.

Richard Morrill, former president of both Salem College and the University of Richmond, warns of this grave prospect. He claims that inertia is a plague on the presidency, reducing the ethical and moral aspects of decision making, teaching, and administration.[15] When this happens, education about values, presumed to be central to mission, is lost in the business of keeping institutions functioning. From experience as a college teacher as well as president, Morrill concludes that administration has become "predominantly managerial, paralleling the disciplinary specialities of the curriculum."[16]

But Morrill is not completely pessimistic. He sees a doubleness in the pressures on presidents: administrative responsibilities and styles can distract them from moral leadership, but society expects them to be moral leaders. The very external environment that can inhibit the moral voice also calls it to lead public discourse about values in a civil society. Morrill observes that "faced with signs of moral disorder and uncertainty, our society has a strong expectation that educational institutions should shoulder much of the responsibility. . . . Colleges and universities have, after all, always claimed a special capacity to influence conduct and to develop moral character. . . . education should address not only the issue of moral reflection but that of moral conduct as well."[17] The enormity of the responsibilities of the office simply do not have to dictate whether presidents are able publicly to articulate opinions and positions, especially those of a moral nature.

A second critical challenge to present and future presidents is their ability to provide leadership about values in education. As president of Johns Hopkins University, Steven Muller presided over the archetypal American research university in the European tradition. In the history of American higher education, the founding of Johns Hopkins marked the beginning of a major shift in emphasis from the British-inspired colonial college to the German research university model. Muller believes that the task of countering this assumption of value-free higher education is made more difficult because modern university leadership "must confront so many value issues, from euthanasia to genetic engineering to weapons that can destroy the world, and we no longer have the strong rallying point that we had in the nineteenth century. We have to develop a new value system."[18]

If anything, ethical and moral issues have become increasingly unavoidable in the research university. In this setting, as well as in liberal arts colleges and other higher education institutions, presidents must refashion moral language that is sufficiently persuasive to address issues of values in the academy and in society.

A third challenge comes from critics of the presidency and the university who believe contemporary presidents are simply inadequate to the task of moral leadership as exemplified by their "olympian" predecessors of decades and generations before. These critics are joined by others who characterize the ills of the American university as being so severe that even heroic moral leadership cannot make a difference. An extension of this argument is that it is no longer possible or desirable for academic communities to rely on the dynamic leadership of a single individual.

For example, Bill Readings, hoping that the trend might be reversed, contends that the chief executive officer of the contemporary university is nothing more than an administrative and managerial automaton. Beginning in the 1980s the attribution "CEO" to college president symbolizes this change. Readings caricatures the president of his "University of Excellence" as "a bureaucratic administrator who moves effortlessly from the lecture hall, to the sports stadium, to the executive lounge. From judge, to synthesizer, to executive and fund raiser, without publicly expressing any opinions or passing any judgments whatever."[19]

These diverse demands on presidents are not really new. Readings argues that the decrease in presidential moral leadership is both a symptom and a result of unresolved problems and issues in the university. But if his assessment of the university is true, then Readings's ironic analysis serves to underscore the importance of reclaiming moral leadership.

Whether the university has for some time, possibly since the middle of the twentieth century, been in a state of disarray and disintegration remains the subject of much debate.[20] We are not primarily concerned here with the alleged failures, however severe, transient, mythic, or profound, of the university. Rather our focus is on the importance of reclaiming the heritage and preeminent role of moral leadership in the presidency.

This story of the college presidency and of profiles in courage in the ivory tower unfolds in the context of changing social and cultural norms and values in American society. This flux, from which the academy is not immune, has intensified in the five decades since the end of World War II. Changes and pressures within the academy include alterations to the presidential selection process; greater expectations of leadership by constituencies such as trustees and governing boards; unforeseen economic conditions and constraints; increased governmental regulations; variations in student demographics; and more management complexity.[21]

As we shall see, presidents have not been silent about these changes in the role of their office and about the need for a moral voice in the academy. As early as the 1950s President Harold Stoke decried the shift from the president as a "Man of Learning" to a "Man of Management."[22] Another president, Harold Enarson, echoes this concern that presidents are now more managers of academic bureaucracies and less moral leaders than was once the case. He further contends that the qualities of character that presidents once possessed as moral leaders are no longer even part of the job description.[23]

This tendency to emphasize the ability and identity of presidents as managers is critical because it has become a self-perpetuating criterion in presidential selection. The capacities assumed to be required for the job tend to define the expectations of searches. As managerial and administrative preparation has become more widely seen as critical to the office, the criteria assumed essential to presidential selection have also changed.

The converse about expectations of moral leadership is also true. Search committees who fail to consider that presidents can or should be moral leaders will have no inclination to select presidents who will be. Enarson recognizes the significant historical shift that has occurred in the expectations and performance of presidents. But he does not think that the presidential roles as moral authority and as manager are mutually exclusive or incompatible.

James Laney, an outspoken and persuasive contemporary president, does not believe the heritage of presidential moral leadership is completely lost or that some erosion of it cannot be reclaimed. He argues that the moral responsibility of the presidency is linked to the moral authority of educational institutions.[24] He believes that presidents are "heirs of a tradition that found in a higher education a high moral calling. . . . part of what we are called to is stewardship of our institutions as a dwelling place for the human spirit."[25] In practical terms, especially in the present era marked by great diversity, Laney's aspiration for community building is a moral imperative. This imperative calls for education to embrace simultaneously the development of practical wisdom and the capacity for moral decency and civic duty.

In the final analysis the forces historically confronting college and university presidents are both within and outside their control. These forces are numerous and varied. Many constraints on the presidential prerogative to take stands on controversial public issues are very real. One irony of life in the academy is that presidents are considered to have vastly less academic freedom than professors. This leads to the conclusion that an "assistant professor can advocate free love, divestiture of South African stocks, abortion on demand, the cessation of all nuclear research, or any number of other things. Chairs and deans have less freedom to say what they think. Presidents have almost none."[26]

Some limitations on presidential prerogatives reflect concern that negative donor reaction to controversial presidential positions could adversely affect fundraising. This perceived pressure forces presidents to be extremely careful in taking potentially unpopular moral stands. Commenting on the difficulty of having to be continually concerned with "tact and diplomacy," Vartan Gregorian, former president of Brown University, agrees "with Lord Chesterfield that wisdom is like carrying a watch. Unless asked, you don't have to tell everybody what time it is."[27]

Even when presidents have something of significance to say, they face difficulties in conveying messages to a wide audience. A century ago the full text of presidential inaugural addresses would be covered not only in campus newspapers, but also in local papers for the surrounding community. On such occasions today, local media normally present only spare coverage, if that. To transmit even the gist, let alone the entirety, of their messages to a broad audience, presidents often resort to internal campus communication through alumni magazines, memos, letters, and bulletins.

There is much debate about whether today's society can be fairly characterized as being devoid of moral leadership. Historically in America, only the expectations of moral voice in the leadership of religious institutions has exceeded that of educational leaders. Presidents have used moral leadership to ensure that the foundations and principles of education would be sustained. They have invoked education's value in inspiring civic duty and the responsibilities of citizenship. And their moral suasion of educational institutions—public and private—has nurtured the common good and enriched the commonweal.

More than eighty years separate the presidential tenures of Horace Bumstead at Atlanta University and John Kemeny at Dartmouth College. The eras of their presidencies—the latter nineteenth and the latter twentieth centuries—and their institutions—one historically black, southern, and poor, the other well-established, elite, and Ivy League—could not be more different. But these two leaders, whose stories are told in greater detail in the subsequent chapters, are united in their courage in the presidential pulpit and in the reach of their voices to their communities and to society. Theirs are only two of many such stories spanning time and place in the following pages.

We arrive then at our purpose and intent. Presidential rhetoric may not always be acknowledged and presidential actions may not always be obvious in today's fast-paced and complex world. In contrast with their predecessors, today's presidents compete for the attention of a populace characterized by transient interests and lowest-common-denominator thinking. Presidents, even when they use the pulpit of moral leadership, often remain unheard.

These voices in the academy starkly oppose the proposition that the moral voice of the contemporary presidency is an oxymoron. Given the crisis of modern society and the university, the past has never looked more relevant.

NOTES

1. Harold Stoke characterizes this change in the college presidency from the time of clerical presidents: "the college president was usually a minister, chosen as the most learned or most zealous among his colleagues. . . . While something of this heritage still lingers about the college president, it is now only a kind of after image of an academic life which has all but disappeared. Higher education has become more secular than religious; it has expanded incredibly in volume and variety; its purposes and intellectual preoccupations are different and more numerous than they used to be." Harold Stoke, *The American College President* (New York: Harper Brothers, 1959), p. 2.

2. Stephen Joel Trachtenberg, "Presidents Can Establish a Moral Tone on Campus," *Educational Record* 70, no. 2 (Spring 1989), p. 9.

3. James Bryant Conant, Introduction to *General Education in a Free Society* (Cambridge, Mass.: Harvard University Press, 1945), p. 169. The Harvard "Redbook," as *General Education in a Free Society* has come to be called, is one of the seminal works in the literature on higher education. The work, including the charge by President Conant in establishing the committee who produced what was originally a report to the president, expresses the tone and concerns of the immediate post–World War II era. Though a major world conflict to maintain democracy had been waged and won, the task of securing the long-range future of democracy remained. Following an American tradition first fully articulated by Thomas Jefferson, Conant argued for the necessity of education to undergird democratic values and institutions. The committee, which included George Wald and Arthur Schlessinger, Jr., wrestled with key issues such as what constitutes education, what education can do, and what it should do. The result of their work is a philosophical and practical synthesis supporting the need for educational thought to focus on moral, spiritual, and ethical concerns.

4. Robert Hutchins, *Freedom, Education and the Fund: Essays and Addresses, 1946–1956* (New York: Meridian Books, 1956), p. 100.

5. Robert Birnbaum, *How Colleges Work: The Cybernetics of Academic Organization and Leadership* (San Francisco: Jossey-Bass, 1988), p. 208. Birnbaum continues by saying that a "college president who reinforces and dramatizes the importance of access, for example, by symbolic acts such as telling stories of underprepared students who 'made it' may have a greater influence on faculty behavior than one who pressures faculty to start a new program."

6. Rita Bornstein, "Back in the Spotlight: The College President as Public Intellectual," *Educational Record* (Fall 1995), p. 58.

7. James O. Freedman, "Our Work Should Not Silence Our Wisdom," *Boston Globe*, January 19, 1997.

8. William H. Honan, "At the Top of the Ivory Tower the Watchword Is Silence," *New York Times*, July 24, 1994. It is important to note that Honan's evidence for his contention that today's presidents compare poorly to the "Olympians" of earlier eras is superficial and pedestrian. He does not explore the state of the contemporary presidency to any degree or depth. The failure to do so, especially in the public press, only contributes to misimpressions and unfounded perceptions about the leadership of colleges and universities today.

9. I am indebted to my dissertation adviser, Professor William W. Jellema, former president of Wartburg College and professor emeritus of higher education at the University of Connecticut, for the notion that today's presidents do not have more responsibilities than their predecessors. Rather, they are merely distracted by pressure, personal choice, or circumstance and thus emphasize certain tasks such as development and academic management and limit or even eliminate an emphasis on moral voice and leadership.

10. Michael B. Katz, *Reconstructing American Education* (Cambridge, Mass.: Harvard University Press, 1987), p. 180. His assessment is that "Universities are less able than ever to define the ways in which they are distinct from other social institutions, how the principles on which they operate differ from those in business and government, and why they should enjoy special privileges. Therefore the *next great crisis of the university* may not be demographic, fiscal, or organizational. Instead, it *may be moral.*" Italics mine.

11. Commission of the Academic Presidency, *Renewing the Academic Presidency*, (Washington, D.C.: Association of Governing Boards of Universities and Colleges, 1996).

12. A. Bartlett Giamatti, *The University and the Public Interest* (Toronto, Ont.: McClelland and Stewart, 1976), pp. 180–84.

13. Lloyd J. Averill, " 'The Sectarian Nature of Liberal Education," in *Colleges and Commitments*, ed. Lloyd J. Averill and William W. Jellema (Philadelphia: Westminster Press, 1972), p. 75. Italics mine.

14. Henry Rosovsky, *The University: An Owner's Manual* (New York: W. W. Norton, 1990), p. 107. Rosovsky's definition of the "moral" component of education quotes in part Harvard's "Courses of Instruction": " 'significant and recurrent questions of choice and value that arise in human experience'—moral issues that are shared by many religious and philosophical conceptions of mankind." Rosovsky concludes by noting that the authors of "Courses of Instruction," presumably representative Harvard faculty members, add that "the courses are intended to show that it is possible to reflect reasonably (deeply and analytically) about such matters as justice, obligation, citizenship, loyalty, courage, and personal responsibility" (pp. 125–26).

15. Richard L. Morrill, *Teaching Values in College* (San Francisco: Jossey-Bass, 1980). This observation is underscored in a valuable foreword by Theodore Eddy, himself a major university administrator at Penn State and former president of the University of Rhode Island, p. x. For additional insights on the role of the moral basis of applied ethics in college and university leadership, see also Richard L. Morrill, "Academic Planning: Values and Decision Making," in *Ethics and Higher Education*, ed. William W. May (New York: Macmillan, 1990).

16. Morrill, *Teaching Values*, p. 118.

17. Ibid., p. 7.

18. Warren Bryan Martin, "History, Morality, and the Modern University," in *Moral Values and Higher Education: A Notion at Risk*, ed. Dennis L. Thompson (Provo, Utah: Brigham Young University 1991), p. 113, quoting Muller from "At 350, the U.S. University Is Vast but Unfocused," *New York Times*, September 7, 1986. In the newspaper article Muller also makes the provocative statement that "we are very good at training new generations not only to function with what we have discovered but to become discoverers themselves. That's the good news. The bad news is that the university has become godless."

19. Bill Readings, *The University in Ruins* (Cambridge, Mass.: Harvard University Press, 1996), p. 55.

20. Readings's book is part of a recent genre spanning the latter portion of the century that includes works such as Thorstein B. Veblen, *The Higher Learning in America* (New York: Hill and Wang, 1962); Robert Nisbet, *The Degradation of the Academic Dogma* (London: Heinemann, 1971); and more recently Charles Sykes, *ProfScam: Professors and the Demise of Higher Education* (New York: St. Martin's Press, 1988); and Bruce Wilshire, *The Moral Collapse of the University: Professionalism, Purity, and Alienation* (Albany, N.Y.: SUNY Press, 1990); not to mention Alan Bloom's *Closing of the American Mind* (New York: Simon and Schuster, 1987).

21. Clark Kerr and Marian L. Gade, *The Many Lives of Academic Presidents: Time, Place and Character* (Washington, D.C.: Association of Governing Boards of Universities and Colleges, 1986). This study exhaustively reviews the background, the expertise, the allocation of time and energy, and the degree of satisfaction with their positions of a contemporary group of college and university presidents. Not surprisingly, the study reveals the extensive demands on presidents in managing and administering their institutions and constituencies, especially faculty and trustees.

22. Stoke, *American College President*, p. 15. The assumption cannot be made that the "Man of Learning" possessed a strong moral voice or that the "Man of Management" is necessarily devoid of one. However, Stoke, then president of Queens College, clearly contends that the change in the types of individuals who were becoming presidents was both dramatic and fundamental: "If I were to make a general observation about the qualifications of college presidents, it would be this: in recent years the factor of educational distinction has declined while factors of personality, management skills, and successful experience in business and administration have increased in importance. This fact reflects the gradual transformation of the college president from an intellectual leader into a manager, skilled in administration, a broker in personal and public relations."

23. Harold Enarson, "The Ethical Imperative of the College Presidency," *Educational Record* 65, no. 2 (Spring 1984), pp. 24–26. In this argument Enarson makes the following comment, which he believes shifts the ground of the conventional view on the matter of the historical perspectives of the moral voice: "Long ago, Thorstein Veblen gave eloquent voice to the fears of many when he wrote contemptuously of presidents as those 'captains of erudition' chosen to reflect the dominant business values of society. However, both the criticism and the defense of new managers miss the point. The present generation can no more evade or ignore issues of value than could earlier generations of presidents, who unhesitatingly articulated their personal values. Today, such effort is considered by many presidents as unnecessary, undesirable, and/or dangerous—except, of course, in safely conventional terms" (p. 25). Enarson agrees completely with a colleague, James

Laney, in believing that these issues are unavoidable, though he acknowledges that many presidents attempt to avoid them. He also appears to indicate that moral concerns are often addressed only in socially correct and acceptable ways. For Enarson the historical moral imperatives of the college presidency must be understood and fulfilled by contemporary presidents.

24. James Laney, "The Moral Authority of the College or University President," *Educational Record* 65, no. 2 (Spring 1984), pp. 17–19.

25. James Laney, "Through Thick and Thin: Two Ways of Talking About the Academy and Moral Responsibility," in *Ethics and Higher Education*, ed. William W. May (New York: Macmillan, 1990), p. 59.

26. Elwood B. Ehrle and John B. Bennett, *Managing the Academic Enterprise* (New York: Ace, 1988), p. 13.

27. Honan, "Top of the Ivory Tower," p. 5.

2

Presidential Perspectives: The Shape of Their Voice

This is a story of the college presidency, a story of the leadership of women and men who have had the honor of serving as college and university presidents. It is a story of what I call the moral voice of presidents and their leadership on campus and in society. These men and women have inspired generations, and their leadership is a unique feature of education in America. College presidents are guardians of the fundamental purposes of a liberal education. They articulate and define the institutional missions of the colleges and universities they lead. The beliefs and wisdom of presidents have traditionally shaped the culture of colleges and universities and of American society. And college presidents can use the pulpit of leadership to address social and political issues within and beyond the gates of the academy.

Presidents carry out their responsibilities in a dynamic culture influenced by the beliefs, mores, and politics of society and by the expectations of higher education. An array of political, ideological, and philosophical forces continually affect the job of president. These longstanding forces are magnified in the contemporary climate. Even as these influences collaborate to question and limit all moral authority, society always has a need for moral vision and leadership. College and university communities have always expected a moral role for their presidents.

A definitive moment for one president exemplified the crucial importance of moral leadership and voice. This example is from the latter twentieth century and is convincing evidence that the moral voice is not yet a lost quality of the college presidency.

PRESIDENT KEMENY AT DARTMOUTH

John Kemeny was inaugurated president of Dartmouth College on March 1, 1970. Just two months later he confronted the reaction of his campus and of the nation to America's invasion of Cambodia and to the murders of four student protesters at Kent State (and subsequent killings of students at Jackson State). Kemeny, relatively young (in his early forties) and new to his presidency, had no previous college administrative or leadership experience. At Dartmouth he had been only a faculty member in mathematics and an occasional department chair. As it turned out, this moment defined a man and a presidency.

Immediately after hearing of the events at Kent State, Kemeny met throughout the afternoon with students, faculty, and administrators of various political persuasions. Feelings were intense and diverse. Kemeny's consultations enabled him to gauge how the college might respond.

As was customary from the outset of his presidency, Kemeny's weekly interview on the campus radio station was scheduled that evening. He went on the air and extemporaneously addressed the national situation and his decision about what the college would do.[1] Kemeny's thoughts reveal major aspects of presidential leadership and the dilemmas inherent in the bully pulpit.

First, presidents must be deliberate in taking stands on controversial issues. The frequency with which they do has a direct impact on their credibility and authority as leaders. Two other concerns are closely related. One is the extremely fine line between conveying positions as personal opinion and the tendency for any public presidential pronouncement to speak *ipso facto* for the institution. The other is the need to recognize the limits to presidential prerogatives for autocratic action. Presidents should consult, but they must also lead, often without a consensus of support.

Kemeny acknowledges there are few occasions for unilateral presidential action without sacrificing confidence in leadership. The reality is that there are limited opportunities to exert decisiveness on the scale he faced in the spring of 1970. As does any leader, college presidents always have a finite supply of goodwill and moral capital. Kemeny also notes that he has "consistently held over the years that while institutions as such cannot effectively take stands on controversial issues, individuals must take stands. . . . no college president can use this prerogative too often or he loses his effectiveness. And yet events have taken place during the past week which make it impossible for me not to exercise this prerogative."

Second, presidential leadership is closely related to institutional saga.[2] The history and culture of colleges—their mottoes, traditions, and ethos—are critical to the foundation of presidential moral leadership. Presidents contribute to but also benefit from the sagas of their colleges. For example, Kemeny quickly discovered a precedent in Dartmouth's history—the action of trustees in response to the "public distresses of the present day" at the beginning of the Revolutionary War in the summer of 1776—to support his closure of the college. Though mentioning this "minute of the Trustees" almost in passing (and with a sense of irony and calculation), he used it to remind his listeners of another critical time for the college and the country.

Third, presidents are responsible for using the leverage of office to urge students and faculty to assume civic and personal moral responsibility. Much of the hope for the development of a personal moral compass is linked to education. This path begins with information and knowledge. Presidents must defend this fundamental principle governing academic communities. The educational foundation of knowledge and wisdom must not be compromised. Herein lies the source of all informed action.

The academy survives because education can transcend ideologies and orthodoxies as the basis of moral insight and responsibility. Presidents must reflect these principles in rhetoric and action and must expect nothing less of members of their college and university communities. Kemeny could not prescribe or predict the outcome of the education he proposed for the college community. However, he clearly believes that education is an essential ingredient in social and political stands.

Next, the presidential moral voice depends on and embraces the highest ideals of education. These ideals must be maintained even when they are in opposition to institutional expectations about educational mission, social conventions, and political ideologies. At times higher learning can transcend the advertised expectations of the institution yet still reflects its truest educational philosophy.

Kemeny cancels the formal academic program because the campus and the nation must inevitably confront grave issues. The education he urges is more informal but nonetheless critical. Kemeny justifies his action because "there comes a time when there are priorities over and beyond that which we have traditionally considered the fundamental purpose of the institution. . . . all of us will be better educated by the end of the week as a result of this action." The campus community is challenged to transcend conventional education. The agenda is guided by Kemeny's moral authority.

Finally, the moral voice of college presidents is expressed both within and beyond the gates of the academy. Though national and international crises of a scope to prompt or demand presidential comment are not regular occurrences, they are moments requiring moral guidance and direction. Such times call for presidential leadership to assume center stage. Generations of college students have interrupted their education because of civil and world wars. Presidents have led campuses to understand national and world events and to suggest the duty of students. College students at the time of the Kent State tragedy faced their own generational crisis. Kemeny's presidential leadership provided students with perspective and counsel.

Kemeny's urging of educational reflection produced results that even he is unlikely to have envisioned. Weeks later a group of Dartmouth Tuck Business School faculty decided to take a stand about the war. They chose to do so on Wall Street as the symbolic center of corporate involvement in the war. When the faculty members delivered a public statement on the Stock Exchange steps, they were given a vociferous, rude, and physically intimidating reception. The faculty made their own choice, but they were clearly affected by Kemeny's challenge to think about the national crisis.

In this brief talk on the campus station, Kemeny displayed a paradigm of the presidential moral leadership. Though seen here in a time of crisis and drama, the characteristics of this paradigm are fundamental to the college presidency.

This story about the college presidency tells of the complicated demands of colleges and universities and of society. Moral leadership requires inspired vision and courage. The moral voice of presidents shows the ivory tower as much less isolated from the world than is often assumed. Presidents shape institutional missions and educational philosophies. They promote the highest ideals of education and its invaluable contributions to society and the world. And lest this important group be forgotten, presidents serve the education of students. These profiles in courage in the ivory tower are worthy of exploration in any time, especially our own.

GENERAL CHARACTERISTICS OF THE MORAL VOICE

The moral voice and moral leadership of presidents is manifest in both rhetoric and action. President George Rupp of Columbia justly criticizes rhetoric detached from the actions of leadership as little more than "public posturing on moral issues."[3] Many factors shape how presidents lead and what they speak about in the complex environment of campus and society. Understanding these factors is essential in understanding the college presidency and its responsibilities.

First, presidents do not have unlimited autonomy and authority. Some limitations create curious paradoxes in the roles presidents must assume. As public figures, college and university leaders are expected to make thoughtful public statements. They are expected, often even selected, to speak from the passion of their hearts and the wisdom of their intellects. However, as with all leaders, the realities and responsibilities of position place real restrictions on the latitude to speak freely of their beliefs.

Presidents constantly confront this dilemma. President Thomas Gerety of Amherst acknowledges that "personal views need to take second place to those views which should be associated with approval and with general support across the constituencies as the views of the institution."[4] But this admission creates its own predicaments.

In theory we believe presidents should be thinkers. We want them to have independent philosophies and views. Some of the best candidates for presidencies are those who possess dynamic reputations as advocates for principles and ideas important to higher education and society. Any inhibition to speak on important matters as presidents contradicts these attractive and desirable qualities.

In order to have presidents who publicly engage beliefs and commitments, trustees, governing boards, and search committees must select leaders who possess these traits. Presidents must have freedom to speak, certainly to be used with great care and discretion, on issues important to campus and society. Without latitude for their voice, moral leadership in the ivory tower is silenced.

Presidents are the major symbolic public figures representing colleges. Unquestionably presidents regularly face the possibility that key stakeholders—donors, potential donors, influential alumni—will be displeased with public presidential positions. Former Brown University president Vartan Gregorian notes that unpopular presidential positions can negatively affect fundraising endeavors when key constituencies become alienated.[5] However, these constituencies should not, on the basis of perceived power, be permitted to compromise and limit presidential moral authority.

The concerns of constituents can be addressed both seriously and pragmatically. To do so, leadership must be attentive to the mainstream interests of the institution. Thus, presidents must balance being educational leaders with the necessities of enlightened politics. This consideration does not mean that they cannot make statements on moral grounds.

There is a question about whether restrictions on presidential leadership are more substantial and intrusive at public than at private colleges and universities. Certainly publicly supported institutions are highly complex and political. The former president of the University of Michigan, James Duderstadt, contends that his job is "on the line" with much greater frequency than are those of colleagues at private institutions. He cites a constant concern about the effect of public statements on the support of his board of regents.[6] This eight-person board is elected by the Michigan citizenry. Recent changes in the social, political, and cultural climate has increasingly politicized the regents' governance of the university. The effect is a significant complication of the Michigan presidency.

Presidents at major private institutions would likely disagree with Duderstadt. They face pressure from constituencies such as alumni, who are often more zealous and influential at private than at public colleges. However, private college and university presidents generally do enjoy sound relationships with their governing bodies. Indeed, private boards are much less in thrall to the political sentiments of the citizenry than are their public counterparts.

Overall, the much more volatile environment of public higher education presents more difficulties for presidential leadership than the environment of independent colleges. But presidents at both public and private institutions do not have unlimited freedom of moral leadership. Both must weigh the cost of public statements on moral issues, especially those on which there is no consensus in or outside the university.

Edward Malloy, president of Notre Dame, has had several major university presidents confide their envy of his freedom as a priest and president of a major religious university to address moral issues. These presidents experience the opposite: no expectation that they take moral positions. This inhibition is coupled with an often unspoken, yet clear, dictum that breaking silence will create difficulties for their leadership.[7] Certainly, Malloy could be viewed as having his freedom restricted by the expectation that he must take certain moral stands.

Very real pressures force presidents to be extremely careful when taking potentially controversial moral stands. Given these pressures, presidents' frequent and full use of their moral voice is all the more remarkable.

A second characteristic of presidential leadership is its capacity to present moral issues to constituents and citizens. There is great concern today about the lack of meaning and spiritual significance in people's lives. The question is rightly asked that if a president will not stand up, who will? Harold Shapiro, who has been president at both the University of Michigan and Princeton University, believes presidents must use their moral capacity to stress the need for meaningfulness in life and for a more profound sense of common humanity. In his last remarks as president of the University of Michigan, he suggests that citizens can help the country face moral and ethical challenges by "reestablishing a sense of moral significance to our lives. . . . that our material progress be invested with meaning and moral significance."[8]

The presidential pulpit is a platform for presenting critical moral concerns to campus (as well as the broader) communities. But doing so is inevitably a choice for presidents, and this choice to speak forthrightly and publicly is made mindful of the limitations on presidential authority.

Shortly after becoming president of Dartmouth in 1987, James Freedman faced such a dilemma regarding the use of his moral authority against forces perceived to wield great power and influence. The *Dartmouth Review*, a polemically conservative student publication not associated with the college, was supported by vocal conservative alumni and friends, including influential national figures such as William Simon, Patrick Buchanan, and William F. Buckley. Since its inception in the early 1980s, the paper issued ad hominem attacks on the political leanings, sexual orientation, and personal lives of many administrators, faculty, and students. The editors also regularly decried the college's continual "liberal" positions.

In this case the *Review* personally attacked Freedman in a front page story, "Ein Reich, Ein Volk, Ein Freedman." The story alleged that conservative students were in the middle of the night being herded onto trains and taken away from the campus.

As president and a man of the Jewish faith, Freedman believed he must make a public statement about The *Review*. He addressed a gathering of nearly three thousand members of the campus community on the Dartmouth Green rallied in opposition to the paper and its tactics. Freedman assailed the *Review* staff for their failures in journalistic responsibility. Trained in the law, he drew a line between freedom of speech and freedom of the press. Outlining the standards to which journalists are accountable, he condemned the actions of the students involved with the newspaper, but not their right to publish. Freedman judges the *Review* and encourages others to join his opposition, but he does so in open debate about free speech, a free press, and the responsibilities of the press and the public.

A third factor shaping presidential moral rhetoric is the search for truth in the academic life. Some academicians argue that the discovery and knowledge of facts is not truth in an ultimate sense. Their view is that education is concerned exclusively with scholarly truth, narrowly defined as the search for knowledge by objective inquiry.

Thus, there is a tension between those notions of truth which presidents must negotiate as they exercise moral leadership. Within the gates of the academy and to faculty colleagues, presidential rhetoric often includes ideas about ultimate truth as well as traditional scholarly learning. At times, presidents underscore the ways in which educational philosophies, the educational experience of students, and the journey of the life of the mind must entail "larger truths." These are fundamental educational principles with which presidents are conversant. For example, Diana Chapman Walsh, president of Wellesley, argues that the moral truths of academic exploration remain hidden by exclusive reliance on traditional assumptions about knowledge and scholarship.[9] Her predecessor, Nannerl O. Keohane, makes the classic argument that the liberal arts produce a liberation of the mind, which in turn leads to a pluralistic understanding of the variety of moral truths.[10]

A final major element of the moral voice of presidents is its emphasis on the personal meaning and moral nature of the individual self. Historically in the West, the relationship of the moral self to life's meaning has been closely connected to Judeo-Christian beliefs. In the search for truth, presidents have cautioned against separating faith and spirituality from the pursuit of knowledge. John Dickey's insistence that education demands competence and conscience is one of the most famous of this genre. Dickey is by no means alone. Decades before, President Caroline Hazard of Wellesley College noted that "trained mind without a reverent spirit is a dangerous product."[11] Nearly a century later in the more secular language of her day, Keohane claims that students must "develop *a strong sense of ethics and personal integrity*."[12]

Religious schools and colleges have exhibited a desire and ability to combine (some would argue always unsatisfactorily) spirituality and faith with the quest for knowledge. However, as Hazard and others warned at the turn of the century, society stands at peril when religious affections wane or die. Many social and cultural critics today issue similar warnings. A major contemporary challenge for presidents is to develop language incorporating spiritual aspects in educational philosophies.

As noted in Kemeny's example and will be seen later in more detail, institutional saga is a valuable platform for the moral voice of presidents. Wellesley College's presidents make full use their motto, *Non ministrari, sed ministrare*: Not to be ministered unto, but to minister. This motto confirms the need to develop the moral self through a call to service in the lives of students.

Preparing students morally for life in the world is a special task of college presidents. In earlier eras, presidents directly touched student's lives through senior seminars in applied ethics and intimate involvement in campus life and discipline. But this task still remains today, often as territory needing to be recharted by presidents. Education must incorporate ethics and the moral demands of human existence. This sense of moral purpose enables students to make the choices and decisions expected of educated people and leaders in the world. Presidents are able to nurture actively this aspect of students' lives.

RELIGIOUS AND MORAL FOUNDATIONS: PRESIDENTIAL REFLECTIONS

In different eras the presidents of Columbia, Notre Dame, Michigan, and Amherst offer distinct yet complementary positions regarding the religious and moral foundations of educational philosophy. With a gap of only seven years the leadership of three presidents, James Angell of Michigan (1871–1909), Nicholas Murray Butler of Columbia (1902–1945), and Theodore Hesburgh of Notre Dame (1952–1987) span over a century. Harold Shapiro of Michigan, Edward Malloy of Notre Dame, and Peter Pouncey of Amherst add their presidential perspective from the mid-twentieth century to the present.

Nicholas Murray Butler at Columbia

Considered one of the giants among college and university presidents, Butler's tenure at Columbia was long and prolific. He embraces the tradition of John Cardinal Newman in arguing for the role of religion and theology in education. Like Newman, Butler believes that theology belongs in the curriculum. He goes even further, contending that the absence of religion leads to an incomplete and unfulfilling education.

Ever the pragmatist, Butler interprets the value of theology and theological education to the university in two ways. First, he is aware of the rapidly increasing impact of scientific and technological progress. Darwinian thinking was largely responsible for the advent of critical biblical scholarship. For Butler, these developments demanded a sophisticated theological education that the rigorous academic and scholarly environment of the university could provide.[13] This required a fruitful connection of theological schools to the educational life at Columbia and other major universities. In light of contemporary concern about ethics, this relationship between theological education and the other academic disciplines and the center of the university is urgently needed.

Second, Butler understands the importance of religion and spirituality to character formation. He does not emphasize institutional religious belief and practice. Rather, his concern is with the critical role of religious orientation, a fundamental sense of ethics, and a comprehension of the place of faith and belief. Butler believes that though the "heart is the ultimate aim of all religious appeals.

... the heart is most easily reached by informing the intellect and fashioning the will."[14] Religious knowledge is instrumental in the formation of character. Religious affections inspire the education of the heart and the will. And these affections are integral to the development of knowledge, conscience, ethics, and conduct—the formation of the student's personality and character. Aware of the historically painful results of religious zealotry, Butler acknowledges that religions have on occasion contributed to evil and immorality, and that "to confuse religion with ethics is to obscure both."[15]

In many ways Butler is truly visionary. In 1902 at the dedication of Earl Hall as the center of religious life at Columbia University, Butler criticizes compelled religious observances (maybe thinking of mandatory chapel). However, he affirms a catholicity of religious practice worthy of contemporary multireligious campus life. He argues that while "Compulsory religion and compulsory philanthropy are of little avail either as motives or as ideals. . . . Earl Hall is, like the University whose instrument it is, truly catholic. Here religion will not be coupled with any particular creed or with any special formula."[16]

A noted national figure in education, Butler courageously uses his moral voice to insist on the cultural importance and vital place of religion in education. For example, he believes the Bible to be crucial to an understanding of Christian civilization.[17] At the beginning of the twentieth century there was concern about erosion of the Bible's value and of its relationship to the future of civilization. In an assessment pertinent to today's world, Butler blames the clash among factions within Christianity and their inability to agree upon interpretation for driving the Bible out of schools and for reducing it as a reference point of knowledge.[18]

Butler decried what he calls the "new paganism." His fear is "that in setting free the individual human being from those external restraints and compulsions which constitute tyranny, he has also been set free from those internal restraints and compulsions which distinguish liberty from license."[19] A religious and moral foundation is the way to balance liberty and necessary limitations on freedom.

In a classical religious response to existentialism and nihilism, Butler claims that "the fool who says in his heart 'There is no God' really means there is no God but himself. His supreme egotism, his colossal vanity, have placed him at the center of the universe which is thereafter to be measured and dealt with in terms of his personal satisfactions."[20] The great moral hope of education is its challenge to individuals to transcend personal wants and needs.

The profound salvific purpose of education is to overcome the ills of the world, to nurture good and oppose evil.[21] It is a philosophy, almost a theology, of education at the foundation of the presidential moral voice.

Later in his presidency, Butler reiterates and expands on these themes. Engaging in a long-standing debate, he maintains the conviction that particular religious and other claims of beliefs should coexist with the educational enterprise in the university.

Butler embraces an ideal of the mission of the university similar to that argued

by Kenneth Minogue.[22] Minogue believes the institutional foundation of the
university must be sustained in a fashion allowing transient ideologies to be
debated without being permitted to gain superiority or control. Minogue feared
the control of the academy by uncontested ideologies. Influenced by events of
the 1960s on campuses in America and Great Britain (where he taught),
Minogue worried that political and other ideologies threatened the very foundation of the university.

However, in the less cynical era earlier this century, Butler is more optimistic
than Minogue about the fortunes of the university. Butler's university is strong
enough to embrace the conflict aroused by a diversity of ideas. Less than half
a century later, Minogue believes the (increasingly) strong force of ideologies
were overwhelming and destroying the university.

Butler's expectation of the university is an important reminder today as we
witness the prevalent battles of multiculturalism and diversity. His notion is that
the university is the institution of society for debate about conflicting viewpoints.
He adds, and this may be lost today, that dialogue among diverse beliefs—
Minogue's ideologies—must be conducted with sincerity, openness, and mutual
acceptance of a commitment to the search for truth. For Butler, "[t]he unhappy
and conflicting diversity of religious beliefs, and the unhappy and conflicting
diversity of social and political theories, find their reconciliation and their unity
in the university, whose frame is so secure, so broad and so generous that there
is room in it for each and all of these *if only they be held in sincerity and
pursued in a spirit of truth-seeking and of service.*"[23]

At least in the university, unlike other arenas of society, differing political,
religious, cultural, and racial beliefs must be debated absent presumptions of
monopolizing truth. Minogue agrees in principle, but he is afraid that the up-
heaval of the 1960s eroded the framework and character of the university to the
point of collapse.

Minogue's contention creates a distinct challenge for college and university
presidents of the latter twentieth and the twenty first centuries. Presidents must
lead in regaining and reaffirming free and open debate in the academy. This is
important ground to be defended. And presidents must regularly remind constituents that no individual or group monopolizes the truth. Presidents must
assure commitment to dialogue among conflicting, even hostile, forces. This
quest is fundamental to the university and is its distinctive characteristic as an
institution of society.

Theodore Hesburgh and Edward Malloy at Notre Dame

Roman Catholic schools and colleges have made great and lasting contributions to the American educational landscape. Their leaders, in this case Notre
Dame presidents Theodore Hesburgh and his successor, Edward Malloy, have
been in the forefront of linking religious mores to educational philosophies.

For example, Hesburgh stipulates a foundation of religious values for Catholic and other Christian colleges. Before a sympathetic audience of educators from church-related institutions of higher education, Hesburgh argues that even "the most dedicated secular humanists" are incapable of incorporating values in education without attention to "the religious realities of faith in man as a child of God and follower of Christ, without prayer, without pondering our profound need of divine grace if we are to transcend our innate selfishness and self-centeredness."[24]

While many secular humanists would disagree with parts of Hesburgh's "religious realities," they would likely concur with his concern about the role of education in overcoming human selfishness. Hesburgh believes the world requires educated people who are prepared to change and improve society. The goal for educators is to "give a vision of truth, a zest for the pursuit of truth . . . to educate persons really capable of shaping the future, not dull and drab practitioners of what is and has been and needs changing."[25]

As his presidential tenure continued, Hesburgh became revered as a "dean" of higher education. With that status he addressed educators at the first joint meeting of the Association of Universities and Colleges of Canada and the American Council on Education. He acknowledges the unpopularity of his position, that universities "consider transcendent virtues like the true, the good, the beautiful, and the moral imperatives that flow from them."[26] These are prerequisite principles of an educational philosophy. And they present a personal challenge for educators. That is, their ability to address the moral dilemmas of human existence is critical to the education they offer students.

But Hesburgh and his successor, Malloy, faced their own difficult task of maintaining Notre Dame's rich and longstanding traditions—its powerful institutional saga—in an ever-changing contemporary era. In celebrating its one hundred fiftieth year, Malloy acknowledges that Notre Dame is a dramatically different institution from that founded by Father Edward Sorin. But he affirms unchanging core assumptions in the Notre Dame education. Among these are human "worth and dignity," "stewardship," and "the sense of beauty" in a world that Malloy views as "God-created" and "God-charged."[27] For Notre Dame students, religion critically influences the expectations of academic and personal life, and of service in the world.

Given its religious heritage, Notre Dame's leaders must be concerned about the university's identity. Malloy pursues the complicated task of maintaining its religious character in an increasingly pluralistic and secular age. He believes that Notre Dame's Roman Catholic character, what he contends is "its greatest and irreplaceable strength" cannot be sustained "without a core group of committed and informed Catholic faculty." Recognizing that the institution will have non-Catholics on the faculty as well, he quickly adds that his stance "does not presuppose a monolithic view of Catholicism." Malloy's educational philosophy and his philosophy of presidential leadership is defined by the assumption that "personal religious identities make a difference, or should, in every dimension of our lives, including our professional responsibilities."[28]

Hesburgh's and Malloy's concerns are much like those of turn-of-the-century presidents in their expression of the need to sustain Christian or at least some religious foundation in their institutions.

James Angell and Harold Shapiro at Michigan

More than a hundred years earlier, James Angell's view of the place of religion was more comprehensive than is normally associated with public universities. Like the warnings sounded by others of his day, Angell was concerned about the erosion of Christian influence on colleges and universities and about the decline in the number of students preparing for careers in ministry.

Angell became the president of a relatively new, publicly supported university already of significant reputation. His rhetorical question was whether state and public universities should have the same deeply rooted concern for religious and Christian purposes as their older denominational college counterparts. In contrast to the appearance of what a public university president can do today, Angell spoke freely about the relationship of the Christian faith to his and other institutions. Angell noted that state institutions were founded and their establishment guided by religious men. He professed that he was "not aware, that in any important particular during its existence, the administration of the College [Michigan] in respect to the moral and religious character of the students has differed from that of the so-called denominational Colleges."[29] Angell's perspective was that regardless of type of school, the essential work of those responsible for colleges and universities remained to ensure that "the life and instruction of the Colleges [is] imbued with a positive Christian spirit."[30] Angell believed that if a positive, symbiotic relationship between the colleges and Christianity was diminishing, then there was cause for genuine concern.[31]

After citing the senior year courses offered by major college and university presidents such as James McCosh at Princeton, John Bascom at Wisconsin, Julius H. Seelye at Amherst, and Ezekial Gilman Robinson at Brown as "the very best corrective young men can have of extreme scientific tendencies of speculative thought," Angell asserted that "whatever science may have to reveal to us of God's truth, we may be sure that it will be reconcilable with Christian truth."[32] Like Butler and other contemporaries, Angell appealed to John Cardinal Newman's contention that Christian (and presumably other religious) beliefs must encounter the tests of scientific methods and thought.

In the closing decades of the nineteenth century, presidents were characteristically unapologetic about religion and religious tradition. However, the Christian founding and purpose of many colleges and universities began to be replaced by new, more dominant secular intentions. The fundamental evolution of secularity and pluralism affected institutional philosophies and purposes. This transition has greatly influenced the moral voice of presidents.

The leadership of contemporary presidents such as Harold Shapiro is affected by this dramatic evolution. After serving as president at Michigan, Shapiro took the helm at Princeton. His inaugural address is a dialogue with his predecessors about tradition and change.[33] This "conversation" with the likes of McCosh and Wilson about the moral fundamentals in individual and university life highlights differences in language and social mores. However, Shapiro's exercise also reveals that the leaders of Princeton in previous generations did not always arrive at perfect answers to pressing problems. These presidents could resort to religious and social assumptions embedded in the culture of their day. Shapiro acknowledges that the solutions of previous eras rarely suffice for succeeding generations. But his address reveals each generation's struggle to address issues of tradition, civility, social cohesion, and change. Shapiro's conversation mirrors the search of contemporary university presidents for the common language and principles essential for a public moral vision.

Peter Pouncey at Amherst

Despite these changes, contemporary presidents use religious and moral principles to create educational philosophies. In his second convocation address, continuing a tradition of Amherst presidents, Peter Pouncey relates a conversation he had with the mother of a prospective student. The mother's worry was that her son would lose his faith at a nonsectarian school such as Amherst. She feared, not incorrectly, that even religion courses would "not teach the truth as truth."

Pouncey's reply is based on personal experience that he believes to be nearly universally shared. Pouncey's early education was at Jesuit institutions in England. It concluded with undergraduate studies at Heythrop and Campion Hall, the Jesuit house of studies at Oxford. In an interview Pouncey says that "his religious beliefs ran up against the 'analytic philosophy' at Oxford—an outlook that is 'agnostic and positivist in tone'—with the result that his 'explicitly religious beliefs came under sharper scrutiny and did not hold up.' "[34] Pouncey's philosophy is that religion cannot avoid encountering the critical domain of intellectual and scholarly pursuit. From that personal experience Pouncey knows that the outcome for one's religion and faith is never certain or assured.

Pouncey addresses this encounter of religious belief with educational inquiry. His conclusion is that the rigors of academia may test formally held beliefs. The good result is that students "would either have confidence in the strength of their beliefs, or else be induced, by correction or qualification, to move them to surer ground."[35] Reflecting on the conversation with the student's mother, Pouncey asserts the continual requirement of the academy for precise thinking that resists "the assumption that truth is something simple, easily stated in a formula or dogma, easily assimilated, and not subject to argument among the reasonable."[36]

Pouncey also believes that religion plays an essential role in the search for truth. He expresses fear for colleges and individuals that if truth is assumed to be unknowable, "the danger is that the point of balance may become a bland

and neutral place, until it represents a studied uncommitment to any conviction at all." For Pouncey the most damaging charge "is not that one is sub-religious, but rather more comprehensively sub-human—that one holds one's intellect poised, but allows all the vital forces of passion and will and creative imagination to atrophy with disuse."[37] Though not pressing a specific Christian belief as might Hesburgh and Malloy, Pouncey believes that convictions, even if not conventionally viewed as religious, are absolutely necessary to the educated life.

Certainly, there is a real danger when the assumptions of religious belief create a refusal to engage education and intellectual inquiry. However, the same could be said of any ideology.[38] What Pouncey rejects is education as a comfortable, middle-ground experience lacking elements of commitment, passion, and change.

THE MORAL BASIS OF THE LIBERAL ARTS

Philosophical discussion about the liberal arts invariably leads to thoughts about the moral aspects of education. Presidential rhetoric is no exception. Presidents advocate the view of education as more than the acquisition of knowledge and the use of information. Ethics and values are an instrumental part of learning, and education encourages the search for meaning.

Because of their comprehensiveness and research orientation, major universities are often believed to deemphasize the liberal arts. But two recent presidents of Michigan contradict this impression.

Shapiro affirms the liberal arts as crucial to the foundation of a civilized society. Liberating individuals and broadening understanding is a moral purpose. Traditionally, and especially in the early twenty-first century, the liberal arts stand as an antidote against the influence of ideology and as a bulwark for civil discourse. In Shapiro's words, the liberal arts function "to substitute reason for instinct and deliberativeness for impetuosity . . . liberat[ing] us from unfounded judgments, from parochial understandings, and from intemperate convictions."[39]

Following his predecessor's lead, James Duderstadt in his inauguration underscores this classical interpretation of the value of the liberal arts.[40] Duderstadt says that undergraduate education at Michigan cannot be "simply aimed at extracting knowledge from the vast information characterizing our society. . . . [T]he goal of any liberal education must be to help our students learn how to extract wisdom from knowledge—and through that wisdom, prepare them to learn the art of life itself. . . . We must enable our undergraduates to find the wisdom in knowledge . . . and hence to find the life that is in living."[41]

Tom Gerety also advocates this connection of the liberal arts to freedom and liberation. Of particular concern is the contemporary climate in which, with increasing frequency, unchallenged prejudice produces tension and division. As an ideal, the moral task of the liberal arts is to free students from this prejudice, what Gerety defines as *"judgment in advance* of persons or ideas: rash unthinking conviction held against evidence and without discussion, without inquiry or reflection."[42] The educational inquiry promoted by the liberal arts is an essential foundation for students to learn how to function in the world. The campus is a laboratory in which ideas are tested in an environment of free inquiry. The moral prospect is a "spirit of inquiry" for students in which they "learn to be confident not so much of their answers as of their questions."[43]

Agreeing with Shapiro, Gerety believes that prejudice is overcome through openness to new ideas. The use of new information is a prescription for avoiding rigidity and orthodoxy. Conversely, all orthodoxies are equally dangerous and equally antithetical to the purposes of a liberal arts. Thus, presidents must exert great care when using the bully pulpit. Gerety's philosophy of education determines his actions as president. His exhortation to himself and by extension to all presidents is that "if my eloquent speech makes it seem as if there is only one attractive position, in my case a liberal orthodoxy, that is really erosive and corrosive of what these campuses are about. The core, the kernel of truth about political correctness is that orthodoxies are always tempting to human beings in groups and singly."[44]

The liberal arts are an invaluable but not foolproof asset against contemporary prescriptions about politically correct and hypersensitive responses to social issues. While conceding that there are right and wrong answers, Gerety invokes the prescient comments of John Stuart Mill about the "strong human tendency 'to extend the bounds of what may be called moral police, until it encroaches on the most unquestionably legitimate liberty of the individual.' " In this vein we must even be able to face the question of "whether the tradition of the liberal arts is itself stifling or repressive. . . . we . . . [can]not shy from that question either, lest we shy from the goal we set ourselves."[45]

Hesburgh's moral basis in the liberal arts develops from classical notions— including Newman's on the study of theology—that specific academic subjects possess the capacity to produce meaning and to develop moral thinking. He criticizes the impact of German universities on American higher education and the influence of scientific methods on educational philosophy. Entering the debate about objectivity versus subjectivity in education, Hesburgh contends that the presumption that science is "value-free" produces a world seriously devoid of humanity and meaning.[46] He warns of the danger inherent in conceiving the university as value-neutral. Colleges and universities are thus challenged "to reestablish the centrality of such subjects as philosophy and theology, literature and history, art and music, and the inevitable value content of political science, economics, anthropology and sociology."[47] The liberal arts are an obvious solution to an overly scientific and value-less education.

Contemporary presidents rely on classical defenses of the liberal arts as one way to underscore the moral fabric of education. Even Duderstadt's description of Michigan as an educational conglomerate,[48] includes the value of the morality embedded in the liberal arts tradition. In the absence of the moral language that

their predecessors had been able to use, today's presidents are able to highlight
the importance of ethics and values by connecting the liberal arts to moral
principles.

EDUCATION AND THE PURSUIT OF THE GOOD

Presidents also link education to the pursuit of the "good." For Hesburgh this
is an obligation of the university and its leadership. Conflating traditional categories, Hesburgh argues that the university is "dedicated to discovering and
transmitting truth—but too long we have harbored a false dichotomy between
the true and the good." His conclusion is that educators cannot "be effective
champions of the truth without some commitment to the good." To the contrary,
the gravely glaring historical example is "Nazi Germany when great universities
allowed themselves to be prostituted to inhumanity in the name of moral neutrality." Prescient about the difficulties of the 1960s, Hesburgh urges fellow
university leaders to be "unafraid to speak out whether it is popular or not,
knowing where we stand and why, unashamed of our moral, as well as our
intellectual, commitment."[49]

Malloy includes faculty as leaders of the university. The development of character in students results not only from the intentions of the curriculum, but also
from the active engagement of faculty. Professors must acknowledge "that ethics
is more than a field of specialization; it is at the heart of our professional commitments and responsibilities."[50] Faculty action on this charge underscores the
place of the ethical good in the university and as a primary purpose of the
students' education. Though universal acceptance of this position is unlikely,
presidents should always encourage debate about the place of values in the
university.

Michael Sovern of Columbia highlights the role of values in the university
in a slightly different way. Outlining a litany of twentieth-century problems,
Sovern contends that "a great challenge for us as teachers is: what shall we do
about the multitudes for whom god is no longer solace but for whom reason is
not enough?. . . . How shall we help them to an ethical system not braced by
hell-fire and brimstone?"[51] While Sovern mourns the loss of belief in God and
the reduced optimism in the perfectibility of humankind, his fundamental question has bearing on moral leadership: are there moral and ethical guideposts in
the university? The essential educational problem is that "Truth seems obtain-
able, definitive. Goodness is elusive, debatable. . . . In an era in which confused
voices impatiently cry for relevance, asking what is good may seem beside the
point."[52]

Sovern is both humble and realistic. His concerns are simple. Acknowledging
that "classrooms are not pulpits," Sovern urges educators to treat the search for
the good as integral to education and therefore that education includes discussion
of ethics and morality. Recognizing its limitations, the task of education is to

challenge students to think, to temper the arrogance of knowledge, and to promote wisdom and the good.

This chapter has outlined the themes and characteristics of presidential moral leadership. In later chapters we will hear the concerns of presidents about the moral basis of education and of the liberal arts, and about involvement in the educational life of students. But first we turn in the next chapter to the moral voice and leadership of presidents in institutional mission and purpose.

NOTES

1. The quotes that follow are taken from Jean Kemeny, *It's Different at Dartmouth* (Brattleboro, Vt: Stephen Greene Press, 1979), pp. 22–24. The complete text as published in her book is worth reading in its entirety. This speech is also published in its entirety in A. Alexander Fanelli, *John Kemeny Speaks* (Hanover, N.H.: Dartmouth College, 1999).

2. Burton R. Clark, *The Distinctive College: Antioch, Reed and Swarthmore* (Chicago: Aldine, 1970). Clark coined the term *saga* as applied to colleges and universities. He describes colleges with sagas as those that develop over time an intentionality about institutional life, which then results in unifying the institution and shaping its purpose as a saga. Clark's view is that "An organizational legend (or saga), located between ideology and religion, partakes of an appealing logic on one hand and sentiments similar to the spiritual on the other" (p. 235).

3. Personal interview with President George Rupp of Columbia University, November 16, 1994. Ellipses have been omitted from all interview citations in the interest of readability. In no case has language or commentary been excised that would have altered the speaker's intent.

4. Personal interview with President Thomas Gerety of Amherst College, July 27, 1994. Elaborating on this idea, Gerety states that presidential utterances "ought in principle to be compatible with the widest possible range of opinions and views on the campus. If the president has strong views on abortion, those views should not be seen as inhibiting students and faculty from having directly opposing or different views on abortion."

5. William H. Honan, "At the Top of the Ivory Tower the Watchword Is Silence," *New York Times*, July 24, 1994.

6. Personal interview with President James J. Duderstadt of the University of Michigan, March 6, 1995.

7. Personal interview with President Edward Malloy, C.S.C., of the Notre Dame University, September 20, 1994.

8. Harold Shapiro, commencement address, December 20, 1987, Harold T. Shapiro Collection, Ann Arbor Commencements, Michigan Historical Collections, Bentley Historical Library, University of Michigan, Box 177, p. 8. Hereafter, Shapiro Collection.

9. Diana Chapman Walsh, inaugural panel at Simmons College, November 5, 1993, p. 5.

10. Nannerl O. Keohane, "The Liberal Arts Today," Rotary Club of Boston, March 2, 1983, Wellesley Archives, Keohane Speeches, 1981–1985, p. 2. Hereafter, Keohane Speeches.

11. Caroline Hazard, 1910 Annual Report, Wellesley College, *Annual Reports*, 1905–1913, Wellesley College Archives, p. 5. Hereafter, Wellesley *Annual Reports*. It is interesting to note the concern of some early twentieth-century presidential commentators about the waning of religious commitment in the life of the nation. An example taken up later in this chapter, James Cavanaugh, "The Religious Life of the Student," University of Notre Dame Archives (UNDA), Notre Dame Early President's Records (UPEL), Box 10, undated, pp. 8–9, hereafter, UND Archives; and James B. Angell, "The Relation of the American Colleges to Christianity," *Quarterly Review of the Evangelical Lutheran Church* 7, no. 1 (January 1878), p. 66.

12. Nannerl O. Keohane, "The Women of the 90s: How Should They Be Educated?" November 15, 1990, Keohane Speeches, 1986–1990, p. 4.

13. Nicholas Murray Butler, essay in the *Churchman*, July 25, 1902, pp 1–2. Columbia University, Rare Book and Manuscript Library, Miscellaneous Addresses and Articles by Nicholas Murray Butler, vol. 1, no. 41, p. 2. Hereafter, Misc. Butler Addresses.

14. Butler, "Religious Instruction in Education," *Educational Review*, December 1899, p. 436, in Columbia University, Rare Book and Manuscript Library, Nicholas Murray Butler Speeches, vol. 1. Hereafter, Butler Speeches. This address was given on October 14, 1899.

15. Ibid., pp. 432–33.

16. Butler, Remarks at the dedication of Earl Hall, March 8, 1902, Butler Speeches, vol. 3, no. 35, p. 2.

17. Butler, "Some Pressing Problems," July 1902, Butler Speeches, vol. 1, no. 38, p. 71.

18. Ibid., p. 73.

19. Butler,"Making Liberal Men and Women: Public Criticism of Present-Day Education, the New Paganism, and the University, Politics and Religion," Butler Speeches, vol. 5, no. 8, p. 12.

20. Idem.

21. Butler's belief is that through education "the heart and mind of man [are] brought back to a comprehension of the real meaning of faith and its place in life. This cannot be done by exhortation or by preaching alone. It must be done also by teaching; careful, systematic, rational teaching, that will show in a simple language which the uninstructed can understand what are the essentials of a permanent and lofty morality, of a stable and just social order, and of a secure and sublime religious faith" (Ibid., p. 13).

22. Kenneth Minogue, *The Concept of a University* (Berkeley: University of California Press, 1973).

23. Butler, "The Mission of the Modern University," November 10, 1923, Butler Speeches, vol. 6, no. 40, pp. 5–6. Italics mine.

24. Theodore Hesburgh, "Reflections on a Church-Related University," June 21, 1979, UND Archives, Theodore Hesburgh Speeches, 1968–1987, Box 142/14, pp. 6–7.

25. Hesburgh, address to the general faculty, October 4, 1983, UND Archives, Theodore Hesburgh Speeches, 1968–1987, Box 142/20, p. 12.

26. Hesburgh, "The Moral Dimensions of Higher Education," October 13, 1983, UND Archives, Theodore Hesburgh Speeches, 1968–1987, Box 142/20, pp. 6–7.

27. Edward Malloy, Sesquicentennial opening Mass homily, President's Office, University of Notre Dame, September 15, 1991, p. 4.

28. Edward Malloy, address to the faculty, October 1, 1991, pp. 14–15. Malloy's approach supports Mark Schwehn's contention that personal faith needs to be taken

seriously in the academy—its institutions and philosophies—and in the learning process. See Mark R. Schwehn, *Exiles from Eden: Religion and the Academic in America* (Oxford, Eng.: Oxford University Press, 1993).

29. James B. Angell, "The Relation of the American Colleges to Christianity," *Quarterly Review of the Evangelical Lutheran Church* 7, no. 1 (January 1878), pp. 76–77. This article was initially presented as a speech to the United States Evangelical Alliance. For a detailed account of the religious aspects of Angell's and his two immediate predecessors' presidencies, see Victor Roy Wilbee, "The Religious Dimensions of Three Presidencies at University of Michigan," Ph.D. diss, University of Michigan, 1967).

30. Angell, p. 66.

31. Ibid., p. 67.

32. Ibid., pp. 73–74.

33. Harold T. Shapiro, "Tradition, Continuity, Discovery, and Change: A Conversation with Princeton's Past" (inaugural address), President's Office, Princeton University, January 8, 1988, pp. 1–12.

34. "The College: Former Columbia Dean to Be President," *Amherst Graduates Quarterly* 36, no. 1 (Summer 1983), p. 5.

35. Peter Pouncey, convocation address, September 5, 1985, pp. 1–2, Peter Pouncey Biographical File (N/A), Archives and Special Collections, Amherst College Library.

36. Ibid., p. 2.

37. "The College," pp. 8–9.

38. This comment acknowledges Kenneth Minogue's thought in *The Concept of a University* about the role of ideology, its anti-intellectuality, and its corrosive and antithetical effect on the aims of education and the purpose of the university.

39. Harold Shapiro, "The Culture of the Intellect and the Culture of the Heart," May 11, 1985, Harold T. Shapiro Collection, Commencement Addresses—External, Michigan Historical Collections, Bentley Historical Library, University of Michigan, Box 177, pp. 7–8. Hereafter, Shapiro Addresses—External. Shapiro's recurrent concern with moral significance and changing concepts of morals and ethics in education are expressed in great detail in his presidential inaugural address at Princeton, "Tradition, Continuity, Discovery, and Change: Conversations with Princeton's Past," noted previously.

40. In an interview, Duderstadt noted the demands on his time and the difficulty of concentrating on the undergraduate life, commenting (almost regrettably) "as president of the university, while I certainly have and should have a concern for the quality and nature of undergraduate education that we provide our students, I also must be concerned about the quality and nature of the medical care we provide almost a million patients a year." Personal interview with President James J. Duderstadt of the University of Michigan, March 6, 1995.

41. James J. Duderstadt, student inauguration luncheon address, October 4, 1988, James J. Duderstadt Collection 1988–1989, Box 217, Michigan Historical Collections, Bentley Historical Library, University of Michigan, 1988/1989, p. 12. Hereafter, Duderstadt Collection. The use of ellipses is Duderstadt's. This is a punctuation device that he uses repeatedly.

42. Thomas Gerety, "The Freshman Who Hated Socrates: Freedom and Constraint in the Liberal Arts," Hartford, Conn., Trinity College, p. 6. Though undated, this address appears to have been delivered as a convocation or as a talk at the opening of the academic year, primarily addressed to first-year students.

43. Idem. In another talk at Trinity, Gerety notes that contrasted with other notions

of education, "we set out on a different path in the liberal arts. We study, as Cardinal Newman once wrote, not for usefulness, or at least not for an immediate and practical usefulness. We study to free ourselves. The usefulness, then the use of these liberal arts lies in preparing the way for that freedom that is their ideal." Thomas Gerety, "Work Hard, Play Hard: Rigor and Joy in the Liberal Arts," Hartford, Conn., Trinity College, President's Office, Amherst College, p. 4.

44. Personal interview with President Thomas Gerety of Amherst College, July 27, 1994.

45. Gerety, "Work Hard, Play Hard," p. 5.

46. Theodore Hesburgh, "The Future of Liberal Education," February 9, 1980, UND Archives, Theodore Hesburg Speeches, 1968–1987, Box 142/15. Specifically, Hesburgh decries the scientific method for producing "a value-free world that is on the brink of destroying itself. . . . It has placed great power in the hands of those who have few priorities beyond their own political, social, or economic aggrandizement. . . . [T]he world is in many ways a technological wasteland today, not because science and technology or the scientific method are bad, but because they can tell us nothing about values, or the meaning of life, or what it really is to be human" (pp. 13–14).

47. Ibid., p. 14.

48. Duderstadt used the terms "international conglomerate" and "entrepreneurial university" to describe the University of Michigan in the mid 1990s. Personal interview with President James J. Duderstadt of the University of Michigan, March 6, 1995. These descriptions may offer an apter understanding of the contemporary university than the notion of the "multiversity" provided by Clark Kerr in *The Uses of the University* (Cambridge, Mass.: Harvard University Press, 1963), over thirty years ago.

49. Theodore Hesburgh, "The University in the World of Change," December 10, 1964, UND Archives, Theodore Hesburgh Speeches, 1947–1967, Box 141/21, pp. 22–23.

50. Edward Malloy, address to the faculty, President's Office, University of Notre Dame, October 3, 1990, p. 20.

51. Michael Sovern, inaugural address, September 28, 1980, the Addresses of Michael Sovern, Public Information Office, Columbia University, p. 5.

52. Idem.

3

Architects of College Mission

THE INSTITUTIONAL VOICE OF PRESIDENTS

Presidential leadership is closely connected to the history, traditions, and purpose of colleges and universities. Many schools have throughout their histories coupled rich institutional culture and the fundamental ideas of mission with the visionary leadership of presidents. The influence of presidents creates and sustains this institutional memory and saga.[1] For many colleges, their saga shapes and unifies the institution. Presidents use this foundation, rooted in saga, to strengthen and further the fundamental principles of the college.

Burton Clark's view is that these sagas are "located between ideology and religion, partak[ing] of an appealing logic on one hand and sentiments similar to the spiritual on the other."[2] Through leadership at their founding, in times of crisis, and in affirmations of institutional mission, presidents provide colleges with ideals and vision. Presidential leadership is thus intertwined with saga and shapes the foundations of the mission and purpose of colleges and universities.

Wellesley College: *Non Ministrari, sed Ministrare*

Institutional mottoes and maxims voice the essence of the purposes of colleges and universities. These sayings tell us why the institution exists, what it hopes to do for its students and the world. Because of their importance to institutional tradition, mottoes and similar statements are closely associated with the character of campus life and are grist for the public rhetoric of presidents. Presidents of colleges with rich histories frequently refer to the purposes and values ordained

by founders and integrated as saga. Wellesley College and its presidents are
outstanding examples.

Wellesley's founder, Henry Fowle Durant, chose its motto, *Non ministrari,
sed ministrare*, not to be ministered unto, but to minister.[3] As did her predecessors for generations, Diana Chapman Walsh draws on this rich tradition of
the founders' vision for the college. In her first opening convocation address,
Walsh notes the revolutionary inspiration of Wellesley's founders who "dedicated themselves to preparing young women for 'great conflicts and vast social
reforms.' "[4]

Occasionally presidents make their own unique contributions to already well-
established sagas. Walsh reinterprets the Wellesley's motto claiming that the
college benefits society not only through the lives of its graduates but also by
making a difference in the world as an institution. Walsh's idea that Wellesley
serves the world as an institution is new. She contends that "Wellesley's mission
has often been defined as 'providing education for women who will make a
difference in the world.' but I think Wellesley itself can and should make a
difference in the world."[5] Certainly, this mission is fulfilled through its graduates, but Walsh also urges a moral voice and purpose in the world for the college
as an institution.[6] Walsh's hope is for the college to be a model of community,
responsive to the perceived demands of a more pluralistic society. She uses
moral leadership to shape the college's purpose, stressing that Wellesley can
and should have an expanded institutional presence in the world.[7]

As noted by Kemeny, a dilemma for presidents is the degree to which a
college can exercise institutional positions in the social and political arena. Kemeny's resolution of this dilemma is that institutions cannot take stands but that
individuals can. However, he takes a stand fully aware that his actions cannot
be totally divorced from his presidential role and may easily be read as representing the institution. Walsh's predecessor, Nannerl Keohane, acknowledges
Kemeny's concern by asking whether "it is inappropriate or even impossible for
a college as such to take a moral or political stand. . . . How can such an institution take a stand on a vexed moral issue without misrepresenting the views of
large numbers of those who would disagree."[8]

Keohane confronted a major ethical dilemma for colleges in the 1970s and
1980s: financial investments in businesses connected to South Africa. What
came to be known as divestment was a call to use institutional investment port-
folios to condemn South Africa's apartheid policies. As a political movement
divestment had its roots during the 1960s when colleges and universities were
condemned for making financial investments in corporations that were benefiting
from business related to the Vietnam War.

Having led Wellesley to its chosen course of "selective divestment," Keohane
countered criticism of that position. She wanted Wellesley to maintain a high
standard of institutional behavior. She proposed that for a college to act on the
basis of moral responsibility, the issue must be sufficiently compelling to demand an institutional response. Keohane contended that a college is not "literally

an ivory tower, cut off from any contact with the outside world. . . . [T]here may be rare issues of such magnitude, so uniquely grave that the college ought to use its moral weight, as a respected institution, to try to make a difference."[9]

The question of whether colleges and universities should take a moral positions as institutions poses interesting problems and can be the crux of many difficulties for presidents. Tom Gerety of Amherst believes that presidents have a responsibility to represent the entire institution and its constituencies. Underscoring the complexity of the issue, Gerety cites a predecessor's involvement in a local demonstration during the Vietnam War. Shortly after his act of civil disobedience, he departed the Amherst presidency. Gerety notes that it is possible to connect these two events. However, from his knowledge of the events, Gerety maintains that participation in the protest did not solely cause the end of his predecessor's tenure. Gerety believes that his predecessor was free as an individual to demonstrate against the war and that this action does not imply that Amherst was thereby institutionally opposing the war.[10]

The University of Michigan: Uncommon Education for the Common Citizen

Presidents of publicly funded research universities inherit institutional missions shaped by the impact of the Northwest Ordinance of 1787 on public education. Contrary to frequent misunderstandings and misapplications of the "doctrine" of separation of church and state, the heritage of these public universities includes attention to religion and morality. James Angell, president of the University of Michigan, believed that the emphasis on religion in the ordinance must be taken seriously. He also thought that religion was as important to the University of Michigan as it was to any of the denominational colleges and universities of his day.[11] Angell equates the university's mission with deeply rooted moral, as well as intellectual, purposes. In his inaugural address, Angell asserts that the state's assumption is that the university will "promot[e] by all proper means the intellectual and the moral growth of the citizens."[12]

For Angell the character of the institution is contingent on the exertion of great care in selecting faculty of outstanding personal, as well as Christian, character. Decisions on faculty hiring were regular opportunities for Angell to use moral leadership. The quality and reputation of any university are contingent on its people—specifically the students and faculty. Angell knows that "as the soul of a nation is in the spirit of the people rather than in the word of their Constitution, so the soul of a University is in the men who compose it rather than in its plan of organization."[13]

Over a hundred years later, President Harold Shapiro described the University of Michigan's mission as filling the role of both "critic and servant."[14] Michigan's purpose, like that of most public universities, is defined by the legislative principles of its founding, affirmed by the periodic interpretations of elected officials, civic leaders, and citizens. Like his predecessors, Shapiro is well aware of the historical expectations of citizens for the social contributions that publicly funded colleges and universities should feel required and accountable to make.

Indicative of the complex and politicized contemporary public environment, Shapiro outlines the universal value of the university. He insists that the university's role and its quest for knowledge include a moral and spiritual component. The coexistence of these roles constitutes a continuous struggle at major research universities such as Michigan.[15]

Debate about the purpose of the university and the meaning of the scholarship it supports is frequently reduced to a mutually exclusive choice. The university and the pursuit of knowledge are either rational, scientific, and objective on one hand, or subjective, human, and spiritual on the other hand. This debate has been persistent for much of the history of higher education in America, but it has been especially noteworthy in the last century.

Shapiro's claim that the university is both a servant and a critic resembles Dartmouth president Dickey's call that education promote both "conscience and competence." Shapiro's university has a "responsibility for providing an education that not only develops an individual's technical expertise, but relates an individual's experience to the broad human landscape of which we are a part, and moves them to a purpose and capacity beyond themselves."[16] Courses in the humanities are important in countering expectations that public research universities must exclusively emphasize scientific and technical education. By underscoring this "positive correlation between progress in science and the development of new knowledge, and progress in a moral and spiritual sense" as fundamental to education and to the life of the university, Shapiro reminds the public that Michigan's importance cannot be valued only by practical service to society.[17]

Sustaining the vision and sense of purpose of colleges and universities as both critic and servant of society is a crucial latter-twentieth-century challenge for both public and private presidents. In the contemporary climate, constituents—citizens, alumni, trustees, and others—demand tangible results and productive value of society's institutions. But, unchecked, this thinking quickly reduces the value of education and progress to the material, at the expense of consideration of the moral or spiritual. What is required and what presidents, in the tradition of Shapiro, must advocate is a broader and more enlightened vision of education and the role of the university. When presidents assume this critical role, they are able to use educational philosophy to shape public understanding of the university's purpose and thereby to contribute to institutional saga.

Edward Malloy and Religious Saga at Notre Dame

The affirmation of religious identity is a cornerstone of religious institutions of higher education. The foundations of religious colleges are characterized by their founders' commitments of faith and belief. The missions developed from these foundations are assumed to be sustainable only by a constancy of religious piety and purpose. Single-mindedness lends great strength and character to institutional identity. However, the religious affections at the heart of these schools can also pose interesting challenges for presidents. The articulation of a mission and identity based on religious beliefs and ideals produces a demanding leadership task at these institutions. In capsule form that task is to uphold a specific religious heritage while incorporating the multidimensional religious perspectives of an increasingly pluralistic society.

This challenge is one of Edward Malloy's major concerns as president of Notre Dame. He acknowledges that the Catholic nature of Notre Dame cannot be merely assumed but can only be maintained by constant nurture. The Catholic identity of Notre Dame must be crucially considered by its presidents in their thoughts about institutional mission. The difficulty is that in the latter twentieth and early twenty-first centuries the type of faculty members and students that Notre Dame must attract to its campus in order to remain a premier and intellectually sound university will of necessity be more diverse and less parochial than at any time in its past.

Malloy publicly recognizes the need for the institution to be more inclusive of diverse religious practices while maintaining its core Catholic identity. This includes integration into the university community of believers from other religious traditions as well as those with no belief at all. While Notre Dame's unique religious character is its "greatest strength," the questions that must be addressed include "How can we preserve a core of committed Catholic scholars while at the same time remaining a welcoming and supportive environment for scholars of other religious traditions or none? How can we provide helpful and competent pastoral care for students, staff and faculty from all faith traditions? How can we celebrate our common life in liturgy with reverence and a proper sense of inclusiveness?"[18]

Because the core values of the institution's saga are at stake, raising these complex questions at schools such as Notre Dame can become highly charged for a president. Malloy knows he must do so if the university is to maintain its historical strength and present reputation.

Considering the relationship of education to society, Malloy presents Notre Dame's distinct point of view. He defends the institution against those who assume that contemporary culture does not accept the basic truths embodied in education at Notre Dame. American society is more secularized, prone to "a weakening of common values, an antipathy to religion, and a resistance to the very notion of underlying truths," but that "The Catholic intellectual tradition and the Western university tradition itself stand in opposition to this contention, as does Notre Dame."[19] His hope and conviction is that both Catholic higher education and the university heritage in Western culture agree that "reason and belief" must coexist in education.

Malloy is a sufficiently modern president and priest to recognize that Notre Dame and the education it offers is not and cannot be changeless. Despite the Church's acknowledged authority over the institution's affairs, Malloy also believes the Notre Dame community must be democratically involved in discussion of the university's mission. To accomplish this end, Malloy initiated a major institutionwide self study in October 1991. His careful planning process included numerous subcommittees representing all university constituencies. But by serving as chair of Committee of the Whole, Malloy ensured presidential imprimatur and declared authorship of the resulting *Final Report: Colloquy for the Year 2000.*

Colloquy for the Year 2000 is Malloy's major statement about Catholic identity and its role in education at Notre Dame for the latter twentieth and early twenty-first centuries. One of its major contentions is that education is "explicitly moral."[20] One of Malloy's goals is to broaden the appeal of the university. In the process he adds to its saga. Malloy argues that Notre Dame's Catholic identity is not exclusionary, but rather provides "a vision that . . . can be comfortably affirmed and participated in by Catholics and people of other faiths alike." With religion declining in influence, especially in the academy, Notre Dame is "evidence that academic freedom and denominational affiliation are compatible and mutually enriching values." But Malloy is quick to make clear that the institution is both a critic of society and of the church by exposing each "to the kind of respectful but critical analysis that is conducive to structural renewal."[21]

Malloy's credo is that only religiously affiliated colleges and universities are able to combine religious questions and concerns with the scholarly requirements of academic inquiry. This includes the frank admission that there are limits to what human beings can know, and thus that there are "truths" beyond the reach of academic inquiry and human knowing. But this unique character of a Roman Catholic or any religious university, especially in the contemporary cultural context of pluralism and secularity, cannot be taken for granted. Notre Dame's historical commitment to maintain a Catholic vision and purpose has become, in Malloy's view, more crucial and pronounced because of expanded secular and reduced religious influence in society.

Horace Bumstead: Atlanta University's Stand on Race

The needs of black education in the South during and immediately after Reconstruction were profound. The South was economically and politically devastated by the Civil War. Intractable prejudice toward blacks continued to impede social progress after Emancipation. On this stage, Reverend Horace Bumstead was Atlanta's second president from 1886, just twenty years after its founding, to 1907.

Horace Bumstead is another noteworthy example of the relationship of the moral voice of presidents to institutional mission. Specifically, Bumstead's story is that of a courageous battle opposing the power of politics and racism. His convictions and those of the university trustees in this watershed epoch were critical to the survival and success of the institution.

The university's poor financial condition and the resulting constant need to appeal for support consumed large quantities of Bumstead's time. Pursuing this task, Bumstead was a profound moral leader and embodied the university's mission and its crucial contribution to the education of blacks. Bumstead made frequent forays to northern churches, using personal contacts with fellow graduates of Yale University and Andover Theological Seminary to get speaking engagements. Tirelessly, day after day, he would give "his address on the 'Higher Education of the Negro' to the morning congregations and his illustrated lecture on the 'Work of the University in the Elevation of the Negro' in the evening."[22] In one appeal quoting from its statement of purpose, Bumstead asserted that the university existed "for the elementary and industrial training of the masses. 'Men of light and leading' in other spheres of activity are also greatly needed by the race that has so long sat in darkness."[23]

Bumstead faced a crisis of great enormity borne out of the racial politics in the South of his day. The battle he waged reveals the depth of Bumstead's moral conviction and courage. Its outcome would shape the future of Atlanta University.

A controversy developed between the state legislature and Atlanta University over what had been an annual allocation of state support. The debate began when some legislators, in a clear attempt to maintain educational separation of blacks and whites, argued that state educational funds should be allocated only to segregated institutions. As the debate proceeded on what came to be known as the "Calvin Resolutions," the university submitted what was to be its final application requesting legislative appropriation.

In making the university's case, Bumstead stood firmly on the charter and reiterated the university's position made clear to the legislature throughout the preceding two decades. He argued that the charter, "granted by the Superior Court in 1867, defined [the university's] work to be 'The Christian education of youth.' It did not limit the word Christian to the tenets of any denomination of Christians, nor the word youth to the youth of either sex, or of any nation or race." Noting that the university's proclamations of its inclusiveness are rooted in the state's imprimatur, he claimed that "In accordance with the freedom thus granted by the charter, the published catalogues of the University from the year of its opening in 1869 contained this announcement:—'The Institution stands on the broadest possible platform and while intended to be thoroughly Christian, is in no respect sectarian. It offers its advantages to all of either sex, without regard to sect, race, color, or nationality.' "[24]

The outcome of this debate between the university and the state legislature reflected the tenor of Reconstruction in the South. The "Calvin Resolutions," mandating that funding appropriations such as those the university had been receiving be used for segregated black education only, were subsequently passed by the Georgia legislature. The university chose to lose the annual $8,000 appropriation that they had been receiving rather than capitulate to the requirements of the resolutions.[25]

The resolutions were a politically motivated state intrusion to restrict its federal funding, which had been designated by Congress through the Freedmen's

Bureau to assist blacks (an action that sheds interesting light on current debates about the equitability of state decisions on federal block-grant allocations). In response, Bumstead staunchly maintained his university's mission to educate both whites and blacks and refused to take money that would compromise that mission.

This was a high-minded stand based on principle. But this stand resulted in severe financial consequences, further testing Bumstead's resolve and the university's principles. Shortly after their passage, Bumstead reports with irony that the "Calvin Resolutions" demanded "that the trustees should bind themselves to receive colored pupils *only* into the Institution. The trustees felt that there would be not merely a compromise, but a sacrifice of principle, in giving a pledge to the state which was in direct conflict with one previously given the National Government, on the strength of which it had received the appropriations of money."[26]

At a practical level, the university's refusal to capitulate to the resolutions was an extraordinary financial sacrifice. Consider the value of that $8,000 in constant dollars one hundred years later. Couple that with the fact that Bumstead was already raising $25,000 annually, mostly from northern churches, themselves not particularly wealthy, merely to keep the doors of his university open to all. Bumstead and the trustees were convinced that something much more profound would be lost if the university capitulated to the prejudice so explicitly embodied in the "Calvin Resolutions." This courageous leadership was a moral inspiration within and beyond the gates of his community.[27]

Before proceeding, an observation about the foregoing presidents deserves comment. We have seen how the moral voice is clearly attached to institutional mission. However, this connection between moral leadership and institutional purpose is even closer for the presidents whose schools have specific missions to educate and serve well-defined constituencies. Institutions such as Wellesley, Michigan, Notre Dame, and Clark Atlanta exist for distinctive purposes—to educate women, to educate and serve the public, to provide education in the context of religious belief, and to educate both black and white in the South. Presidents of schools such as these have an institutional obligation to emphasize their distinctive educational missions. This means securing their foundations against forces that might undermine fundamental principles. Presidential convictions and a moral voice also enrich the saga embedded in core institutional values and purposes.

FASHIONING THE VALUES OF THE COLLEGE

Contemporary social critics and theorists argue that institutions must assume social responsibility about issues of economic justice. Colleges and universities are no exception, and some presidents—including contemporary presidents Edward Malloy, George Rupp, and Diana Walsh—have exhibited leadership in institutional economic responsibility.[28]

Malloy believes Notre Dame has an institutional obligation to compensate employees at or above local salary levels. The university's ability to do so is clearly related to its ability to maintain balanced budgets.[29] Attention to financial stability has enabled Notre Dame to make sound decisions among competing demands such as plant maintenance and student aid and to avoid reducing its number of employees. To Malloy, economic justice is a moral issue. Thus, economic stewardship is a presidential and institutional moral obligation. Institutional financial decisions are "moral decision[s] in economic terms, part of the mechanism by which we live our own internal life."

Walsh is likewise quite specific in connecting Wellesley's financial decisions to its institutional values. The college's fiscal choices are clearly linked to its moral obligations.[30] It is crucial for the institution to determine its values *a priori* to making financial decisions. Walsh also acknowledges the important connection between the college's fiscal decisions and the financial aid needs of students. Sensitive to the financial plight of many parents and students, and well aware of the difficult decisions about financial aid and college cost facing educational leaders, Walsh admits that "tuition can't just keep going up, financial aid can't keep going up. We [need to] have a process that really reflects our values."[31]

Rupp believes that the obligation for stewardship of Columbia's financial affairs is an inseparable aspect of presidential leadership. His commitment to maintain the university's fiscal stability and future became a major issue during the early months of his presidency.

When he began as president, Columbia was in the last year of a planned multiyear reduction of expenditures. Shortly after his arrival, faculty began pressuring to extend for two additional years the completion of the plan and its fiscal goals. Rupp refused to capitulate to the faculty arguments, contending that it would be fiscally irresponsible of him as president to do so. The basis of his argument was that "one of the most fundamental moral issues that any president has to engage is to balance the claims of the future against the needs or wants of the present." Though not necessarily "expressed rhetorically," these decisions are an "important part of the actual work [of] priority setting that presidents do." For Rupp, the question at stake was responsible stewardship for the university, a responsibility that he defined as "restraining self-indulgence" to ensure future security. He self-revelatorily and self-reflectively concludes that "partly because I am a Calvinist, I see that as a moral issue."[32]

Rupp's Calvinism directly shapes his opinions and values and influences his leadership. As a further example of his convictions about fiduciary responsibility, Rupp cites his departure from the presidency of Rice University. He had disagreed with the Rice trustees about their decisions to spend money that they were not committed to raise. While "that issue played itself out without a lot of moralistic rhetoric," it contained for Rupp "a deeply ethical set of issues." Rupp concludes that even though public rhetoric by presidents is often described "in moralistic categories" there are no greater moral issues "than the basic ones of the distribution of goods within a community, which is what a university is."[33]

Rupp, along with Walsh and Malloy, use moral leadership to support values not stated as institutional mission and purpose, but which undergird the principles for which any a college or university stands.

INTERPRETING EDUCATIONAL MISSION

Presidents not only influence institutional mission but also use moral leadership to shape their colleges' educational philosophy. For Peter Pouncey at Amherst, the challenge to make a personal statement about his institution's mission was neither a welcome nor an easy task. He did so only at the urging of his trustees and faculty, dedicating his 1992 convocation address (which coincidentally was to be his next to last as president) to an analysis of the college's mission.

Pouncey was highly skeptical about the successful completion of the task and candidly expressed his apprehension, defensiveness, and resistance. He was critical of the contemporary fad that compelled many colleges and universities, often with repetitious frequency, to define, restate, or reinvent institutional missions. Unconvinced of the value of the endeavor, he noted in an ironic preface that "after 171 years of a notable school's existence, it seems late in the day to be deciding what its mission is, and perhaps arrogant to be offering it a mission." Nonetheless, Pouncey offered his beliefs about Amherst's principles. Acknowledging the shoulders on which he and his Amherst colleagues stand, he averred that "there is a real sense in which, whether we are just arriving, or have been here for ever, as so many people seem to have been, we should not be here at all, if we do not know what this school is about, and what we have come to do."[34]

For Pouncey, there was at Amherst an apparent contradiction between the strong missionary roots at the foundation of the college and its charter's statement that there shall be no religious tests applied to faculty, administrators, or students. He believed that this tension is resolved in the founder's commitment to liberal learning. As a preamble to his credo, Pouncey quoted Amherst graduate Daniel Bliss, who in 1871 founded a college in Beirut based on his understanding of Amherst's mission: " 'A man white, black or yellow; Christian, Jew, Mahommedan or heathen may enter and enjoy all the advantages of this institution . . . and go out believing in one God, or in many Gods, or in no God. But it will be impossible for anyone to continue with us long without knowing what we believe to be the truth and our reasons for that belief.' "[35]

This philosophy of liberal learning has continued to undergird an Amherst education. Amherst's educational philosophy and core principles are determined by a response to the question, "what is it that you believe, which the students intrusted to you cannot leave without knowing? And what are the reasons for that belief?" His personal belief is, "against dark patterns of evidence about human nature, that a college, whatever its religious affiliation, is pledged to a special faith of its own—that men and women can live together in a community where they teach and learn from each other."[36]

Pouncey presented five articles of faith, a credo of his moral voice, universally essential to education and particularly crucial to learning in the Amherst community. Pouncey claims that teaching and learning communities are characterized by creativity, intellectual groundbreaking, self-improvement, preparation for life, and moral decency. He cited teaching and learning as "creative activities, in the sense that they make something where there was nothing before—knowledge out of ignorance, structure out of disorder, particular skills to advance further, where there was only fumbling for a beginning." Aware of the way in which ideologies can be intellectually stifling, he qualified his position by adding that teaching and learning "are only creative activities when those involved in them are both passionate and disarmed—passionate in the sense of desire, energy and focused concentration, and disarmed, in the sense of stripped of prejudice, of any preconceived views of what is in the material before them, and of what is in the minds of those around them."[37]

This concern about the damage to learning as a result of prejudice is not a new one. However, it is an increasingly frequent topic of discussion in the academy, sparked in large part by debate about politicized curricula and the related ideological campus battles about social action, discrimination, and values. These matters create moral dilemmas for presidents. Pouncey shifted the ground by outlining what he believed to be the countervailing claims of a college education: prejudice has no place in a learning community.

Pouncey challenged the Amherst faculty to generate new ideas and learning by overcoming academic and scholarly rigidity. Pouncey asserts that "a community of teaching and learning only reaches the highest power when those who teach are committed to think new and break new ground, to see further and deeper, within a discipline or across disciplines."[38]

This article of belief led Pouncey to a moral claim about education: that this "community of teaching and learning challenges itself with a reality principle beyond all pieties—to this effect: does the education the community offers its students prepare them best with the necessary skills to make sense of the world they will live in—to hear and answer the conflicting voices, to probe the rhetoric, sift the evidence and offer solutions that reach further?"[39] The result is a learning community dedicated to the improvement of all members, in spite of "conflicting voices," and to the betterment of those in society served by Amherst graduates.

Pouncey's use of "pieties" reenforced his concern about artificial scholarly boundaries and the antithetical effect of ideologies on education. He amplified this position in his final assertion that "an excellent community of teaching and learning stands for certain decencies both for itself and for its students to carry out into their lives. Our predecessors in this chapel believed it passionately and their lives and actions, often of great sacrifice, show they believed it beyond piety. This can be embarrassing to certain temperaments, but it should not be."[40] All pieties—Amherst's founding religious ones and their contemporary heirs— must be transcended by common decency, civility, and the moral elements of teaching, learning, and living.

In a reference to Martin Luther's historic ninety-five theses, Pouncey stated that he was prepared to nail these five articles to the door of the chapel in which the address was given. His use of religious language—higher power, pieties, belief—and reference to the religious and pietistic foundation of the college are not accidental or coincidental.

Despite his initial reluctance about the task of discussing Amherst's mission, in the tone of a preacher, Pouncey unapologetically stated his beliefs. Pouncey purposefully challenged his faculty and students about the value of the educational life. He absolved his audience of any embarrassment they might have felt about allowing passionate and strong beliefs to lead to commitments to knowledge and public action. He also built his argument on a strong Amherst tradition of presidential calls for decency and civility and about the difficulties presented by prejudice in academic communities.[41]

This rich tradition is linked to moral and social realities and responsibilities. Pouncey believed that while "Amherst has had a great tradition of moral and social urgency . . . [what] would have seemed self-evident to our early predecessors that a liberal education should equip a man and woman to see further and broader, to know themselves and to see and care beyond themselves," these assumptions could no longer be taken for granted. Pouncey answered the challenge of defining the meaning of an Amherst education in the latter twentieth century. By doing so he contributed to Amherst's saga about the value of its education.

In similar fashion, one of Father James Cavanaugh's primary presidential responsibilities was to maintain the prominence of religion at Notre Dame. The institution's identity has always hinged on self-consciousness of its religious heritage. As other presidents of Notre Dame, Cavanaugh drew on the saga begun by Father Sorin and his fellow founders. Cavanaugh claimed that "If our work here is not a missionary work it is worse than nothing, if students of Notre Dame are not more religious men, more virtuous men, more true to the sacred loyalties of life than the students of other schools then the dream of Sorin and the brothers was an illusion, their sacrifices were folly, their aspirations a barren hope."[42]

This memory is crucial to Notre Dame's saga. Sorin and his party of priests came to America as missionaries. After struggling to survive in the wilderness during their first winter at what was to become the site of the Notre Dame campus, they founded the university.

Cavanaugh used Notre Dame's founding ideas about institutional purpose as a platform to contribute his educational philosophy to the university's mission. His early-twentieth-century understanding of a Notre Dame education arose from the value he attached to personal morality and character formation. Cavanaugh believed that education must distinguish between "right"—what is good, correct, and moral—and "wrong." Education is "growth towards the right point of view of what in the narrow sense is termed personal morality.... Education primarily means not the acquirement of knowledge or skill, but the development of the mind towards the right point of view and the practice of the will in the right course of action."[43] Education possesses a clear and strict moral component. As a university, Notre Dame "is based upon the theory that education is chiefly moral; that character is more than culture."[44]

Cavanaugh believed in a partnership between students and the university, but that it was a partnership in which students had to submit to the demands of a Notre Dame education. The result of this partnership is the character formation of students. Traditionally at Notre Dame the partnership between the university and the student emphasized the student's responsibility. A university, even one with a strong religious and moral purpose, can do only so much in forming the character of its students. The student must do the rest. But Cavanaugh added the institutional responsibility to support and assist the student, thereby broadening Notre Dame's understanding of its mission.

Cavanaugh did not fear publicly using of his university's fundamental values as a platform to stress the importance of a greater commitment to religion in education at other schools and throughout the land. He initiated a debate with Charles Eliot sparked by a 1909 speech on religion Eliot made shortly after leaving the Harvard presidency. In a sermon to students and other members of the Notre Dame community, and with clear passion, Cavanaugh stingingly rebuked Eliot. For Cavanaugh the substance of belief at Notre Dame would always stand in marked contrast to Eliot's notion about religion. He assailed Eliot's argument that "the religion of the future ... would not acknowledge the providence of God; would not profess belief in prayer or in heaven or hell; the religion of the future would be a religion without mystery and without miracle, without altar or priest or sacrament." Then Cavanaugh made a rather unprecedented (at least for college presidents of his day or our own) personal attack on his former presidential colleague. He asserts that Elliot, "After a long life spent in the work of university education, after long study and much refinement and accomplishment, after having received loyal and loving veneration as a leader in great schools, all this pathetic old man could leave the world as his final message was a thin and arid philosophy—not a religion, observe, for a religion without miracle or mystery is an absurdity—a rare and attenuated philosophy which deprives God of personality, religion of grace and humanity of prayer."[45]

While relying on religious faith, Cavanaugh also argued that Notre Dame's mission does not divorce faith from intellectual and scholarly life. Sharply critical of Eliot, Cavanaugh distinguished between his view of true religious belief in education—the foundation of Notre Dame—and his interpretation of Eliot's view—a secularized religious philosophy fashioned to coexist with the university, with education, and with scholarship. Cavanaugh's Notre Dame stood in stark contrast, "a protest and a challenge" to "schools where everything in the

universe may be studied save the Master of the universe, where every name in
history is mentioned save that of Christ." But, in the tradition of Newman, this
education is in no way inferior because "no fragment of human knowledge must
be withheld from its students; here learning must be as broad and deep and
strong as elsewhere. In so far as this school should attempt to withhold or darken
or attenuate any particle of human knowledge, this school would fail and fall
short of her duty not alone to science but to that God whom she professes to
worship and to serve."[46]

Cavanaugh used this debate over the role of religion in education to argue
that religious beliefs can be integrated into the life of a university and must be
tested by scientific and other scholarly propositions in the academy. Religious
beliefs and scientific discoveries mutually benefit the quest for knowledge and
the life of the mind. Cavanaugh's stand was taken in an attempt to secure Notre
Dame's mission in the increasingly secular world dawning at the beginning of
the twentieth century.

Presidents have always faced the perpetual leadership challenges to institutional mission created by continual changes in society. Cavanaugh confronted
changing social and religious mores as he worked to maintain the religious and
moral foundations of Notre Dame's philosophy of education.

Despite the differences between Notre Dame at the turn of the century and
Amherst College decades later, Pouncey quite similarly defended Amherst's
chartered purpose in the face of the challenges brought about by political correctness. He acknowledges that American society is divided along political and
ideological lines, and that this fragmentation is manifest on college campuses.
Pouncey fears that Amherst has fallen short in addressing forthrightly the dilemmas caused by diversity and political correctness. Speaking of an Amherst education, Pouncey argues that "it is not enough that we reflect the fragments and
divisions, and cover them all with an academic politeness that everyone is free
to do his or her thing, in his or her place, making whatever connection he or
she can find."

Like Cavanuagh's invocation of Notre Dame's founders, Pouncey invokes
Amherst's motto, "Shedding our light across the earth," to justify how an Amherst education stands in opposition to contemporary ideas about individualized
learning (i.e., students being able to do what they wish). At its best, an Amherst
education answers the ideological problems of diversity. This part of the college's mission is rooted in its heritage: an institution committed to being a true
learning community.

This means that mere politeness (read "political correctness") whether in or
outside the classroom is not sufficient to addressing differences opinion and
thought. Pouncey's criticism is that "we have yet to achieve common, intellectual ground together, not reductively, leveling the differences, or watering them
down, but celebrating them, and teaching and learning with insistence and urgency the many languages that express them. That way we enlarge our vision,
we extend politeness to active collaboration, and in an amplified sense we fulfill

our chartered mission to shed our light across the earth."[47] What Amherst stands for and what the challenges of diversity demand is transformation into a collaborative learning effort. Only such a renewed sense of the meaning of education will allow Amherst to fulfill its charter and its principles designed to export enlightened knowledge to the rest of the world.

We have previously observed some of the ways in which education is itself a moral endeavor. Presidents are aware of and capitalize on these moral aspects of the educational experience. Some presidential interpretations of the relationship of institutional mission to philosophies of undergraduate education are based on assumptions about the moral foundations of education. A number of today's presidents offer interesting commentary.

Thomas Gerety suggests that "the entire enterprise" of education "seems to have important intrinsic moral aspects and has its moral consequences."[48] Elaborating on this theme, he makes the oft-cited comparison between the manifestation of moral concerns in the academic and in the nonacademic—i.e., residential—life. A fundamental value of life together in a residential community is that it complements other moral aspects of the college experience, resulting in an education that is in its totality profoundly moral. Gerety believes the entirety of the educational experience both in and outside the classroom is moral and concludes that "residential life seems to be where emotions and passions come out strongly. Anger, hatred, fear, a misunderstanding, all those things seem to get piled together more dramatically in the residential things that happen at a college. The whole enterprise is moral, but certain things stand out as engaging us in moral conflict and moral crisis."[49]

Diana Chapman Walsh makes similar claims about education. Reflecting on Wellesley's purpose and the challenges presented to students, she states that the education offered by the college is deeply rooted in "our fundamental purpose and has to do with educating the whole person." This education is further grounded in "a moral imperative."[50]

But Walsh acknowledges a difficult dilemma that can arise from making a moral imperative the basis of an education. She found herself to be struck by comments made by Wellesley alumnae in a Public Broadcasting special on members of Hillary Clinton's class of 1969. A large number of these alumnae expressed their experience of the college's motto—not being ministered unto, but to minister—as a lifelong burden. They described it as an unreachable ideal that they felt themselves incapable of fulfilling. There is then a dangerous irony when well-meaning moral imperatives, in this case one embedded in the grand language of the college's motto, become an apparent requirement to be perfect. The presidential task, as Walsh conceives it, is to create a moral education that addresses "what is the good life, what is the whole life, what is wholeness" but that does not equate wholeness with perfectionism.[51]

The high ideals of college mission can be grand and glorious. A task for presidents is to make those moral ideals a set of principles that graduates can carry throughout their lives rather than a cross to bear.

One way in which students can be exposed to the ideals of their education in practical ways that may remain with them throughout life is from involvement in community service. Opportunities for service have become an increasingly important part of many college and university campuses in the last decade and a half. Students are, in increasing numbers, showing strong interest in participating in service activities. Edward Malloy believes that community service is an important out-of-the-classroom aspect of moral education and learning. To John Sloan Dickey's attributes of "competence and conscience," Malloy adds compassion as a critical element of education. Involvement in social concerns and community needs is significant for the moral growth of students because their "compassion [is] being touched by something, the plight or dilemma of some group of people."[52]

The student's compassion, stimulated and stirred through community and volunteer service, is then brought to the academic and classroom setting, which in turn enriches and makes more whole the student's education. These experiences in and outside the classroom are complementary and essential to a complete and moral education. Malloy contends that at Notre Dame "the value formation which goes on to some extent in the classroom is enhanced if not initiated in experiential educational opportunities." Volunteer service forces students "to clarify their own values, test out things, and then to bring it back into the classroom for more rigorous analysis of what options might be."[53]

Another president, Thomas Cole of Clark Atlanta University, also views the education of students as transpiring inside and outside the classroom and as being strongly linked to student engagement with the needs of others. Like many of his predecessors at historically black colleges, Cole is keenly aware of the disadvantages experienced by African Americans. He is also committed to the crucial educational and social role played by predominantly black institutions. Discussing education at Clark Atlanta, Cole claims that higher education is "one of the major opportunities for disadvantaged or nonadvantaged individuals to improve the quality of their lives and that of the larger African American community. Access to almost anything of substance and equality depends on having quality education."[54] Given the importance of service and providing students the opportunity to give of themselves dictates that the educational purpose of Clark Atlanta extends beyond learning technical knowledge to a "particular focus on [the] ethical and moral, a sense that there is a right and a wrong, and that there is a companion obligation once 'they get theirs' to reach back and be helpful to others."[55]

Cole believes that education has three major components. First, students should integrate the moral ability to make reasoned judgments. Second, they should learn to conduct themselves in the light of those judgments. Finally, they should be challenged to make contributions to society. Such an education features clear distinctions and choices between right and wrong for students. Cole's responsibility as president and Clark Atlanta's as an institution is to draw these distinctions and to provide an education that guides students in their moral choices.

Though not formally categorized as a religious college, Clark Atlanta is affiliated with the United Methodist Church. While the church influence differs quantitatively and qualitatively from that at some religious colleges and universities, Cole believes that the Methodist connection has an impact on moral and ethical education at the university. This tie is sufficiently significant to create "an environment [which] recognizes the importance of the Judaeo-Christian ethics and [the] endeavor to infuse some dimension of that as part of the culture and as part of [the] learning process."[56] He elaborates that in order to incorporate ethics and values the school must provide "nurturing, support and sensitivity" to students, the goal being to offer students the best possible preparation for their lives beyond the university.[57]

Like the descriptions of the ethos of their campuses by other presidents, Cole's view is that much of the student's moral formation and discussion of ethical issues occurs outside the classroom at Clark Atlanta. Though there are numerous examples, one in particular is the frequent effort to remind students through discussions, presentations, and lectures about the history of the civil-rights movement, its importance to the lives of blacks, and its significance to current undergraduates. This commitment has been a tradition at Clark Atlanta and other black colleges. Black leaders such as Cole and his predecessor, Elias Blake, believe it is critical for black students to understand this history.

Prior to his presidency, Blake offered thoughts similar to ones made later as president about the meaning of the historic struggles of black people to contemporary black youth. He was direct in his observation that they "must not be pandered to under the banners of any 'Black ideology' that does not demand of them they work . . . as their past eight generations did, even when the pay was short and the day was long. . . . If our black college students do not understand history in the context of their historical responsibilities then we must tell them in no uncertain terms whether they like it or not."[58] This attention to the history of black people and its importance to successive generations of black students is a recurrent theme of the moral leadership of black college presidents such as Cole and Blake.

Finally, a portion of the institutional saga at Clark Atlanta is to introduce students to the expectations of them as they emerge from the institution to life in the world. This is accomplished in two ways. One is through a community service requirement that is designed to remind students of the needs of the communities from which they have come. Second is a required "language and culture" course to make certain that the students leave Clark Atlanta with a firm grasp of what will be demanded of them in a predominantly white world. This course is an "effort to sensitize them and expose them to cultural things, but also behavior and expectations, and the importance of reaching out and dealing with other cultures."[59]

George Rupp views Columbia University's curriculum as being an important aspect of moral education for Columbia students. Here there is a direct connection between institutional mission and a philosophy of undergraduate education. Uniquely, particularly in the age of multicultural ideologies and in the face of numerous critics, Columbia has remained committed to a required core curriculum featuring a traditional, Western culture, Great Books approach. For Rupp, the value of this aspect of a Columbia education is not that it directly develops "an ethical dimension" in students, "but through the curriculum they learn to understand themselves and also be open to others in a way that they could not if they did not go through that process." Rupp believes this "process is intrinsically, at least potentially, a moral one, because it gives them the kind of capacity to both understand themselves and identify with others that is a capacity of the moral imagination."[60]

If the Columbia core is performing the task of enriching the ethical sensitivity and development of Columbia students, the question arises whether faculty who teach "Lit Hum," as it is fondly known, believe this to be the case. Reflecting on this question, Rupp does not think that either students or the faculty are aware, at least directly, of the value of the core courses to the moral development of students. Rupp's conclusion is that "Hegel was right in talking about *die List der Vernunft*—the 'cunning of reason,' as it is translated. It does not matter whether they know what they are doing or not. The impact of it is moral upbuilding or building of *moral imagination* quite apart from what any given professor thinks he or she is doing in any given course or what the students think is happening in the course. When they get done, they are different people. Many of them would deny that they are more moral people, but they can be."[61]

Two Columbia alumni have underscored Rupp's judgment. More than two decades after first taking "Lit Hum" as an undergraduate, alumnus David Denby retook the course several times. One faculty member with whom he took the course, himself a Columbia alumnus, acknowledges that "the course had driven me to become a professor of literature, and for twenty years I had been wrestling with the intellectual and ethical questions that the syllabus had first forced upon me."[62] While not claiming that this course absolutely makes every student a more moral person, Rupp finds this curricular requirement to be crucial to Columbia's philosophy of education. The core curriculum creates an ideal impact of the academic life of the institution on students. This education is a contemporary manifestation of the notion of character formation through "moral upbuilding" or, as Rupp puts it, inspiring the "moral imagination." The "moral imagination" as the moral dimension of academic work reflects Rupp's moral leadership and is a contemporary way of thinking about the moral basis of institutional and educational philosophy.

These five presidents—Rupp, Cole, Malloy, Walsh, and Gerety—emphasize the ways in which a college education is a moral endeavor. They contend that there is a vital link between the moral development and the way in which we view educational philosophy and institutional purpose. These presidents share assumptions that the education offered to students is holistic, that experiences in and outside of the classroom are complementary, and that moral conscience and value formation are essential goals of the educational experience.

INSTITUTIONAL DIFFICULTIES

Thus far in this chapter we have explored the moral voice in the context of the ethos of colleges and universities. In most cases this ethos—the principles and mission of the institution—serves to support the moral voice and provide occasions for its expression. However, on other occasions expression of the moral voice by presidents becomes complicated in connection with particular intra-institutional dilemmas.

First, some of the difficulties James J. Duderstadt faced at the University of Michigan are linked to the realities already discussed regarding the institution's size and scope. Duderstadt's presidency was conducted as Michigan continued to become more profoundly complex as an institution. One effect was that this institutional ethos generated a degree of confusion about the institution's purpose and coherence. This, in turn, caused difficulties for Duderstadt's moral leadership as president.

For example, defining a mission for an institution with the breadth of the University of Michigan is difficult because one of its primary characteristics is that it is a "collection[s] of thousands of people [who] are doing what they want to do, but they define the mission of the institution."[63] On the question of developing a philosophy of education with some moral basis, Duderstadt remarks that "part of the difficulty that one has in grappling with these issues today is that these institutions that we call universities have evolved in such a way as to become so complex, so broad, involved in so many activities that certainly the various constituencies we serve do not understand what we are. Our faculty no longer understands what we are. And I think, in many cases, the leaders of these institutions don't really know what they are."[64] While delivered with a degree of humor, Duderstadt's comment, combined with his description of the university as an "international conglomerate" and an "entrepreneurial university," support the suggestion that Michigan's institutional definition is probably less coherent and more fluid than that of many colleges and universities.

In light of the unified institutional mission implied by Burton Clark's concept of saga, several significant implications arise regarding the university's sense of purpose and Duderstadt's ability to have his moral voice influence institutional mission. By contrast, though Columbia may have as many competing interests striving to offer disparate definitions of mission, Rupp can at least use the core curriculum as evidence of educational coherence at Columbia and as a platform for moral expression.

However, Duderstadt does not view the potential difficulties created by a vast, multifaceted university as insurmountable for presidents or as an excuse to avoid or neglect moral leadership. Discussing university issues in which he has been actively engaged such as affirmative action and student life, Duderstadt concludes that "to change an institution in a fundamental way, the President has to get out on the front line."[65] This statement conjures up Clark's concept of the "long shadow of a man," the notion that presidents can leave distinctive marks on a college's saga. Duderstadt is also affirming the potential for one individual, even as the leader of such a large educational institution, to make a difference.

In spite of his assessment that the many constituencies of the university offer competing missions, Duderstadt nonetheless provided a presidential moral voice for the University of Michigan. An example of his practical application of leadership is his use of principles in the governance of the university's athletic program. Collegiate athletic programs are frequently viewed as creating profound challenges, sometimes of great consequence, for college and university presidents. However, at universities such as Michigan, the profile and culture of the institution is closely connected to highly visible athletic programs. Furthermore, university participation in major intercollegiate sports often leads to significant institutional and administrative problems, many of which are ethical and moral.

Prodded by his conscience (and mindful of his undergraduate experience as a football player at Yale), Duderstadt wrote and circulated internally to colleagues, administrators, and others at the university a draft of a paper entitled "The Thrill of Victory . . . The Agony of Defeat . . . and the Gnashing of Teeth . . . As College Presidents Attempt to Reform Intercollegiate Athletics." The thinking revealed in this essay is exemplary of Duderstadt's engagement in the ethical concerns of the university and the revolutionary aspects of his voice.

Duderstadt outlined in great depth the abuses in intercollegiate athletics, the treatment of college student athletes, and the corrupting influence of money. His proposals included a one-year moratorium on televised intercollegiate sports. During this time the universities participating in major athletic competition, guided by presidents, would review the relationship of their institutional missions to their athletic programs in order to bring the latter more in line with the former. Following this there would be more selective television coverage and greater revenue sharing among all institutions regardless of NCAA division status. He also commented at length on the manner in which, with little or no regard for their academic progress or long-term futures, student athletes are recruited and treated.

Underscoring his and the university's stance and the practical leadership exercised, he noted that "Each year I . . . meet with all of the coaches in order to stress to them the importance of the integrity of our programs. I take great pains to point out to them that in my many years at the University there has never been a coach who has been released from the University because of their win-lose record. . . . if in fact coaches or staff were found bending or breaking the rules, then dismissal is almost certain."[66] True to his concern for integrity, in the spring 1995 Duderstadt dismissed Michigan's head football coach on grounds of socially unacceptable personal conduct while intoxicated. Major university sports can create difficult issues. Incidents in athletic programs and involving student athletes are accompanied by a high degree of public visibility and significant potential for causing notoriety. This is a reality for presidents of large universities. Duderstadt provided leadership in this arena of university life in which presidential stands can be critically important.

Likewise, Clark Atlanta presents a unique context and challenge for Cole's leadership in relation to institutional saga. One year after Cole became president of Clark College, a trustee-initiated consolidation of Clark and Atlanta University was begun. Cole would assume the presidency of the merged institution. He was forced to confront the significant difference between a presidency of two merged schools and what would be the case had he "inherited a single institution that had its mores and its culture, its rhythm of activities and events already decided."[67]

The merger posed a twofold problem for Cole. First, the management demands of the Clark Atlanta merger created the need for Cole to be significantly and unavoidably involved in numerous administrative details. His experience offers a warning about the possible consequences for presidential leadership when major administrative responsibilities exceed the normal expectations on presidents, thereby overtaking other concerns at the heart of institutions.

Second, as a "new" institution, Clark Atlanta had yet to form a saga of its own. Rather, it had two distinct sagas that Cole needed to join and blend into one. Though he could exercise moral leadership to accomplish that task, he did not inherit the luxury of a core, coherent institutional saga as a context. This unique situation presented an opportunity for presidential leadership. But it was also perplexing for Cole as he was forced to appeal to two histories, traditions, alumni interests, and campus cultures.

Commenting on the development of a coherent university culture that could be called a saga at Clark Atlanta, Cole remarked that "this environment is not yet at that point. We are not a mature university. We do not have these things that everybody recognizes [should be] part of the course of events here and the culture of this place. We're still trying to develop that."[68] Cole was presented with the leadership opportunity of creating this new culture and thereby of shaping the saga of new-formed Clark Atlanta.

In this chapter we have observed how presidential leadership and its moral voice is able to contribute to and to shape the saga of colleges and universities. Presidents do so in a variety of ways. They can influence the understanding of institutional mission. They are able to enlarge the purpose of the college through the application of the moral voice in the development of the institution's philosophy of education. And they can provide moral guidance in their practical leadership of institutional affairs. We have also noted the impact on the moral voice of the dilemmas and difficulties presented by particular institutional contexts. One of these is when the mission of the college is not coherently or commonly understood. Another is when the institution has yet to develop a saga. We turn next to the specific elements of moral leadership and moral voice as presidents speak within the gates of their colleges and universities.

NOTES

1. I am indebted to Clark's concept of saga. See Burton R. Clark, *The Distinctive College: Antioch, Reed and Swarthmore* (Chicago: Aldine, 1970). See also Louise Joyner Butler, *The Distinctive Black College: Talladega, Tuskegee and Morehouse* (Metuchen, N.J.: Scarecrow Press, 1977). Butler demonstrates the applicability of Clark's notion of saga to three historically black colleges.

2. Clark, *Distinctive College*, p. 235.

3. *Wellesley College* (Louisville, Ky.: Harmony House, 1988), p. 85. Durant's philosophy on the education of women as embodied in the motto is reflected in an 1877 sermon in which he asserted that "the higher education of women is one of the great world battle cries for freedom, for right against might. . . . I believe that God's hand is in it; that it is one of the great ocean currents of Christian civilization; that He is calling to womanhood to come up higher, to prepare herself for great conflicts, for vast reforms of social life, for noblest usefulness."

4. Diana Chapman Walsh, "Why Are We Here?" September 7, 1993, p. 4.

5. Phyllis Meras, "A Morning with a President," *Wellesley*, President's Office, Wellesly College, Fall 1993, p. 7.

6. Personal interview with President Diana Chapman Walsh of Wellesley College, November 28, 1994. Of note is her indication that the presidential search committee agenda included this interest in expanding the moral voice of the college beyond the presence of its alumnae in the world. Most colleges hope that alumni involvement in the world will reflect positively on the institution. For example, Duderstadt points to Jonas Salk, an alumnus of the University of Michigan, as an example of how the institution makes major moral contributions to the world through its graduates. Personal interview with President James J. Duderstad of the University of Michigan, March 6, 1995.

7. Diana Chapman Walsh, Friday All College Reception, August 6, 1993, p. 2. Expounding this theme of reshaping the purpose of the college, she contends that the institution "can articulate forcefully and well what the essence of a liberal education is—the most potent antidote any democratic society has against parochialism and divisiveness. . . . We can develop new vocabularies, relationships and social mechanisms that will help lead the way out of the current period of suspicious ethnic divisions and isolated enclaves toward truly nurturing, trusting, and respectful multicultural communities."

8. Nannerl O. Keohane, convocation address, September 5, 1985, Keohane Speeches, 1981–1985, p. 7. See both Kenneth Minogue in *The Concept of a University* and A. Bartlett Giamatti in *The University and the Public Interest*—especially Giamatti's chapter "A Coda: The Codification of Us All"—who wrestle with this issue against the backdrop of their concerns that the university not be subject to political and social pressures lest it become less than a university, that in so doing it would risk becoming no different from other institutions and organizations.

9. Keohane, convocation address, pp. 7–8.

10. Personal interview with President Thomas Gerety of Amherst College, July 27, 1994.

11. At the 1887 ceremony commemorating the fiftieth anniversary of the University of Michigan's founding, James Angell cites the language of the ordinance "placed here upon our walls. . . . 'Religion, morality, and knowledge being necessary to good government and the happiness of mankind, schools and the means of education shall be forever

encouraged.' " James Burrill Angell, *Commemorative Oration* (Ann Arbor: University of Michigan, 1888), p. 4.

12. University of Michigan, *Exercises at the Inauguration of President Angell* (Ann Arbor: Courier Stearn, 1871), p. 6.

13. *Inauguration of President Angell*, p. 16.

14. Harold Shapiro, inauguration address, April 4, 1980, Shapiro Collection, Box 178. The title of his address is "Critic and Servant: The Role of the University."

15. Supporting this assessment, Duderstadt notes that the demands of administering the institution divert his attention from concern about the quality of the undergraduate experience and from time to reflect on the moral aspects of his role as president. Personal interview with President James J. Duderstadt of the University of Michigan, March 6, 1995.

16. Shapiro, inauguration address, pp. 10–11.

17. Ibid., p. 9.

18. Edward Malloy, address to the faculty, President's Office, University of Notre Dame, October 3, 1990, p. 11.

19. Edward Malloy, "Notre Dame: The Unfolding Vision," unpaginated.

20. Personal interview with President Edward Malloy, C.S.C., of Notre Dame University, September 20, 1994.

21. Edward Malloy, *Final Report: Colloquy for the Year 2000*, President's Office, University of Notre Dame, May 7, 1993, p. 38.

22. Myron W. Adams, *A History of Atlanta University* (Atlanta: Atlanta University Press, 1930), p. 2.

23. *Atlanta University Bulletin* no. 113 (November 1900), p. 1. The *Atlanta University Bulletin* regularly recognized the university's donors. In this issue Caroline Hazard, though serving as Wellesley's president, is listed through her affiliation with the Peacedale Congregational Church as having donated $50, one of two donors from the state of Rhode Island (p. 4).

24. *Atlanta University Bulletin* no. 9 (April 1889), p. 2.

25. A detailed account of this controversy is found in Myron W. Adams, *A History of Atlanta University* (Atlanta: University of Atlanta Press, 1930), pp. 24–28.

26. *Atlanta University Bulletin* no. 20 (June 1890), p. 4c. Responding to the passage of the resolutions, Bumstead summarizes the university's position by reviewing the history of the university's principles in relationship to national and state authorities. In a statement noteworthy in its own right, but also bearing great resemblance to ensuing and present debates about federal versus state jurisdiction on appropriations of federal funding, Bumstead notes that "before donating any money the Bureau (of Refugees, Freedmen, and Abandoned Lands) required and secured from the trustees the passage of certain resolution forever binding themselves to keep the doors of the Institution open to the two races represented in the operations of the Bureau."

27. Fortunately for Atlanta University and for Bumstead, their stand produced support from various quarters. Bumstead is able to report that "The New York *Nation* of the current week says: 'The Atlanta University was not founded to raise or to force the issue, but it has, by a simple observance of Christian and democratic principles, called attention to the repudiation of these by its persecutors.' " Commenting on the broader social implications underlying the challenge presented by the resolutions, Bumstead adds that "possibly the adoption of a policy which the *Nation* thus implies to be un-Christian, undemocratic and un-American might, for a time, increase the influence of the University

among those who now insist on such a policy." Then taking the argument to an even higher moral plane, he concludes that "there can be no doubt that this would be done at an immense sacrifice of influence among the colored people, who feel their humanity recognized and honored by the refusal of the University to treat them as educational lepers whose training must be conducted apart from pupils of all other races than their own." *Atlanta University Bulletin* no. 20, p. 4c.

28. For a discussion of the issue of institutional fiscal responsibility and other moral choices faced by colleges and universities, see Noel B. Reynolds, "On the Moral Responsibilities of Universities," pp. 91–110 in *Moral Values and Higher Education: A Notion at Risk*, ed. Dennis L. Thompson (Provo, Utah: Brigham Young University, 1991). For additional background, see James B. Angell, *The Higher Education: A Plea for Making It Accessible to All* (Ann Arbor: Michigan Board of Regents, 1879), pp. 7–11.

29. Personal interview with President Edward Malloy, C.S.C., of Notre Dame University, September 20, 1994. In the interview, Malloy discusses at great length the economic realities of Notre Dame and the surrounding geographical area. For example, he notes specifically that "a very fine moral thing," often overlooked by many people, is that the institution's stability as an employer "brings a degree of prosperity to this community that wouldn't exist otherwise. Everything that we do in terms of having balanced budgets and running an efficient operation contributes to that, but most people would never praise it in moral terms."

30. Personal interview with President Diana Chapman Walsh of Wellesley College, November 28, 1994. Walsh expressed a major goals for her presidency as a commitment to work in the area of "fiscal effectiveness and accountability [so that] decisions in the way we allocate our resources are truly driven by our values."

31. Ibid.

32. Personal interview with President George Rupp of Columbia University, November 16, 1994.

33. Ibid.

34. Peter Pouncey, convocation address, September 1992, p. 2 in Peter Pouncey Biographical File (N/A), Archives and Special Collections, Amherst College Library.

35. Ibid., p. 4.

36. Idem.

37. Idem.

38. Idem.

39. Ibid., pp. 4–5.

40. Idem.

41. For example, see *George Harris, Amherst Student* 45 no. 62, (June 10, 1912), p. 1.

42. James W. Cavanaugh, C.S.C., "The Spirit of the Founders," UND Archives, Box 10, undated, p. 6.

43. Cavanaugh, "Life and Duty," UND Archives, Box 10, p. 6.

44. Cavanaugh, *The Conquest of Life*, ed. John A. O'Brien (Paterson, N.J.: St. Anthony Guild Press, 1952), p. 9.

45. Cavanaugh, "The Price of a Soul," in *The Conquest of Life*, ed. John A. O'Brien (Paterson, N.J.: St. Anthony Guild Press, 1952), pp. 16–17. Cavanaugh's position reflects a discussion beyond his disagreement with Eliot. For example, a few years earlier, in an address to a Sunday school convention at Kings Chapel in Boston, Caroline Hazard

commented that "with our more modern views of education, with the idea of imposing less and less from without and developing more and more from within the reverence for any one book or series of writings has most sensibly diminished" (Caroline Hazard, *From College Gates* [Boston: Houghton Mifflin, 1925], p. 104). Hazard and Eliot may reflect a changing point of view among New England colleges as well as a difference between the Protestant and Catholic points of view of their day. Though Hazard's comments might not appear as radical as Eliot's in the eyes of Cavanaugh, they still represent a departure from his staunch position quite specifically rooted in Christian and Catholic belief. Despite this statement, Hazard held her own brand of strong Christian assumptions that shaped her educational philosophy and her understanding of Wellesley's mission.

46. Cavanaugh, "Price of a Soul," p. 19.

47. Peter Pouncey, "Dialectics and Dialectic," p. 12, Peter Pouncey Biographical File (N/A), Archives and Special Collections, Amherst College Library.

48. Personal interview with President Thomas Gerety of Amherst College, July 27, 1994.

49. Ibid.

50. Personal interview with President Diana Chapman Walsh of Wellesley College, November 28, 1994.

51. Ibid.

52. Personal interview with Edward Malloy, C.S.C.

53. Ibid.

54. Personal interview with President Thomas Cole of Clark Atlanta University, February 16, 1995.

55. Ibid.

56. Ibid.

57. Ibid.

58. Elias Blake, Jr., "Preventing a Backlash in Higher Education for Black Education," the Black Conference in Higher Education, February 1974, p. 11. See also his Founder's Day Address, From the personal papers of Elias Blake, February 19, 1980, pp. 3–5.

59. Personal interview with Thomas Cole.

60. Personal interview with President George Rupp of Columbia University, November 16, 1994.

61. Personal interview with George Rupp. I have italicized "moral imagination" as a term that Rupp shares with two other college presidents, Richard Morill of the University of Richmond and James Laney of Emory. All three use this term to describe one of the primary tasks of education. Of interest is the fact that all three are graduates of Yale Divinity School. This not a coincidence. Though the precise source has yet to be located, a Yale graduate of the same era (1950s and 1960s), Professor Louis Hammann of Gettysburg College, believes it to be in the lectures and writings of H. Richard Niebuhr, then of the Yale faculty (personal communication).

62. James Shapiro, "David Denby's Return to 'Great Books,' " *Chronicle of Higher Education* 18, no. 3 (September 13, 1996). Denby's book is *Great Books: My Adventures with Homer, Rousseau, Woolf, and Other Indestructible Writers of the Western World* (Boston: Simon and Schuster, 1996).

63. Personal interview with President James J. Duderstadt of the University of Michigan, March 6, 1995.

64. Personal interview with James J. Duderstadt.

65. Ibid.

66. James J. Duderstadt, "The Thrill of Victory . . . The Agony of Defeat . . . and the Gnashing of Teeth . . . As College Presidents Attempt to Reform Intercollegiate Athletics," James J. Duderstadt Collection, Box 248, folder 1, Michigan Historical Collections, Bentley Historical Library, University of Michigan, unpaginated.

67. Personal interview with President Thomas Cole of Clark Atlanta University, February 16, 1995.

68. Personal interview with Thomas Cole.

PART TWO

WITHIN THE GATES

4

Shaping Student Character

The campus community is a major arena of influence for presidents and the expression of moral leadership. The presidential voice within the gates embodies a college's mission and realizes its most fundamental educational ideals. Historically, presidents have had timeless impact on their campus, especially in shaping the character of their students. While there is a role for presidents in the world beyond their gates, their leadership within the gates is clear and can be of critical importance. Contrasting the realm of moral leadership on and off the campus, Thomas Gerety notes that for a president to "[speak] out is all right as long as you keep that tether, that sense of groundedness back home. Your most important crises are going to be those that happen here. *Your greatest moral authority is about what's going on here.*"[1]

There is a continual flux to the issues and debates of different eras on campuses and in society. Every college has its unique problems and needs. But despite the distinctiveness of the challenges confronting presidential leadership, there is also a timeless quality to the concerns of campus communities. Presidents share similar and characteristic responses to the common elements they face in the lives of their campuses. In many different times and moments, presidents must ensure that education has meaning and that the academic, intellectual, and social life of the campus, whatever else it does, contributes in some way to moral learning and reason.

THE MORAL FOUNDATIONS OF THE EDUCATIONAL LIFE

Presidents frequently are called upon to defend and justify the intrinsic values of education. When they do so, it is common for them to address the moral aspects of education. Presidential affirmations about the importance of education and about the responsibilities of students for their own education reveal philosophical and practical qualities in presidential moral leadership. This is especially true in justifications of the value of a liberal arts education to students and society.

Responding to this issue, James Cavanaugh affirms the inherent value of education as a good to be attained rather than for its material benefits. To those who question education's value, he simply suggests that education is the basis for the development of meaning in life and for the betterment of culture and society. His conclusion contends that "the centuries have taught me that the heart of culture is culture of the heart, that the soul of improvement is improvement of the soul, that the making of a life is incomparably more than the making of a living."[2]

For Cavanaugh religion was a critical part of the students' education. Religious belief and practice were to have an established role in the daily lives of students. Their lives "must be challenged by the standard of religion and conscience." This foundation was terribly important because it enabled students "to see things aright, and . . . do things aright." Cavanaugh's concern for students was clear: even with a secure faith "the influence of the easy-going, self-indulgent, corrupt world may easily enough affect your morals."[3] Notre Dame's presidents regularly underscore the university's philosophy that connecting the students' religious affections to their education develops conscience and forms character. These guides then enable students to face the challenge posed by the hostile and corrupting influences of the secular world.

Cavanaugh was greatly concerned about practically applying this education to the lives of students. He did not want students to so fear the challenges and demands of society that they would be unable to use their gifts to meet society's needs. Failure to overcome this fear, he surmised, reduced the great potential afforded by education and diminished education's true value in the lives of students. At a profound level learning and knowledge must prepare students to educate and to lead others. In a baccalaureate sermon, he challenged students to embrace education because "the world is perishing today for lack of courageous and generous men." A college education is an antidote to this situation. For Cavanaugh, the "ideal college man," presumably a Notre Dame graduate, "is the exact opposite of all this. Empowered by education with skill and strength to exercise his faculties, to use his knowledge, to discover truth for himself and to uncover truth for others, he is naturally called to intellectual leadership in the world."[4]

These responsibilities of the educated person were to be taken with the most ultimate seriousness. Cavanaugh believed that church, state, home, and the university were joined in admonitions about the formation of character and about *noblesse oblige*—the expectations of students resulting from education. Lest the students required a reminder of the expectations on them, Cavanaugh noted that "The Church demands it of you as a religious duty; the state requires it as a service of citizenship; your parents hope and pray for it for the honor of their old age; Notre Dame expects it as the vindication of her teaching and her influence."[5]

These high-minded hopes of education and expectations of students are not the exclusive province of a bygone era—Cavanaugh's days as a president at the beginning of the twentieth century. Decades later, Nannerl Keohane, president of Wellesley College, asserted similar focus on the moral value and meaning of education. Keohane was also interested in the important connection between courage and education. For students this includes being prepared for the discomforts and difficulties of living according to moral convictions. The road students must travel is not easy because "education . . . means being willing to risk being disagreed with and argued with when your views about important topics like politics, morals, religion, science, don't square with those of your friends and colleagues." She adds further that "education also takes the courage to stand out front and be counted for your beliefs, to argue for things you have come to know and hold dear, to have faith in yourself."[6] This counsel is particularly important given the pressures of political correctness, which tend to stifle open debate and discussion on many campuses.

Like many her presidential counterparts, Keohane believes that one obligation of educated people is to use their educations to provide leadership in society. Education is essential "because only educated people can live in such a complicated world, can continue to change it and harness it, understand it and soften it for human use."[7] Educators frequently make this contention that society's needs can be met only by the ranks of the educated.

The assumptions underlying this stand present their own set of difficulties. An obvious charge is that of elitism. At a deeper level, the roots of this assumption about the educated class reflect a recurrent tension in American education. This tension results from a desire to balance a belief that society, while fundamentally egalitarian, must also rely on the *noblesse oblige* of an educated, even if allegedly meritocratic, elite. Education produces superior citizens but they must use the advantages of learning and knowledge to promote human progress and good. Keohane stresses this important responsibility. American democracy maintains the belief, even if at time illusory, that the civic order is founded upon and stresses equality, at its best even equal opportunity. However, those who pursue education will always lead the less educated. In their moral rhetoric, presidents urge that the educated must avoid elitism and must provide leadership committed to the commonweal.

Peter Pouncey, president of Amherst and a contemporary of Keohane, justified the value of education on two major accounts. First, he believed that education must lead students to a core set of beliefs. The ability to develop and to defend core beliefs are goals of education. Courage and the ability to be true to oneself—elements often associated with character formation—are essential qualities of the educated person. Pouncey conceived these beliefs as being derived from the educational life rather resulting from religious faith, as might his predecessors at Amherst. But regardless of the source of inspiration, the development of beliefs that shape and define life remains a crucial and fundamental purpose of education.

Discussing *The Education of Henry Adams*, Pouncey used what he viewed as the pathos of Adams's wife's suicide, and contended the tragedy is that all Adams's "knowledge seemed to have no relevance . . . because it did not help him keep her."[8] From this sombre example, Pouncey challenged students to recognize the transformative power of education. His assertion was that as well as sharpening the student's intelligence, "your heart should be informed as well, and you should form beliefs you care for, and learn to have the courage to stand behind them." But this is only part of the transformation.

Second, Pouncey adamantly resisted the conventional dichotomy between the ivory tower and the real world. Pouncey concluded that students have in themselves the power to construct and develop their own lives, that they "do not come to Amherst to become more like us (whoever *we* are), but to become the most completely fulfilled version of [themselves]. There is not radical discontinuity between here and any other world; real or unreal, this is it, just as much as the place . . . left behind."[9]

There are other examples of Pouncey's desire to resist what he considers to be a false dichotomy between the real world and the ivory tower. Previously, he connected the question of whether college is an ivory tower to the students' application of learning and knowledge in the world. His clear philosophy was that "the life of the mind . . . can never be a cloistered, solipsistic activity. In fact, the reason we come to a liberal arts college is precisely because we know that it is the interaction with teachers and students which tells us what exactly our talents are, what problems we can best address, what more we need to make sense of them, what individual insights we can bring to their solution." This education is "real world" in the sense that "these are not lessons to be learnt for a grade in a course, but lessons to be learnt and continued for a life-time."[10]

Finally, both of Pouncey's assertions—that the development of beliefs is a critical result of education and that education is not an isolated, ivory tower experience—are brought together in his final comments on this theme. His aspiration is that the education that young people receive as college students consists of "interactions in class and out of class, which help us achieve some self-knowledge, of where we stand in ourselves," and these elements "should also help us plot our position and make us certain of where we stand in relation to others, and what we stand for—what kind of generosities, of sympathy and respect, what kind of decencies and principles do we offer the world and insist on for ourselves."[11] A college education results in moral demands and learning is a lifelong process. Personal convictions developed by students enable them to discover what they will stand for in life.

Presidents Thomas Gerety and George Rupp believe that intellectual dialogue—the conversation of academic communities—is critical in the creation of moral features in educational life. Gerety's commitment to this educational conversation reflects Amherst's rich liberal arts tradition. Gerety views "the moral core" to be "teaching as conversation—a conversation about ideas." Taking on the narrowness and intolerance resulting from attitudes rooted in political correctness, Gerety admonishes that "The liberal arts means the most radical ideas, even ideas that are inimical to the liberal arts as a tradition, [for example] that the tradition is oppressive, should be embraced with joy." In a unique conception of presidential responsibility, Gerety asserts that "the morality of the president [is] to keep the conversation going. [It is] more fundamentally about the entire set of relations that makes up the university or college. It is a set of relationships designed to facilitate, in a metaphoric sense, conversation, inquiry. A president should speak out first and foremost on that morality, the morality of conversation."[12] Gerety's presidentially conducted educational conversation is a significant way for presidents to concentrate moral attention within the campus communities.

This notion of presidential moral leadership has its roots in Robert Hutchins' understanding of the Great Conversation. A campuswide educational conversation has a purpose that is at its core a moral proposition, a belief that dialogue and discourse about ideas and relationships—moral at their core—should permeate the campus. Gerety desires to establish and maintain this conversation as a presidential responsibility. Declaring this as part of the moral voice of the president, Gerety views this as "the moral voice of a teacher, but a teacher of very complex class. The role brings with it a certain kind of teaching responsibility that is necessarily suffused with moral questions about how human beings live." Finally, the president must actively support the proposition that the "whole liberal arts tradition is built around [this] fundamental principle: what [are] the most important and difficult subjects for human beings to know about. And that's what we're teaching."[13]

Gerety understands that, though as president he must exhibit extreme care in presenting personal beliefs, there is no reason that he should avoid expression of beliefs completely.[14] The student–teacher relationship he envisions as the ideal will be a major force to shape and form students through mutual interaction with teachers, including the president as teacher, and through relationships with fellow students.[15]

Gerety's predecessor, Pouncey, understands the Great Conversation as a bridge between scholarship and research on one side and teaching on the other. The apparently mutually exclusive nature of these two fundamental faculty responsibilities has grown in recent years. The notion frequently associated with major universities that faculty cannot simultaneously be both outstanding classroom teachers and committed scholars has gradually seeped into the culture of much smaller colleges as well.

To underscore the traditional importance of teaching at Amherst, Pouncey convinced his board of trustees to support publication of faculty commitments to teaching.[16] In the book and wearing his hat as a professor of classics, Pouncey discusses what he believes students gain from being taught the ancient texts of the classics. Pouncey's philosophy was that these texts contribute to the liberating nature of liberal education. Such an education challenges students to examine their ideas, to develop their thinking in response to academic material and scholarly knowledge, and to integrate into their lives what they learn. From ancient and classical texts students learn "to read narratives with intensity and sympathy, and then to engage the rhetoric, reflect hard on the judgments it offers, and work out what they will accept, what they will leave behind, or what alternative judgments they will pass on their own." As a result, students "will be deepened by connections with the past, but in a way that does not hold them back, but releases them, from a stronger base of understanding, to dare brave new departures for themselves."[17]

For Rupp a portion of the moral core of educational life is located in Columbia University's curriculum. This core curriculum engages students in Hutchins's notion of a Great Conversation.[18] Rupp is highly critical of much of what he sees in collegiate education. Contrary to the contemporary tendencies, he believes a college or university education should "provide students with better grounding in facts, more competence in dealing with the world, preparation for what they are going to do later." Rupp insists that "the fundamental moral issue for a university is to provide outstanding education in just those mundane terms. Very many of our institutions are failing to do that." Providing a sound education is a critical presidential responsibility within the gates of the institution. Rupp views this failure as "a moral problem" adding that "if universities and colleges and schools aren't doing that they are abdicating their central responsibility. The moral texture of an institution is shot right through it. This moral texture is not [only] a function, but should be woven through the institution's life."[19]

This belief that the moral life of the university is not marginal but rather must be conceived as central to institutional purpose is one of Rupp's core contentions. Despite the contrary opinions of numerous vocal critics, Rupp believes that there is a moral basis for grounding education in Western traditions. The encounter with these intellectual traditions, complemented by insights gained in a requirement rooted in non-Western cultures, provides an opportunity for students to learn about themselves and others. Describing the educational life at Columbia, Rupp remarks that "what we do with undergraduates in the core curriculum is work with our students so they understand themselves in their own world, [so] they are grounded in Western traditions." The moral value of this education is that students "learn about themselves in a quite fundamental way, not themselves only as individuals but as part of the society, the basic traditions that have shaped Western ideas and values. And then we also require that they learn about others in a major cultures requirement."[20] The value attached to student engagement with traditional Western thought leads Rupp to this broader contention that the entire educational life is a moral endeavor.

Rupp knows that education is not morally perfect; it can be used for destructive and negative purposes. Therefore it is the ends of education that make the difference. In its ideal form "liberal education or liberating education is, [though] it doesn't always take, a moral enterprise." The purpose of this education "is to have the individual both understand himself or herself and be able to see relationships to larger wholes, whether communities or whole societies, to understand himself or herself in a context wider than just very provincial interests." Education does not guarantee that provincialism and self-centeredness will be suppressed. Rupp is fully aware that "it is not salvation that is achieved through this process." But he strongly believes that the "process is enlargement of the self through education, is a moral process that does not inevitably have positive effects but the enlarging process itself is a moral enterprise."[21] Rupp's pragmatism and self-confessed Calvinism leads him to point out that education will not produce an always perfect, moral outcome. Nonetheless, he views education as fundamentally a moral endeavor. As president he bears personal moral responsibility to secure that foundation.

EDUCATION AS SPIRITUAL AND SOULFUL

In a few instances, especially at the turn of the century and at religious colleges, presidents have invoked specific language about the soul and spirituality in their attempts to influence the formation of student character. These references differ from presidential references to religion and morality, especially in the articulation of educational philosophy. Caroline Hazard was a lifelong member and active lay leader of the Congregational Church. She revealed affection for the spiritual aspects of life on numerous occasions during her presidency. One was in her last annual report in which she requoted a statement from her acceptance of the presidency a little over a decade before. She captured the solemn responsibility of the presidency by claiming that "it is because I believe in divine life among men, in the direct and personal connection of each soul with its Maker that I dare to take up the great work you are committing to my care. Humanity without Divinity is of the dust that perishes. Humanity joined to Divinity can compass the impossible."[22]

As did many presidents of her era, Hazard had weekly contact with students through Sunday evening chapel talks. In these short sermons, Hazard admonished students to take seriously the importance of the soul in daily living. The soul is active in people's lives and forms character by helping the individual to resist the conformity of external forces.[23]

Hazard's philosophy of education contains two assumptions about spirituality. One is that "spiritual experiences are not necessarily divorced from common life."[24] The other is that the "supreme task of all education [is] the training of the soul."[25] Individual souls are created (and, Hazard contends, remain) equal. For Hazard all "souls" are equal and the educational search for wisdom is a spiritual quest.[26] But because education produces knowledge, individuals differ in their capabilities. Those with greater knowledge have greater social responsibilities. We will observe recurrent presidential emphasis on this *noblesse oblige* as a way of resolving the tension between democratic equality and the meritocratic differences that result from education. Hazard's reliance on the soul and spirituality contributes to our understanding of the moral leadership of presidents.

Hesburgh's concept of the soul reaches beyond its importance to the students' identity and what they are able to become in the world. For Hesburgh, educators and the mission of the university itself have a moral battle to wage and win for the souls of students. In this way, students will then move into the world better prepared to improve the lot of others and of society. This recurrent theme of the role of the university in improving the world through the lives and work of its students is captured in Hesburgh's suggestion that "in the realm of truth . . . is the mission of the university manifest. If our graduates are to have a vital part in the struggle for men's souls, they must begin by achieving true wisdom and freedom in their own souls. . . . A University today will have an impact on the progress of man and human society, in direct proportion to the truth of the heritage it imparts to its students."[27]

THE FORMATION OF CHARACTER AND MORAL VALUES

Throughout the history of higher education in America and in a variety of institutional contexts, presidents have been attentive to character formation— the moral life and development of students. Circumstances, student attitudes and values, and religious, cultural, and social assumptions have changed. And these changes have produced concomitant changes in presidential rhetoric. But there remains a remarkable consistency in presidential concern about student moral issues and dilemmas and about the moral contingencies of college communities.

Citing Henry Fowle Durant's founding charge that Wellesley would educate women to "have lives of noblest usefulness," Keohane describes how that can be done.[28] Keohane understands that the academic aspects of a Wellesley education do not by themselves lead the student to moral insight and understanding. Mandatory Bible courses and required chapel attendance performed some of this task for earlier generations of students. Though much of Durant's goal continues to be fulfilled through academic learning and the classroom experience, Keohane knows that "something beyond this is necessary. If we want students to develop a sense of responsibility for leadership and service, intellectual stimulation alone is not enough. We also have to develop moral sensibility and a sense of purpose."[29]

For Wellesley students of the latter portion of the twentieth century, Keohane suggests that out-of-the-classroom experiences provide some of inspiration that fulfills Durant's hope of "noble usefulness." She believes that opportunities such as community service, symposia, political involvement, and campus discussions of important issues and events are the way to develop a moral sense in students.[30]

But Keohane's thought also reveals the struggle of many contemporary presidents to find substitutes for the traditional ways such as required chapel, senior seminars in ethics, and religion—especially Bible—courses that provided at least structure for students to develop moral meaning. Keohane and her contemporaries face the realities that the world has changed and that once-accepted structures and expectations are no longer viewed as reasonable or possible. The void is easily identified. The dilemma is to discover or uncover contemporary ways in which character can be formed and moral conscience instilled. Though the jury remains out on their effectiveness at filling the void in moral development, public, community service, and similar outside-the-classroom experiences are frequently employed today to inspire moral values in students.

The problem of locating ways to shape the character of students is not, as is often thought, merely a contemporary phenomenon. Presidents in earlier times confronted similar difficulties. For example, Caroline Hazard of Wellesley provides insight into the concerns facing college leaders of her turn-of-the-century era. In her 1910 Annual Report, Hazard reviews the fact that years before, in her first year as president, she proposed and the trustees allowed the abolition of compulsory morning prayers. In hindsight, Hazard notes that the change to the nonmandatory services presented "the difficulty [is] that the students who most need such a service are not there."[31]

One of the continuing dilemmas facing college and university leaders is how much freedom to give to students. Commenting on student behavior and the expectations of undergraduates, Hazard asks "is there not danger in giving untried young people too much liberty, of expecting them to decide for themselves questions of life-long importance, without guidance of those who ought to guide?" Then linking her thoughts to the history of her home state, Hazard continues: " 'Here liberty of conscience is carried to an irreligious extreme,' one of the early divines wrote of Rhode Island. Is the same indictment true, in part, of the modern college?" At the beginning of the twentieth century, political, cultural and religious changes were underway and were producing an impact on college campuses. In the face of increased freedom for students, especially in morals and religion, Hazard raises concern about what may result: "there is no greater good without lesser benefits, and the sense of solidarity, of community life, of college loyalty which is fostered by such a service is something which no college can afford to lose."[32]

One of Hazard's contemporaries, James Angell of Michigan, was concerned about the formation of moral character of students throughout his lengthy presidency. Like many presidents of his era, Angell is concerned about the entire generation of college students. The importance of character formation is that it changes the individual. Angell believed that he and his contemporaries were obligated to create a more profound moral complexion for an entire generation. This obligation would be fulfilled by making changes in the lives of a sufficient number of students.

Angell believed that there was a balance in life between forces over which people have little or no control and those areas in which they need to be active agents not bound by convention. In the face of the conflicts and dilemmas that accompany life, students must possess the basic qualities essential to live productively and well in the world. Concerned about the ease with which anyone can justify means and ends, Angell warns that individuals cannot "sacrifice . . . moral integrity to the attainment of . . . ends. This moral integrity must be paramount."[33] He adds that "if one is to exert a permanent and benign influence, is to fill up the measure of his opportunity to bless mankind and be honored by mankind, one must have those high moral traits and purposes which give weight to whatever one says and does. This power of moral personality is by far the most important of all the qualities essential to the highest success in moulding one's generation."[34] Angell believed that he and similarly concerned fellow educators must as educational leaders inspire values in students, thereby shaping the moral character of generations of students passing into the walls of the academy.

As noted, Angell was ever emphatic about the role of the Judeo-Christian heritage in the life of the University of Michigan. Character formation was grounded in the Judeo-Christian tradition. Discussing the academic development of students, Angell contends that "what I have said of intellectual development may be affirmed equally of moral development. To attain moral strength, that moral vigor and firmness, which we call weight of character, it is not sufficient to be convinced what we ought to do nor even to write it down in a statement or to sign a pledge to do it. . . . we must be rooted and grounded in habits of right action." This mark of character that colleges or universities were responsible for instilling in students was too precious and fundamental to be left to chance or fortune. For Angell the challenge was that the student's "character must often be transformed in order to be rightly formed. We cannot extemporize preparation for the moral exigencies of life."[35]

Angell was not naive about the scholarly and social changes already multiplying at the turn of the twentieth century. He did see a parallel between the Temptations of Jesus and the temptations of scholars, calling them "to cherish some aim lower than the one true christian aim in life," and deterring them from the challenge of involvement in "some battle for righteousness," and from the value to the self of service to the community and the wider public.[36] However, he realistically acknowledged that changes in biblical scholarship and new archeological evidence created a situation in which "the transition for this generation from the old conceptions to the new truth is a difficult process, and not unattended with some temporary discomfort and even danger."[37] But for Angell the Judeo-Christian basis in the formation of character remained beyond compromise. It was a tradition for him and for the university that could be ignored only at the peril of education itself and of the lives of students as well as their teachers.

A contemporary of Angell's, William Crogman, was also committed to his human responsibility for the moral formation of character. While a faculty member at Clark College and prior to becoming president, Crogman remarked on the degree to which human beings must be responsible for themselves. Discussing the wrongs done to his African-American race, Crogman is quick to refute the all-too-human tendency to place blame externally. Alternatively, he proposes that "in truth, many of the so-called worries and vexations of life are but the legitimate offspring of our own shortsightedness or neglect of ignorance or indifference or recklessness. As finite beings we shall, of course, never be able to foresee all things, nor make adequate provision for all contingencies." The problem is "that we often blame one another, blame society, blame government, blame the Almighty himself for afflictions and calamities, both personal and national, which might have been averted by the exercise of forethought on our part, or by a little deeper investigation into the nature of things."[38] Crogman refused the simpler course of declaring himself and those of his race merely victims of evil. The frailties of human beings, even their capacity to mete out evil, is tragically universal. Crogman's students are urged to draw themselves out of the comfortable position of laying blame for their victimization to a more difficult but necessary position as responsible moral agents.

Crogman did not deny that students will encounter racial hatred and bias but urged them to live despite these barriers. Aware and concerned about the racial divide in the nation, Crogman had direct counsel for students. His plea was that "when you go into a strange community," avoid the tendency that you must "inform the people how wise you are, and what vast store of learning you possess. Too many are doing that now, wasting precious time and life. Life was not made for that. Life hath a deeper meaning." Crogman emphasized the importance of good works and the knowledge that one's reputation proceeded from participation in the life of the community. A segment of character formation is that students learn to value their lives and make their best contribution to the lives of others unimpeded by racial discrimination. His straightforward advice was that "if you know anything, if you are of any value to the community, the people will discover it in time, and give you credit for it; and if they do not, you can better afford to go without such recognition than not to have merited it."[39]

The last few years of Horace Bumstead's presidency at what was then Atlanta University overlapped with Crogman's at Clark College in Atlanta. Bumstead had a philosophy remarkably similar to Crogman's about the character of students and about their expectations of the world after college. On one occasion he used Acts 1:6–8 as a text in a talk to students. Counseling students against feelings of entitlement, Bumstead urged: "Do not ask to have a kingdom bestowed upon you because you are graduates. Seek rather to use the power, which as graduates you should possess, to achieve your own kingdom."[40] He noted the important distinction between having a titular position of power and having the truer power of the self. This power is most important and "such power will either give you all the position you can rightfully desire, or if not that, surely a sufficient opportunity for its exercise in doing good to the world."[41]

Reflecting his era, Bumstead grounded this advice to the graduates in Christian belief and imagery. And, like Crogman, Bumstead desired that his students avoid racializing their lives and their relationships in society. He encouraged students to view education as preparation for a broad mission, transcending self and race. He wanted Atlanta students to be blind to matters of race. Concerning their racial heritage, Bumstead's moral message urged that students not "go from Atlanta University with too much thought about the African race *as such*. If you plan to help them, as of course you will, plan to help them for the manhood and womanhood that dwells in their souls rather than for the race blood that flows in their veins."[42] Freeing themselves from racial expectations and assumptions would enable students to develop character and to pursue their mission in the world.

These presidents of black institutions in the South in the latter nineteenth century understood the unfortunate fact that racial discrimination would force some, maybe many, of their graduates to take jobs beneath their skill and training. Despite these potential barriers and frustrations, their presidential counsel was that students use their education fully and refuse to allow social conventions to deter contributions to a needy world. Bumstead, in advice not likely easy for the students to accept, confronted them with the reality they faced. When discriminated against, Bumstead wanted students to "seek the welfare of the *whole* community, take an interest in *all* the people and, so far as you may, in all public affairs. . . . Adopt as your own the thought of [William Lloyd] Garrison when he uttered the words engraved upon the pedestal of his statue in Boston, 'My country is the world—my countrymen are all mankind.' So be ye witnesses unto Christ even unto the uttermost part of the earth."[43]

Crogman and Bumstead were in unique positions as college presidents: they were compelled to encourage their students to overcome the racial prejudice of their time. In an unfortunate paradox, the students were gaining an education in part to improve their status in the world, but their presidents simultaneously had to prepare them for the hostilities awaiting in society. Crogman and Bumstead are also exemplary of presidential expressions of moral voice by calling upon commonly held beliefs, in this case the traditions of the college's ethos of resisting racial prejudice and segregation.

No discussion of presidential exhortations about the character formation of students would be complete without mention of Nicholas Murray Butler. As noted, presidents frequently refer to the formation of character when discussing the moral assumptions and expectations of education.

In one commencement address, Butler used classical and theological assumptions about human nature and the role of freedom to elaborate the connection between education and moral principles. Acknowledging that the liberty of free will forces individuals to be responsible for their choices, Butler maintained that education and the culture of the university are essential ingredients in character formation. For Butler "Character is not the mechanical resultant of blind forces; rather it is the product of choice. Were there no freedom of choice there would be no such thing as what we now call character."[44] He believed that freedom and liberty, preserved by subduing the forces of tyranny in World War I, have always been essential to education. For Butler, "the university is the natural home of liberty. . . . [and] has no higher lesson to teach than the significance of liberty, the importance of liberty, the worthy use of liberty to the end that character may be built constantly stronger and firmer."[45]

Another major concern for presidents during the late nineteenth and early twentieth centuries was the importance for students to resist the temptations of youth. Cavanaugh, an early twentieth century colleague of Butler, relates this concern to the moral development of students. In a sermon opening a school year, Cavanaugh assessed the problem of temptation and its fearsome challenge to students. He contends that "against the theory that a young man must 'sow his wild oats,' that there is one law of conduct for young men and another for your sisters, that sin is merely experience, such a college as this stands in absolute and uncompromising protest." In uncompromising language he adds "that weakness is as pitiful as ignorance; that conduct is four-fifths of life; that if you cannot decently restrain passion, your talent and your wealth and your social position merely make you a tenfold more damnable failure." Cavanaugh does not hedge his convictions. Notre Dame has an unbending and unrelenting stake in the character development of its students. Cavanuagh's warning is one of hell-fire and brimstone. The moral demand for responsible behavior leaves no doubt or question about the correct path for students. His stark conclusion is that "For the earnest young man who is seeking seriously in spite of human frailty to upbuild character, this college is a tender and forgiving mother; for the sunken and sodden libertine who does not desire to rise out of his sensual life, she is an avenging goddess, angry-eyed and armed with all the lightnings of heaven."[46]

In another sermon Cavanaugh reiterates these demanding beliefs and concerns about student behavior and development. He remarks ironically that "men sometimes talk lightly about the thoughtlessness of youth as if that were a sufficient excuse for neglecting life's serious duties; but if you are ever to be thoughtless would it not better be in old age, when your work is done and the years are not so heavily freighted with destiny?" But Cavanaugh was not naive about the realities of college student life, agreeing that "Recreation and entertainment, then, there must be for youth."[47] Proper formation of character is possible only when student outlets for personal growth occur within a university-defined environment of moral constraints. Cavanaugh views it as his presidential responsibility to maintain Notre Dame as such a preserve for students.

The early twentieth century featured significant debate about the teaching of moral values both in higher education and in American society. Students had begun to experience newfound freedoms. Presidents then as now struggled to balance the liberating nature of education with the structure and values of traditional moral supports for the development of young people. This tension between the doors that education inevitably opens and the growth it inspires in the young, and the desirability of traditional mores and values presumed to be of special importance to youth is an enduring challenge facing all educators, especially presidents and their moral leadership.

We have observed certain timeless themes and expectations in the culture of campus communities. However, time has brought about necessary and detectable changes in the presidential voice. Even at a school as fundamentally religious as Notre Dame there is a difference between Cavanaugh's statements about student behavior and Malloy's approach less than one hundred years later in how the university should address moral issues. Certain realities of the late twentieth century argue for changes in Notre Dame's posture. Malloy is aware of the limitations imposed on the institution as a result of attempts to remain attentive to its Catholic heritage. Assessing the impact of constraints created by the Church, Malloy argues that "as a Catholic university, we have retained certain policies in the area of student life and conduct that distinguish us from many of our peer institutions. The closer these policies are to the core of our Catholic identity and value system, the more resistant the Trustees, Fellows and officers of the University will be to their alteration or abandonment." However, accompanying this realpolitik of the relationship between Notre Dame and Church authorities and influence, Malloy expresses confidence "that all of the participants in the conversation about these matters of fundamental policy will remain open to good arguments for change and to the need for periodic review and further articulation of the values that are thought to be at stake."[48]

This presidential call for members of the campus community to participate in discussions and to be prepared to alter positions signifies a more collaborative, democratic approach than normally imagined in Cavanaugh's era. Then the presumed expectation was that the president would more autocratically assert strong and vastly less flexible moral positions on behalf of the university. In the present climate, Malloy believes that even those policies held most strongly on the grounds of their importance to Catholic morality should nonetheless be subject to review and to potential change through rational discourse.

One of the major changes from the early twentieth century to the present is the increased freedom experienced by students in college. Addressing the behavioral choices of students, Gerety argues for the need to maintain a moral basis within which these expanded freedoms are exercised. During his presidency at Trinity, Gerety warned students that "college will be a kind of freedom time for you. So much that was fixed before in your lives will seem now unfixed, open, up for grabs. . . . There is a danger in so much freedom of drifting aimlessly, like a dilettante, or, on the other hand, of going off in directions that betray what you stand for." Gerety urges students "to experiment, to venture out, to risk both a little and a lot. But never, ever, leave your good sense and moral judgment far behind. These are guides you will need now as never before."[49]

Since it cannot be assumed that students come to college with some "good sense and moral judgment," Gerety is realistic about the difficulties of making moral judgments in the practical setting of campus life. Being stretched and growing are an integral part of the college experience. These aspects of student life are best accomplished when accompanied by sensible moral understanding and constraints.

One of Gerety's contemporaries, James Duderstadt, commented to the Michigan Senate Assembly about constraints on student behavior and moral development, especially in a changing social climate. His thoughts arise in the context of discussing violations of expected social civility and in response to external criticism (no doubt conveyed by citizens to their legislative leaders) of student behavior. He extends Gerety's concern about student responsibility, suggesting the responsibilities of the university in providing essential constraints on student conduct. Duderstadt develops a framework for student behavior now that the *in loco parentis* era is past. He calls for "a new respect for limits that carries with it concern for the moral values and restraints that unify communities and keep human conduct within acceptable bounds. Universities cannot avoid the task. Like it or not, they will affect the moral development of their students by the ways in which they administer their rules of conduct, by the standard they achieve in dealing with ethical issues confronting the institution, by the many who counsel their students and coach their athletic teams."[50]

Duderstadt was concerned about the university abandoning the playing field of student moral behavior. For him and his fellow educational leaders the issue of institutional involvement in the lives of students was a difficult dilemma. The problem is exacerbated by the fact that the university "community is so diverse, set in a society so divided and confused over its values." The too frequent result is that the university that "pays little attention to moral development may find that many of its students grow bewildered, convinced that ethical dilemmas are simply matters of personal opinion beyond external judgment or careful analysis." To stem this tide, Duderstadt urges that "universities should be among the first to reaffirm the importance of basic values, such as honesty, promise keeping, free expression, and nonviolence, for these are not only principles essential to civilized society; they are values on which all learning and discovery ultimately depend."[51] Though the topic is not frequently discussed, there is a direct connection between the values university communities wish to inspire and maintain and the purpose of teaching and learning. Linking life outside to life within the classroom, Duderstadt reminds us that the commonly accepted values held to be important for social interaction on the campus are also fundamental to the academic aspects of student life.

Another contemporary president, Elias Blake of Clark College, makes a forthright comment about the values of college students. Like other presidents, Blake was concerned about the need to create complements to academic life and norms for student behavior and moral development. He urges that Clark and its sister black colleges "must recognize that to compete and survive, . . . [they] must exert some impact on the ways in which academic performance and the student culture interact. Over the last decade patterns of student life have developed that we must take a stand against, however unpopular or seemingly conservative. It is clear from our historic obligations and what our students are up against for the future that we need a system of support for academic and overall personal development."[52]

Education must also incorporate the highest ideals as a source of inspiration to students. For the goal is that "new generations of Clark graduates will not forget that humanism, the concern for the value of the individual, whatever his social, economic or racial definition, is the challenge for the creation of a society we have not yet seen."[53] Blake has his own version of John Dickey's "conscience and competence." Like other contemporary presidents, he remains aware of the need for new ways to develop "traditional values and principles that are timeless," adding that "If we do not find contemporary ways to achieve more than competence and proficiency, we may train narrowly and not educate broadly, make professionally profound but shallow in the potential for wisdom, reflective thought and creative leadership for our unfinished agenda as black Americans."[54] Blake's point is that black students and the colleges that educate them can ill afford to ignore building a lasting foundation of character. Though not a simple task, character formation is a significant challenge for all higher education.

Differing in significant ways from the present, concern about student behavior in the 1960s arose primarily from student involvement in political and social protests and other forms of campus disruption. The student generation of that era was a great challenge for presidents such as Theodore Hesburgh and other college leaders. Frequently, the political activities and the social consciousness of students directly questioned the moral authority of anyone in a position of leadership. Notre Dame was no exception and experienced the tensions that developed between students and administrators at many campuses during the 1960s. Hesburgh's reflections on dealing with student protests acknowledge the profound difficulties frequently encountered during this period. His perspectives provide interesting insight about the likely mindset of other presidents (though we can only speculate on how many) serving during the 1960s and early 1970s. Hesburgh's response to these social and political concerns reveals his moral leadership, especially in the formation of character and the moral life of the campus.

Addressing fellow educators, Hesburgh expresses earnest and heartfelt feelings for students. He contends that students are "always the most exciting and the most difficult part of any educational discussion today. Here, change is not only rampant, but galloping. First let us say, God bless them, these difficult, demanding, revolutionary students who are the reason and often the despair of our educational existence." It is as though Hesburgh was preaching to himself. However, a more important point is that he offers an appeal and encouragement to fellow educators. He wants them to embrace students despite the developing walls of separation between young people and their elders—whether parents, teachers, or other authority figures such as Hesburgh and his fellow presidents. Expressing the tension many educators often experience, Hesburgh adds that

"We find it difficult to live with them, but without them, there would be little reason for our institutions. They are the wave of the future that threatens to engulf the present, namely us. But we have to understand them, even more, to love them—else we should abandon the whole endeavor."[55]

Other of Hesburgh's thoughts about the tension resulting from changing student attitudes reveal hope that solutions could be found. In the absence of historical precedents or guides, he searched for a way through the difficulties and divisiveness of the time. However, though his context was different, some of the basic qualities—honesty and nonviolence—Hesburgh invokes are identical to those often suggested by presidents in other situations. Hesburgh appeals to a belief and a hope that if we "can agree on these basic values that make human life worth living, then perhaps we can pool our efforts, young and old, to redeem the times. It still won't be easy, but it can be done."[56] Certainly, regardless of era and of the difficulties engendered by student behavior, student activism is a reality of university life and thereby a challenge to the moral leadership of presidents.

Finally, Hesburgh stresses the need for courage from those involved in the education of students. Hesburgh directly challenges the Notre Dame University community and its students, but also faculty and administrative colleagues. His theme stressed the connection of conscience and competence in education and of students and teachers to the concerns of the world. He suggests that students "must be taught values as well as skills, and we must teach the values by courageously exemplifying them. It takes courage to say that there is no easy path to truth, and competence, and wisdom, and that each of these is far more important than false, but easy victories, moral ambiguity or neutrality, and cunning deceit in life." With a passion befitting his identity as priest and preacher, Hesburgh adds that "In a world where so few of us can glory in freedom, it takes courage to use our freedom to promote justice, even when justice is unpopular; to reject falsehood when everyone else says that the naked emperor is well clothed; to unmask the shoddy, the superficial, and the ersatz when others are applauding it because it happens to be in vogue."[57] Hesburgh's reflections about the tensions and difficulties of the 1960s and 1970s remind us of the importance of moral leadership in the relationship between students and administrators, especially in times of significant mistrust and cynicism.

In a commencement address at Dartmouth College, Hesburgh used the adage that the unexamined life is not worth living to underscore the combined importance of conscience and competence in education. His distinction is similar to then Dartmouth president John Dickey's concern about the need for both "compassion and competence."[58] Hesburgh's Dartmouth address centered on values in the formation of character, on the development of identity as an individual, and on the moral basis of an education. Hesburgh contended that "values, consciously examined and adhered to, are extremely important to the examined life that alone is really worth living. I know of no greater obstacle to the good life than the attitude of denying the importance of values, or of equating all values, good and bad, or, what is perhaps more prevalent in our day, just taking good values for granted." Against the backdrop of the many ethical dilemmas that were becoming increasingly pronounced in the post–World War II world, Hesburgh drew the critical distinction that "We hear more praise of talent today, than of values. Talent, however, is useless, even dangerous, without values. A man of great talent and no values is like a powerful sports car without a steering wheel—there is no direction for the power and no meaning to its journey."[59]

In discussing the role of education in character formation, presidents acknowledge that certain values are crucial to life, that education (especially the liberal arts) includes moral aspects, and that education is related to the pursuit of "the good." Occasionally, presidents will also argue that religion has a role in education. Such commentary is frequently found in the turn-of-the-century era, when presidents tended to develop philosophies of education based on theology and on the language of faith. One example is George Harris of Amherst, who fashioned a religious and moral foundation for the character formation of students.

Harris believed that certain guideposts were critical in the lives of students and graduates. He repeatedly stressed the need for those who became educated to apply moral perspectives in the social order. In this way human beings could fulfill their responsibility to create a decent society. Harris highlighted moral and religious insights by using biblical language. Elaborating a reference to the prophet Isaiah, Harris says that for Isaiah, "There is a vision of rectitude, of a right man, of the nobility of righteousness, of a man making his way through the world, with never a mean, low, base or petty action or thought, doing his whole duty to himself, to his neighbors and to God." In terms of the character of students, the example is "a vision of honor, of a self respecting man. We have no better word for honor than the word gentleman, which . . . does really signify character, a character of magnanimity, a man who is more than decent, who is sensitive to the feelings of others, a man of generosity, who thinketh no evil."[60]

Harris also cherished a strong theology of the Kingdom of God and he believed this "age to come" was essential to the formation of the life. The Kingdom defines for students who they are, shapes their view of the world, and directs them to contribute to society. For him, there are high ideals that must become embedded in the way one lives. Though the language is high-sounding, Harris had an extremely practical regard for the crucial role played by educated people in society. This practical vision emphasized the task of doing right because "it is the faithful picture of the career of a right man. . . . Performance is the realization of the ideal."[61] Without the application of these ideals into practice in society, there is no social improvement, no movement, in Harris's terms, toward the Kingdom of God on earth. Harris applied this vision to the lives of students and the formation of their character. It was a vision that contrasted with the mundane ideologies of the reformer who "thinks the world can be made perfect by some one device, as temperance, or socialism, or universal suffrage. . . . The ideal of rectitude and honor is not an ideal of the person isolated. Rectitude is in the relation of man to man, and so is honor."[62]

Presidents as well as most educators regularly face the criticism that education exists in an "ivory tower" far removed from the real world that students enter upon graduation. Harris took issue with this presumed separation, arguing that there is no difference between the world of undergraduates and the world they enter upon graduation. He believed that an Amherst education conveyed a clear message of *noblesse oblige* to students, ensuring their recognition of responsibilities to the world. Speaking to graduates, Harris argued that they stood "on a threshold, passing from one abode to another, not from seclusion into the world, for the college is a place in the world, where you have known the outside world, where the currents of thought and anticipation have not been detached from the common life of men." The collegiate experience was a meritocracy in which the students "have measured one another up, and can forecast the future of each one, judging not by what each has, but by what each is—the person."[63] Harris possessed a clear vision of the *next world*, but it was a vision whose power shaped and informed the character of individuals, their relationship to each other, and the contribution they can and must make in *this world*.

Harris believed that at the core of the formation of character was what he called "personality"—the source of other values.[64] It was the college's responsibility to instill these moral values, values embodied in the students' educational experience. But the relationships engaged during college also served the formation of character. What college offered the student was "a place where sincerity, honor, and magnanimity are fostered." This environment developed students whose "power of success . . . lies in personality." Truly successful students were those who were "upright, honorable, and magnanimous."[65] The vitality of the each student's personality would then sustain these values throughout life as graduates.

In recent years Amherst College has continued a tradition of its presidents delivering opening convocation addresses. In Peter Pouncey's first such address, he described the tension between what is known—the habits and rituals of existence—on one hand and what is unknown—what is new and what is yet to be explored—on the other. Setting a tone for the academic year and for his presidency, he identified a recurring struggle at the heart of the academy and in the lives of its members. The contrast within places of learning is that "on the one hand we build seasonal rituals and ceremonies and habitual values into our life to give it dignity and the poise of continuity; on the other, we seek to refresh ourselves with new sensations, ideals and experiences, to break out of the rut and to shatter the mold. It is the tension in us between the time-honored and the time-worn, between the tradition that dignifies and the habit that dulls."[66] Pouncey concluded that the heart of the matter for education is that "when all is said and done, it is the application of a living spirit and intelligence that transforms a tradition that can be stagnant and limiting, into something vibrant, sustaining and progressive."[67] Pouncey believed that life should not be lived in an unchangeable past and that education's challenge is to bring the values and ideas of the past into the present in ways that are born out of "a living spirit and intelligence."[68]

Peter Pouncey shared the views of his successor, Tom Gerety, about presidential responsibility as a teacher for maintaining educational dialogue on the campus. The connection between these two presidents reflects an institutional predisposition at Amherst to have leaders who strongly value teaching. Pouncey believed that teachers should present their human side to students as teachers. He also believed that the historical understanding that professors are individuals who profess their subject matter needed to be taken with greatest seriousness.

Exhibiting thoughts similar to Hesburgh's, Pouncey reflects on the values and moral positions of teachers especially in their relationships with students. In an address while dean at Columbia prior to becoming Amherst's president, he discussed the faculty and student relationship. Pouncey claimed that students "have a right to know where we stand and what we care for, not merely what we know about what we teach. To withhold this larger view, formed from our own more extensive experience, is a kind of betrayal, and reduces our influence on their lives to a mere grade in a transcript, a few more intellectual hoops to jump through, or a bibliography to be forgotten."[69] As president at Amherst, Pouncey publicly expressed personal beliefs and concerns and urged students to consider important matters. In this way he and other presidents, both as teachers and leaders, influence the lives of the students.

Nothing exemplifies this philosophy and approach to moral inquiry sparked by the presidential pulpit than one of Pouncey's convocation addresses in which he presented a classic moral dilemma to students.[70] This speech is profound evidence of the contemporary existence of the moral voice. Pouncey's choice of title—"Abraham and Isaac"—for a major address at a nonsectarian college and before a pluralistic audience that included believers and nonbelievers is in itself interesting. We thus close this chapter and our discussion of the shaping of student character with an outstanding example of presidential commitment to moral matters and Pouncey's profile of moral courage in the ivory tower.

A classicist, Pouncey began not surprisingly by engaging in a critical, scholarly, textual examination of the Hebrew scripture account of Abraham and Isaac. But in spite of this academic and intellectual approach, the address could easily be mistaken for a sermon on the ancient biblical story. While Pouncey developed a number of moral points about violence, the crucial question he posed was simply what would happen if God had not intervened to stop Abraham's sacrifice of his son?

Pouncey cited two of the multitude of historical occasions when there was simply no divine intervention to prevent human tragedy. First he noted that one way for Abraham Lincoln to understand the deaths of so many young soldiers on both sides of the Civil War was to rationalize their sacrifice as an atonement for the sins of slavery. Next, he commented on the conclusion of Wilfred Owen's World War I poem, which uses the Abraham and Isaac story:

Behold a ram caught in the thicket by its horns;
Offer the Ram of Pride instead of him.
But the old man would not so,
but slew his son,
And half the seed of Europe,
one by one.

The imposition and the unreason are all Abraham's now. God is really not a presence at all, any more; He can only hover, anxious and unavailing, in the background.[71]

Pouncey challenged students to realize that human beings cannot rely on the intervention of a god (or, presumably, even other human beings) to solve moral problems and to absolve themselves of moral responsibility. The Abraham and Isaac story concludes happily only because God intervenes. But students, regardless of their belief or unbelief in God, cannot presume that this is the way their moral difficulties will be resolved. In the face of this dilemma, Pouncey urged students to engage in serious reflection. To underscore the educational importance of Abraham and Isaac, he reminded the audience that such stories should not be seen as "shelved in the mind, to gather dust and die."[72]

The Abraham and Isaac address, or sermon as it might more properly be called, is profound evidence of the existence and quality of the contemporary moral voice. One speech by one president certainly does not refute the notion held by many that presidents no longer speak about moral issues or possess moral convictions. However, Pouncey's address is symbolic of what presidents are actually doing and of the contemporary ways in which their moral leadership is exercised. In the next chapter we will review three specific issues that presidents regularly face within the gates of the academy—freedom of speech, academic freedom, and diversity—issues especially pronounced in the contemporary climate and issues that command the attention of the moral leadership of presidents.

NOTES

1. Personal interview with President Thomas Gerety of Amherst College, July 27, 1994. Italics indicate my interest in emphasizing this point, about which Gerety was equally emphatic.
2. James W. Cavanaugh, C.S.C., "Saint Paul, Apostle of the World," in *The Conquest of Life*, ed. John A. O'Brien (Paterson, N.J.: St. Anthony Guild Press, 1952), p. 67.
3. Cavanaugh, "The Religious Life of the Student," UND Archives, Box 10, undated, pp. 8–9.
4. Cavanaugh, "The Tests of a College," in *The Conquest of Life*, pp. 133–34.
5. Cavanaugh, "The Day of Visitation," September 20, 1908, UND Archives, Box 10, pp. 5–6.
6. Nannerl O. Keohane, "The Founding Enterprise," September 14, 1984, Keohane Speeches, 1981–1985, p. 4.

7. Keohane, "Educational Futures," September 25, 1986, Keohane Speeches, 1986–1990, p. 6.

8. Peter Pouncey, convocation address, September 4, 1989, Amherst Archives, p. 11.

9. Ibid., p. 12.

10. Pouncey, convocation address, September 5, 1985, Amherst Archives, p. 12.

11. Ibid., p 13.

12. Personal interview with President Thomas Gerety of Amherst College, July 27, 1994.

13. Ibid.

14. Ibid.

15. As president at Trinity, Gerety likens the personal quality of the teacher–student relationship to Buber's notion of I/Thou: "Martin Buber, the great Jewish theologian spoke of the relation between us and God as an 'I/Thou' relation, one in which we know one another intimately, personally. For Buber this was an ideal in all our interactions, human and divine. Teaching here at Trinity is an I/Thou relation, certainly not to a god, but to someone learned, expert, in a field" (Thomas Gerety, "Work Hard, Play Hard: Rigor and Joy in the Liberal Arts," Trinity College, Hartford, Conn., p. 3).

16. Peter R. Pouncey, ed., *Teaching What We Do: Essays by Amherst College Faculty* (Amherst, Mass.: Amherst College Press, 1991), p. xii.

17. Peter R. Pouncey, "Ancient History and Ancient Morals," in *Teaching What We Do: Essays by Amherst College Faculty*, ed. Peter R. Pouncey (Amherst, Mass.: Amherst College Press, 1991), p. 103.

18. Personal interview with President George Rupp of Columbia University, November 16, 1994. Though Rupp does not use the term "Great Conversation," his remarks throughout the interview, as the portions that follow indicate, support this assertion.

19. Ibid.

20. Ibid.

21. Ibid.

22. Caroline Hazard, *1910 Annual Report*, Wellesley *Annual Reports*, 1905–1913, p. 16.

23. Caroline Hazard, *The College Year* (Boston and N.Y.: Houghton Mifflin, 1910), p. 86.

24. Caroline Hazard, address to the Congregational Conference in Rhode Island at Peacedale, May 23, 1905, Caroline Hazard, Personal Papers, Addresses, 1905–1916, Wellesley College Archives, p. 8. Peacedale, Rhode Island, was Hazard's hometown and this meeting likely took place in the Peacedale Congregational Church in which she was raised and in which she played an active role.

25. Caroline Hazard, *Some Ideals in the Education of Women* (New York: Thomas Y. Crowell, 1900), p. 23. This work, published at the end of the first year of Hazard's presidency of Wellesley, presents a broad outline of her philosophy of women's education. While it appears based in part on her experience as president, given the publication date, undoubtedly much of the material was well formulated prior to her appointment as president. Indeed, it is likely that Hazard's ability to articulate the importance of the education of women was a significant factor in her selection. It must be borne in mind that Wellesley, as one of the "experiments" in women's higher education in America, was only a quarter of a century old at the time of Hazard's inauguration, a point noted on that occasion by speakers such a President Charles Eliot of Harvard.

26. For elaboration of this belief, see Caroline Hazard, *1910 Annual Report*, Wellesley

Annual Reports, 1905–1913, pp. 15–16. Here Hazard contends that "the college should teach true values. Every man is 'as good as' another as an individual soul; he is not as a thinking mind. . . . To discriminate, to distinguish, to choose, is the duty of every educated person. To do this there must be a basis of knowledge which the College must impart. But beyond this, it must point the way to wisdom; it must never let its students rest in the letter; it must always point to the spirit which alone can make alive."

27. Theodore Hesburgh, sermon opening the school year, September 25, 1955, UND Archives, 1947–1967, Box 141/7, pp. 10–11.

28. Nannerl O. Keohane, convocation address, September 5, 1985, Keohane Speeches, 1981–1985, p. 6.

29. Idem.

30. Idem.

31. Caroline Hazard, *1910 Annual Report*, Wellesley *Annual Reports*, 1905–1913, p. 4. Previously noted is Hazard's concern about whether the religious vitality of the nation was ebbing. However, we have previously observed that she was less worried than contemporaries such as Cavanaugh about the state of religious belief. In the above example, she is partially critical of the outcome of her proposal abolishing morning prayers. It is an opportunity to view Hazard's internal debate of moral voice between freedom of religion and the freedom that ought to be permitted in the liberal arts on one hand and her personal beliefs and convictions about the importance of religion to the lives of individuals on the other.

32. Ibid., p. 5.

33. James Burrill Angell, *Environment and Selfhood* (Ann Arbor: University of Michigan, 1901), p. 6.

34. Ibid., p. 8.

35. James Burrill Angell, "Lessons Suggested by Christ's Life to the Scholar," *University of Michigan Bulletin* 4, no. 13 (July 15, 1903), pp. 2–3.

36. Ibid., pp. 4, 6, 7–8. For additional examples of Angell's moral voice on character formation, especially concerning wisdom and one's relationship to God, see his baccalaureate address, "Knowledge and Wisdom," *University of Michigan Bulletin* 5, no. 20 (July 15, 1904) pp. 1 and 9; concerning the highest moral demands of professional life, see "The Heroic Spirit of Life," *Unitarian*, 1890, pp. 5–6.

37. Angell, *Environment and Selfhood*, p. 10. The impact of this change on religious faith is a significant aspect of the debate and discussion among Cavanaugh, Eliot, and Hazard mentioned previously. Presidents are challenged by such issues in expressing their moral voice, and, the evidence suggests, on occasion may alter their assumptions and rhetoric accordingly.

38. William H. Crogman, "Life's Deeper Meanings," in *Talks for the Times* (Cincinnati: Jennings and Pye, 1896), p. 20.

39. Ibid., p. 42.

40. *Bulletin of Atlanta University* 1, no. 11 (June 1889), p. 2c.

41. Ibid., p. 3a.

42. Ibid., p. 3b–c.

43. Ibid., p. 3c.

44. Nicholas Murray Butler, "Character Building," June 4, 1924, Butler Speeches, vol. 6, no. 79, pp. 1–2.

45. Ibid., pp. 3–4.

46. Cavanaugh, "The Function of the Religious College," in *The Conquest of Life*, p.

78. This is not an isolated example of Cavanaugh's strong position. In a sermon delivered on September 26, 1909, he warns that "God pity the clean-hearted boy on the day when he begins to think of evil merely as 'getting experience' or 'knowing the world'! Do those who babble of 'sowing wild oats' ever stop to ask themselves, 'What shall the harvest be?' Do they remember those terrible words of the Apostle: 'The wages of sin is death.' " James W. Cavanaugh, "The Perfect Service," UND Archives, Box 10, p. 7. To strengthen his case further, Cavanaugh often links these urgings to the sacrifice made by parents to enable their children to attend Notre Dame, the implication being that the student who misbehaves is wasting parental support and violating parental expectations. For example, see James W. Cavanaugh, "The Religious Life of the Student," UND Archives, Box 10, pp. 2–3. For Cavanaugh's comments on the related issue of the relative financial worth of parents, see "The Day of Visitation," UND Archives, Box 10, pp. 3–4. He contends that students from poorer economic circumstances are more serious and disciplined as students than those who come from wealthy backgrounds.

47. Cavanaugh, "The Conquest of Life," in *The Conquest of Life*, pp. 4–5.

48. Edward Malloy, C.S.C., President's Address to the Faculty, President's Office, University of Notre Dame, October 12, 1993, p. 20.

49. Thomas Gerety, Trinity College Convocation 1993, President's Office, Amherst College, August 28, 1993, p. 5–6.

50. James J. Duderstadt, untitled speech, senate assembly, March 19, 1990, JJD (Duderstadt) Speeches, James J. Duderstadt Collection, Michigan Historical Collections, Bentley Historical Library, University of Michigan [Hereafter, JJD Speeches], Box 235, p. 3. Duderstadt credits Derek Bok for a portion of these observations.

51. James J. Duderstadt, "Ethics in Higher Education," JJD Speeches, Box 248, unpaginated.

52. Elias Blake, Jr., Founder's Day address. From the personal papers of Elias Blake, February 19, 1980, p. 18.

53. Elias Blake, Jr., inaugural address. From the personal papers of Elias Blake, October 27, 1978, p. 13.

54. Ibid., p. 14.

55. Theodore Hesburgh, "The Changing Face of Catholic Higher Education," April 8, 1969, UND Archives, 1968–1987, Box 142/2, pp. 16–17.

56. Theodore Hesburgh, "The Student Today," April 7, 1970, UND Archives, 1968–1987, Box 142/3, p. 8. Specifically, he suggests that "perhaps we might begin by establishing certain givens—such as human dignity and liberty, the open society, the quality of life characterized by a few fixed values, such as honesty, love, peace or non-violence, competence as opposed to dilettantism, rationality as opposed to blind feeling, spirituality as opposed to materialism, civility as opposed to incivility and vulgarity, respect as opposed to contempt for persons."

57. Theodore Hesburgh, opening Mass homily, September 11, 1977, UND Archives, 1968–1987, Box 142/11, pp. 6–7.

58. Hesburgh also quotes Dickey toward the conclusion of the address (see below).

59. Theodore Hesburgh, "The Examined Life," June 8, 1958, UND Archives, 1947–1967, Box 141/12, p. 5.

60. George Harris, "The Ninety First Commencement," *Amherst Graduates Quarterly* (November 1912), p. 27. This address, Harris's last baccalaureate sermon, is described as "worthy of its unique occasion. But it was not pitched to the key of farewell or

sadness" (p. 26). It is an exegesis on his text, Isaiah 40:31, and is, as is often the case with Harris's rhetoric and moral voice, biblical and theological.

61. Ibid., p. 28.

62. Ibid., p. 27.

63. Ibid., pp. 28–29.

64. George Harris, "Values of Life," *Amherst Student* 45, no. 62 (June 10, 1912), p. 1. Harris argues "there are other values which might be enumerated, but all spring from the same source—personality. Culture is a value. Culture is stored up. . . . A degree of culture, even slight, is the salvation of men from narrowness, selfishness and pettiness. The cultured man has resources. He has knowledge from art, history, religion and science and those are real values."

65. Ibid., pp. 1, 7.

66. Peter Pouncey, convocation address, September 4, 1984, Amherst College Archives, Peter Pouncey General File, p. 2. Hereafter, Pouncey file.

67. Ibid., p. 15.

68. Idem.

69. "The College: Former Columbia Dean to Be President," *Amherst Graduates Quarterly* 36, no. 1 (Summer 1983), p. 8. This address, "Can Virtue Be Taught?" was given to a conference on values in education at Horace Mann School in 1978. Prior to this statement he reveals the relationship of moral values to the life of the teacher and scholar: "We must beware of banishing our values, by process of mental departmentalization to some minimal or marginal area of proper behavior, which we hope will be socially graceful, or at least not disruptive. This kind of reductionism is an evasion or distortion of what a moral sense really is; a moral sense is not merely a series of do's and don'ts, building fences for all our original and creative impulses, but a capacity to relate a particular action, work, or attitude to a larger view of mankind, and its place in the order of things" (p. 8).

70. Peter Pouncey, "Abraham and Isaac," September 1990 convocation address, Pouncey file. To be fully appreciated the address should be read in its entirety. His message is provocative, especially for first-year students suddenly exposed to the challenge of his remarks after being on campus for only a few days.

71. Ibid., p. 12

72. Idem.

5

Critical Issues in the Academy:
Free Speech, Academic Freedom,
and Diversity

The distinctiveness of America's colleges and universities as institutions in society is shaped largely by the fundamental principles of the academy, which in turn are uniquely embedded in the character of individual institutions. The primary features traditionally defining the nature of colleges include commitment to civility, justice, diversity, and the value of free discourse. Two crucial and related principles—academic freedom and free speech—are critical premises of any college's educational and organizational life. Notions about campus community, individual freedom, and both individual and corporate responsibility derive in large measure from these basic principles. The level of currency commonly bestowed on academic freedom and free speech results from the expectation that these pillars of the life of the mind are closely connected to the moral and ethical fabric of campus life. In turn, and for sound reasons, these freedoms and the importance of rational discourse are major issues, often creating enormous difficulties, for presidents. But they are also among the most fundamental values that presidents are responsible to uphold.

The qualities of free and open inquiry in academic communities have a long history. They were also the center of major debate in the early 1950s when the political climate characterized by the charges and countercharges of McCarthyism set in motion the rationale on campuses for academic tenure. Contemporary discussion about educational and scholarly freedom occurs in a no less politicized climate. Its characteristics are increasing pluralism and diversity and heightened rigidity of ideological positions in academia and American society. The resulting debates, issues, concerns, and incidents facing contemporary presidents demands their moral leadership, leadership that must understand and be informed by free speech and academic freedom.

RUPP'S FUNDAMENTAL PRINCIPLES

The principles of academic freedom and diversity, held to be of great importance by many in the academy, are often fraught with increasing misunderstanding and misapplication. Many critics, commentators, and ideologically driven constituencies at both ends of the political spectrum view the demands of academic freedom and the ideals of diversity as mutually exclusive and, almost by definition, in opposition to each other. In order to make a firm and clear position at the outset of his presidency at Columbia, George Rupp used part of his inaugural address to discuss the linkage and resulting tension between academic freedom and diversity.

Rupp fashioned a series of assertions to address the delicate balance between the commitments to freedom that colleges and universities must uphold and the potential that speech and scholarly inquiry will become offensive to some members of academic communities. He outlined three aspects of this balance and in so doing delineated the fundamental values and established the guideposts without which the academy qua the academy simply cannot flourish. In this address, Rupp alluded purposefully to the numerous debates in higher education about multiculturalism. He wanted to affirm the university's support for particularity while at the same time emphasizing that the commonweal demands, if not positive relationships, at the least respect among diverse, at times combative, constituencies.

As a first principle, Rupp pointed out the significance of human interaction to teaching and learning. In Rupp's mind "our collective aim is not homogeneity and reinforcement but interaction. We nurture particular traditions even as we encourage their interrelationship in this shared space." In Rupp's mind "this commitment to fostering interaction indicates that we should continue to allow the full exercise of free speech on this campus." The necessary dose of realism, lest his audience misperceive the difficulty of maintaining these commitments, leads to the conclusion that "The struggle among alternative positions and perspectives will continue to be a defining feature of this community. But—to adapt . . . [President Michael] Sovern's formulation—the right to free speech does not mean that every exercise of this freedom is right."[1]

Underlying this principle is the realistic recognition that freedom of expression sometimes results in harmful and divisive speech. Building on this notion, Rupp's second critical idea is affirmation of the right and responsibility of community members to condemn offensive speech. Most colleges and universities have advocates for the development of policies to prevent any offensive speech. In the last two decades these advocates have led campuses to experiment with the implementation of speech codes. The frequent result has been tedious battles about the legality and constitutionality of the codes, and concomitantly innumerable practical problems involved with enforcement.

The approach Rupp fashioned was founded on his beliefs about basic and transcendent values of the academy. Rather than arguing that some speech should be prohibited because of the rights of those who feel offended, Rupp supported the absolute importance of free speech. Defending his position on these rights and anticipating his critics, Rupp stressed that, as has been the case in the past, "There will surely be further occasions when speakers offend the deepest sensibilities, and also the common sense, of many Columbians. While we are committed to allowing the exercise of free speech, we certainly do not need to welcome every utterance." With this as a common starting point, Rupp turned his attention to individual responsibility, the "collective obligation to criticize deficiencies, to correct errors, to set the record straight, to defend members of this community who are unfairly attacked, to advance more adequate interpretations, and to press for responsibility and civility in the expression of differences."[2]

Using the power of his presidency at the outset of his tenure, Rupp's third assertion urged the Columbia community to agree that inevitably there will be speech perceived to be harmful, upsetting, and divisive. The crucial principle is to avoid prohibiting such speech, lest all speech be subject to infringement. He enjoined members of the university to accept personal responsibility and accountability, to take stands, to use their right of free speech, to engage in civil discourse, and to protect those who consider themselves to be the victims of attack.

In this speech, Rupp made a strong attempt to convince his university community to abide by these principles and values. However, he and his audience knew well that complex and portentous problems will remain. Free, even potentially harmful, speech and the commitment of the academy to unfettered scholarly inquiry, teaching, and learning must always remain hallmarks of the academy. But maintaining these fundamental values is made more difficult in university climates that are highly charged due to pressure for increasing diversity and multiculturalism in curriculum and campus life.

In addition, Rupp wanted to make certain that the audience understood his and the university's certain response to situations where free speech appeared to attack or harm. To avoid any misunderstanding of this position, Rupp asserted unqualified support for free speech. Basing his stand firmly in educational principles and the Constitution, he argued that "our response to speech we find objectionable must be more speech, more responsible and civil exchanges, not enforced silence."[3]

As a guide for the university community, Rupp offered a reasonable and academically justifiable way to maintain both free speech and the rights of all, including minority members of universities. He freely acknowledged that conflicts inevitably resulting from commitments to multiculturalism, but he remained true to the fundamental and transcendent aspirations of the college and university. Reminiscent of Kenneth Minogue's concern about the future of universities if they permit themselves to be subject to ideologies, Rupp believed that "more speech" was the best way to counter hateful and harmful speech, thereby letting the university be the university.

Later in his first year at Columbia, Rupp reiterated his concern about the value of free speech in a democracy. He joined his understanding of allowing the university to be what it should be to a Jeffersonian belief that rights and freedoms in a democracy are the foundation of the Republic. On this occasion, Rupp remarked that "Where there is silence, there is repression. Where there is the clash of ideas, the quest for truth goes on."[4] He acknowledged "that the full exercise of free speech on the American campus is not universally accepted. Yet it is a principle we believe to be integral to higher education in a democracy. The struggle among alternative positions and perspectives, and a preference for tough interaction rather than tranquil homogeneity, should be defining features of the American university."[5]

THE CRUCIAL ROLE OF FREEDOM IN THE UNIVERSITY

Harold Shapiro, a contemporary of Rupp's and president of both the University of Michigan and Princeton University, believed in the crucial link between academic freedom and the capacity of institutions to take stands on controversial political and public issues. Part of his concern centered on the practical arena of universities "taking a stand on some moral issues such as affirmative action and research on human subjects." For Shapiro the values of academic communities "include the value of knowledge, the benefit of fair and open inquiry, respect for other points of view, and the possibility of human progress." But Shapiro also knew that these values can become a slippery slope leading to quagmires for universities. Thus, institutions need to "be very cautious about adding to this list." His fear was that in the absence of "developing a means of distinguishing ideas from ideologies we risk the possibility of undermining the environment that supports our principal commitments and responsibilities." The inherent danger is that the university will allow its unique identity to be swallowed up by ideological battles. However, Shapiro believed that some ways proposed to prevent ideological battles from overtaking the university were worse than the disease. For example, simplistic suggestions of a return "to an earlier model of moral, political, and scientific orthodoxy would, however, undercut academic freedom and open discourse, transforming the character of contemporary higher education and undermining the university's capacity to make positive contributions to society."[6]

However, Shapiro was understandably ambivalent. He recognized the appeal of a return to a more orthodox, more homogeneous era in which ideology and politics were more clearly defined. He also understood the danger of orthodoxy as antithetical to the goals of the academy, especially in a more pluralistic world.

There is no easy way out of this conundrum. The dilemma is rooted in two competing, and often mutually exclusive, demands. One side is characterized by the expectation that higher education can and should make contributions to society. The other side warns of the danger that the philosophy and purpose of colleges and universities can be controlled by political and social forces.

These competing demands led Shapiro to share Rupp's concern about the commitment necessary for the university to maintain its fundamental moral principles and values. Such concerns require universities to make careful choices when taking public positions. Care is essential because the self-interest of radically competing constituencies pressures university endorsement of their particular ideological agendas. These competing interests are normally only marginally capable of grasping the bigger picture of the university. In search of a middle ground, Shapiro stands between critics who believe the university has already gone too far in asserting moral stands and those who believe that institutions of higher education should be more engaged in political and social concerns.

Shapiro is not alone in these fears. They are echoed by his colleagues Stephen Trachtenberg of George Washington University and Thomas Gerety of Amherst College. Trachtenberg agreed fully about the danger of competing ideologies and of the battle for values in higher education. His views provide an important perspective on the issues presidents face in attempting to exercise the moral voice.

With experience as president of two major universities, previously having been president of the University of Hartford, Trachtenberg focused on the contemporary political climate, especially in the battles about morals and values. Replying to critics such as Charles Sykes,[7] Trachtenberg dramatically warned about the demands on contemporary presidents who "need to keep their eyes and the eyes of their audiences fixed on the dangerous potential of a movement of this land some of whose caricatures are not altogether different from the scapegoating of the 1920s and '30s." In this environment, "today's president must be prepared to deal with a new ideological edge that has entered American discourse and may well intensify in the 1990s." The clear danger for Trachtenberg is that "in its beneficent guise, it is often called a 'search for values.' In its more ambivalent guise, it seems also to be a longing for authority and discipline."[8] His thinking suggests that those who wish to embed values into the framework of campus life are in reality attempting to control the free inquiry and expression essential to the academy.

As Trachtenberg describes it, this debate about values further complicates presidential moral leadership. In the highly politicized climate, presidents must be extraordinarily careful and skillful in commenting on moral and ethical issues. Their thoughts about education must focus the attention of institutional and public constituencies on fundamental concerns about the value and significance of education. But presidents must also be wary of reducing their voice solely to pleas for a "search for values" or calls for social controls as the only remedies for halting the social disintegration of values and morals.

The moral voice of college presidents is complex, timeless, and fully integrated into the fabric of educational life. True moral leadership cannot be narrowed to a role of providing transient solutions to every contemporary social problem and moral dilemma. A great challenge for presidents, especially in the present social and political climate, is to find ways of responding to the guises of ideology and to the demands of constituencies for specific ideological stances. Addressing this challenge is critical if presidents are to avoid rhetoric and action leading, even if in some cases unintentionally, to positions antithetical to the purposes of the academy.

At the close of the twentieth century, presidents of colleges and universities face critical and unavoidable moral dilemmas posed by freedom of speech. Free speech is integral to academic communities as well as being an instrumental part of the foundation of democratic society. Thus, the voices of college and university leaders become an essential and, one would hope, enlightened guide for society and its citizenry.

Another aspect of the problem faced by presidents in dealing with orthodoxies is particularly troublesome: the pressure to be "politically correct." Thomas Gerety warns of this danger in academic communities of conforming and capitulating to political correctness and other forms of political pressure. Large segments of contemporary campus controversies are spawned by those who label as "politically correct" many decisions of colleges and university leaders. These judgments, many of which center on values, diversity, free speech, and freedom of academic inquiry, lead critics to accuse universities of pandering to ideological interests. The resulting allegation is that the university has become a distorted version of itself because of capitulation to ideological demands for "correctness."

Gerety cuts through the superficialities of the contemporary debate by declaring that political correctness is nothing more than an attempt to gain political advantage. The danger is that presidential acquiescence to calls by proponents of new orthodoxies to instill their values succeeds in undermining important principles in the life of the academy. To Gerety "political correctness" is essentially a trap. Confronted by the complexities, dilemmas, choices, and learning characteristic of a college education, college leaders must resist simplistic, though alluring, calls for values and moral security. Tackling the dangers inherent in this ideological debate, Gerety asserts "that the core, the kernel of truth about political correctness is that orthodoxies are always tempting to human beings in groups and singly. In the case of the undergraduate population, the late adolescent, early adult, orthodoxies are doubly tempting because of the insecurity about their adult selves, their adult roles and their adult personalities."[9]

Historically, the moral leadership of presidents is rooted in values, many of which were and are based in political and cultural assumptions and many of which are arguably ideological. Today's presidents often find that they must lead in response to these controversies and battles about values. Their leadership becomes even more essential as constituents advocate diametrically opposed and highly passionate positions about whose values should predominate. But in their responses, presidents cannot themselves become inflexible or ideological. Contending with the current ideological debates within and outside the academy, presidents must continually refashion and refine their moral positions.

THE TONY MARTIN AFFAIR AT WELLESLEY

One such ideological situation confronted President Diana Chapman Walsh at Wellesley College when she responded to a campus crisis regarding academic freedom and free speech. Just as John Kemeny was thrust into a crucial leadership role as a result of the Kent State slayings in the spring of 1970, having been president of Dartmouth for only two months, Walsh was in office for a similarly brief time when she faced a defining moment for her presidency.

Walsh assumed the full-time duties of the presidency in October 1993, having completed the transition from her previous responsibilities at the Harvard School of Public Health in the six weeks following the announcement of her appointment. In December, one of her faculty, Professor Tony Martin, had his book, *The Jewish Onslaught: Despatches from the Wellesley Battlefront*, published. In it he recounted his personal experiences of events (detailed in a moment) from the previous spring at the college. He thus created a major issue for the campus and for Walsh's presidency.

To understand fully the crisis Walsh confronted, we must go back to the previous spring, in 1993. Martin, a tenured professor of African and Afro-American Studies, had placed on a course syllabus a Nation of Islam publication citing evidence of the Jewish involvement in the slave trade. Within academic circles, the book's scholarship had been widely debated, questioned, and distrusted, though some, including Martin, believed its primary contentions to be true. Martin's course requirement that students read the book sparked a highly charged campus controversy regarding his judgment in using the book. In heated discussions with fellow faculty members, Martin argued that substantial scholarly evidence corroborated the book's contentions.

These tense and racially charged arguments pitted black and Jewish members of the community—students, faculty, and alumni—against one another. The college community became seriously fragmented, fractious, and contentious. Faculty members questioned Martin's scholarship and his right to do as he wished with this course and presumably others he taught. Faculty seriously considered (though never approved) a proposal to establish a committee charged with reviewing and approving all course syllabi for all faculty. Though that step was not taken, the history department decided to discontinue giving credit toward its major for Martin's history courses offered through Black Studies. Following this acrimonious campus discussion, the issue quieted down as people left for the summer.

However, during the summer Martin continued to be on the receiving end of epithets and charges. He believed the abuse to be racially motivated. Martin primarily blamed Jewish members of the college community for inspiring the insensitivity and invective that had been directed toward him. After pondering and assessing his avenues of recourse, Martin began writing and subsequently published his book as an exposé of these recent events at Wellesley.

Following her appointment, Walsh was briefed by the college's attorneys on the events of the spring. This review included the public statement on the Martin affair released by her predecessor, Nannerl Keohane, and the potential for legal action that might result from the campus turmoil.[10] The lawyers' assessment and belief was that little or nothing was likely to happen and that Walsh need not be concerned.

These advisers failed to anticipate what was about to happen. A short time later, Walsh received a promotional flyer indicating that Martin's book was to be released later that fall. Only a few months into her tenure, Walsh was confronted with a difficult and complex, not to mention potentially explosive, issue.

Because of the nature of his attacks both on the college and on individuals, the release of Martin's book immediately raised the question of how, if at all, Wellesley would respond. The extensive media attention during the early stages of the episode in the previous spring had subsided. But some of Walsh's inner circle of administrative advisers correctly concluded that the book's publication would spark renewed media coverage. Walsh realized that action was required. She engineered a process to shape and fashion a public institutional response, subsequently articulated in a letter to the entire Wellesley College community. She chose a path exemplary of moral leadership.

Walsh began by directing her office to purchase copies of Martin's book and distribute it to senior staff and faculty leaders. She requested that this group read it and meet with her to provide counsel. Walsh wanted her advisers to be knowledgeable in their impressions of the book in order to provide informed analysis and advice on a course of action. When the group gathered a few days later, their discussion generated agreement that Walsh should issue a statement as quickly as possible. Their hope was to head off outside pressure, which would then force the college to be reactive and make it "harder to find the moral high ground." Walsh also consulted with Afro-American and Jewish leaders on and off campus, colleagues from her days as a Kellogg Fellow, and fellow current and former college presidents.

Her colleague presidents urged caution. They counseled that any response Walsh might make would have to cite appreciation for the value of academic freedom, confirmation of faculty support of the position, and a claim that the book was an extraordinary publication. Because presidents do not normally comment publicly and in detail on faculty publications, Walsh's challenge was to affirm faculty freedom of speech and to address the content of the book without censoring it.

Following these discussions, the advice of colleagues, and additional personal reflection, Walsh developed the rhetoric defining the college's stance. She expressed this position in a presidential letter to the entire Wellesley community:

over forty thousand alumni, friends, benefactors, students, and faculty. The letter captures the essence of Walsh's moral voice articulated in the context of debate about free speech on campus. Her response is grounded in principles of freedom of speech, in the academic integrity that must characterize a learning environment, and in the importance of condemning speech deemed offensive.

She began the letter by affirming the fundamental values of the community. These values, she argued, were jeopardized by the book's publication. The situation demanded a presidential response because "occasions arise in the life of any community when it becomes necessary to reaffirm values so essential that they must not be left to chance."[11] These values were inspired by the heritage of the college as a scholarly community whose fundamental individual freedoms also entail individual responsibility to the whole. Thus, Walsh affirmed that "we will continue to defend the rights of all faculty members to express themselves freely, without fear of reprisals. Despite Professor Martin's incendiary words, and his attempt to portray Wellesley College as a repressive institution bent on silencing him, we will continue to recognize his right to express himself." Avoiding language that would imply censorship of Martin, Walsh argued that "the principle of freedom of speech is a bedrock value in a democratic society, the more so in an institution of higher learning. As Justice [Oliver Wendell] Holmes emphasized, society should 'allow the expression of opinions that we loath' because 'the best test of truth is the power of the thought to get itself accepted in the competition of the market.' "[12]

Her position was based on one of the fundamental principles for which colleges and universities must stand: speech, no matter how detestable, is best and most properly contended openly in the marketplace of ideas. While the inherent risks and difficulties of this approach are obvious, the existence and uniqueness of academic communities are sustained precisely by such principles. College and university leaders must rely on the essential necessity and wisdom of placing the highest value on the free exchange of ideas. Walsh did precisely that by engaging a public argument about what Martin wrote, while not challenging his right to do so.

Concluding the letter, Walsh focused on the specific problems that resulted from the book's publication. It is at this point that she censures Martin, claiming the necessity to "speak out against the content of this particular book." Her rationale is straightforward and based on the fact that the book has "violated the basic principles that nourish and sustain this college community and that enable us to achieve our educational goals: norms of civil discourse, standards of scholarly integrity, and aspirations for freedom and justice." Adding specificity to this charge, Walsh maintains that "the recurrent and gratuitous use of racial or religious identification of individuals makes it impossible to address substantive claims and ideas. Standards of reason and logic demanded in academic discourse cannot be met through stereotyping and group ad hominem argument. Rhetoric of this kind undermines the force and critical exchange of ideas on which teaching and scholarship rest." Embodying the principle of free speech, Walsh asserted presidential responsibility by contending that "Professor Martin's book crosses the line from simply unpopular or controversial argument to unnecessarily disrespectful and deeply divisive speech that must be countered, however strong the temptation not to dignify it with a response."[13]

Walsh used the counsel she received from other presidents regarding the need to portray Martin's book as "extraordinary" by judging the book as "cross[ing] the line" between what might normally be ignored to something that demands response. She takes the courageous risk of publicly condemning Martin for his action in publishing the book. Walsh's argument rested on Wellesley's heritage and mission, which embody principles integral to inquiry and discourse. Citing her comments from an interview in *Newsweek* at the time of the incident, Walsh noted that the care undertaken in developing this approach allowed her to walk a critical and fine line: censuring the content of Martin's publication, but not censoring the book or his right to speech.[14]

FREEDOM OF SPEECH: A NATION OF ISLAM SPEAKER AT TRINITY

Walsh is certainly not alone in facing as president a difficult situation regarding free speech. Following the announcement of his appointment to the Amherst presidency, Gerety reflected on a free speech controversy in which he became embroiled while president at Trinity.[15] His is another story of presidential leadership, significant for its impact on a campus and the surrounding community.

The story begins somewhat innocently. A group of students had invited a Nation of Islam representative to speak on campus. Prior to the visit, Gerety had condemned anti-Semitic aspects of the Nation of Islam agenda. Gerety's condemnation pleased members of the College's Jewish community. But he strongly resisted their pressure to prohibit the speaker from coming on campus. Further displeasing the Jewish community, Gerety made a commitment that similar speakers would likewise be permitted on campus for public presentations in the future. However, he did so with a caveat.

Because threats of violence were rumored to be associated with this event, Gerety mandated that attendance at future appearances of any such speakers be restricted to members of the college community. This stand sparked outrage from black community leaders. They accused Gerety of racism by unfairly preventing young black males from hearing the Nation of Islam message of empowerment. They further alleged that his assumption that blacks from the surrounding community were interested in perpetrating violence additionally confirmed Gerety's racist motivation.

Following the attack on him by both the Jewish and black communities of Trinity and Hartford, Gerety spoke to a group of fellow lawyers about the thinking behind his position. Like Walsh, he grounded his action on the principles of the academy. Gerety claimed that while he "feared that *provocateurs* might

seek entry to the talks. . . . I upheld the right of the speakers to speak on our
campus and of our students to hear ideas that I and many others found offensive.
But I maintained as well a prudent regard for the safety of all concerned—
students, faculty and staff, and the speaker—whatever the content of the message." He added that "our allegiance to the free exchange of ideas is linked to
our commitment to the *liberating value of education*. . . . In part we resist the
temptation to ban speakers or ideas because we cannot devise a fair procedure
for doing so. But we also resist it because, in the act of banning, we would
forego the opportunity to examine, and thus to educate ourselves." With a sense
of humor and confidence about what he believed had been accomplished, Gerety
described the principles of free speech in the academy: " 'Homo sum,' Terence
said long ago, 'human nil a me alienum puto'—'As a human being nothing
human should be alien to me.' If to be human means to face up to all that is
human—including hatred—then Trinity has held firm this winter as a free and humane institution. Ideas, good and bad, have been heard and debated. Some of
these ideas, we reject as hateful. To be free, though, we must continue to listen,
to reflect and decide for ourselves."[16]

   In a fashion similar to that faced by Walsh at Wellesley, Gerety responded
to a clash between free speech and significant political differences of opinion
between African-American and Jewish members of the community. On matters
of speech in the academy, presidents are tested on their ability to uphold the
principle that ideas, even when distasteful or harmful, must be able to be freely
expressed. At first glance this position would appear to be expected and beyond
question in the academy. Support for free speech should be the right thing to
do and certainly can be defended on grounds of educational principle. However,
in the midst of the contemporary climate, such seemingly reasonable principles
can easily be overwhelmed by ideological critics. Presidential courage is required if these fundamental values of the academy are to be sustained. Such
presidential stands assume greater importance in the face of the critics driven
so thoroughly by narrow agendas that they minimize or ignore the fundamental
values of the academy. In fact, many of these battles affect the meaning of the
academy itself.

CONFLICTING VALUES OF CHURCH AND UNIVERSITY

   At Notre Dame, academic freedom has traditionally been debated in the context of Roman Catholic expectations of higher education. Academic ideals must
satisfy the religious beliefs of the Church and its notions of authority over
Catholic universities. But Notre Dame still shares with other non-Catholic universities the central ideal of the academy to maintain a climate of free, open,
and independent academic and scholarly inquiry. However, historically, conflicts
between the authority of the Church and the defenders of traditional academic
freedom have been inevitable.
   Edward Malloy faced precisely such a conflict at Notre Dame in 1990 when,

after ten years of planning, the Pope signed the "Apostolic Constitution on Catholic Universities." This document is a major statement reaffirming the Church's relationship to Catholic universities. As the document was being written, Catholic educators were apprehensive about whether it would impinge on core principles such as academic freedom. In the latest in a long history of debate, faculty were concerned about Church attempts to restrict academic and intellectual inquiry. The battleline is clearly delineated. On one side are Church leaders who have a responsibility to assure Catholic priests and laity that the university has a religious center and focus. On the other side are Catholic university faculty who, regardless of their personal beliefs in Catholicism, are equally insistent on the necessity of freedom and independence. External authority, whether the Church or other, cannot (or at least should not) prevent the university from being true to its mission.

In this instance, Church officials had offered Malloy and other Catholic educators the courtesy of the opportunity to present their ideas in the formulation of the Apostolic Constitution. However, the dilemma for these presidents and their faculties is that they know the difficulties inherent in confronting the Church's authority. Like his colleagues in and out of Catholic education, Malloy was faced with affirming principles of academic freedom in the face of both internal (from his faculty) and external (from the Church) pressures.

Because of the scope of this 1990 papal document, Malloy took the lead in offering an interpretation designed to allay faculty fears. He reassured the faculty by suggesting a liberal interpretation of the Church's document, especially as it relates to Catholic theologians. Responding to faculty concerns, Malloy focused on the document's statement about academic freedom. He contended that the crucial part of the text is that "Freedom in research and teaching is recognized and respected according to the principles and methods of each individual discipline, so long as the rights of the individual and of the community are preserved within the confines of the truth and the common good" (Article 2, #5). Though the notion of the truth and of "the common good" is subject to diverse interpretation, Malloy believed this language provided some latitude. He believed that the leaders and faculties of Catholic universities could defend any questionable instances of academic freedom as not violations of the common good. He added that a "subsequent text on Catholic theologians (Article 3, #3) may seem more restrictive, but I believe can be properly glossed to be included under the fundamental claim about academic freedom."[17]

Malloy believed that the Church decree does not infringe academic freedom at Notre Dame and he made a convincing argument to that effect. However, merely the official authorization of the document by the Church served as yet another reminder of their interest in asserting province over Catholic universities. The response of the Notre Dame faculty and Malloy's interpretation of the document were designed to affirm the university's preeminence in matters of governance and academic principles.

DUDERSTADT AND DIVERSITY AT MICHIGAN

James Duderstadt's leadership on issues of diversity at Michigan is an example of a contemporary president acting on the basis of deeply felt personal commitment. His concern about civil rights, race relations, and diversity began in the formative years of his undergraduate experience at Yale. In an address to first-year students, Duderstadt offered insight into the foundation of his commitments, developed when his "college generation of the 1960s was ignited by the spirit and leadership of Dr. Martin Luther King, Jr., in his effort to blaze a new path of opportunity for all peoples." Reflecting on the impact of King's honorary degree at his Yale commencement in 1964, Duderstadt urged students to take seriously King's crucial message, which "conveyed a sense of love and appreciation for one another, regardless of our differences. He taught us to replace confrontation with cooperation . . . to replace distrust with respect . . . to replace ignorance with understanding. He also taught us that we can only make progress toward his dream if we move forward together."[18]

King's legacy inspired Duderstadt, leading him to promote a significant civil rights agenda as president. At the outset of his tenure, Duderstadt initiated the Michigan Mandate, a major initiative to expand diversity through a program of commitments and goals for the university. Duderstadt shared the accountability of the institution for these efforts with the entire community through annual progress reports. Capturing the essence of his hopes, Duderstadt claimed that the mandate "reflects our commitment to make the University of Michigan a national and world academic leader in the racial and ethnic diversity of its faculty, students, and staff. . . . [It] is our plan to link academic excellence and social diversity."[19]

Using his presidential office, Duderstadt worked to gain publicity and support for the mandate's goals. He was particularly eager to communicate the university's aspirations and efforts with the greater Detroit area. Thus, Duderstadt accepted an invitation to preach at the Hartford Memorial Baptist Church, a major inner-city Detroit church. Using Isaiah 43:18–19 as a text, his sermon addressed the importance of educational opportunity, the hope of making the world a better place, and the role of education in that future.

Reflecting the intensity of his personal commitment, Duderstadt candidly admitted the failure of the nation's colleges and universities to do their share in fulfilling promises of justice and opportunity. He acknowledged that "as a nation we have been spending our children's future to pay for greedy consumption and quick fixes. Instead of investing in our schools we have squandered our money on junk bonds and leveraged buyouts, on payouts and write-offs to people who already have enough—or more than enough."[20] After indicating the ways in which Michigan was attempting to serve the people of the city and the state, Duderstadt noted the standard against which colleges and universities must ultimately be judged. In short, he contended that academic leaders and institutions "must come to terms with our historical failure to live up to our own ideals and to the democratic principles of our nation. It has to be said honestly and forthrightly that we have failed to provide equal educational opportunity to African Americans through much of our history. There is no way to gloss over this. It is a fact—a blot on our otherwise proud record of contribution to American life."[21]

Duderstadt was committed to alter a tradition of neglect of racial problems that Michigan shared with fellow higher-education institutions. To underscore the serious public investment demanded of universities, Duderstadt cited the injunction found in Luke 12 that of those to whom much is given, much more will be asked. In a pledge, he remarked that "at the University of Michigan, we accept this challenge—this public trust."[22]

PRESIDENTIAL LEADERSHIP WITHIN THE GATES

In Part 2 we have observed the moral voice within the gates, the context of the life and times of the campus. College and university presidents have forever faced intrinsic moral demands as they have affirmed the principles governing the academy, addressed a constant array of campus issues, and shaped the future of their institutions. The fundamental values about which presidents must be concerned include arguing for an education that has purpose and meaning, encouraging the formation of individual student character and of community values, and challenging students about social responsibilities. Presidents throughout American history have borne a responsibility to lead their colleges and universities in the crucial role of developing the minds and the hearts of students. Whether explicitly stated as a purpose or merely implied as an understood aspect of education, the development of students takes place inside and outside the classroom, and in structured and unstructured ways. Though not alone, presidents are presumed to be one of the primary guardians of the moral standards that their institutions are responsible for impressing upon students. Inevitably, students will fall short of ideals. But the expectation nonetheless is that education, the life of students in the academy, shapes and forms their character.

Citing the value of the core curriculum at Columbia, George Rupp reminds us of the portion of student moral development accomplished in the classroom. In spite of continuing criticism about the efficacy of requiring study of an intellectual tradition dominated by white males, Rupp believes that the content of Columbia's core courses, even as a source of reaction, forces students to develop moral conscience and moral imagination. In addition to placing a high value on the ability of the curriculum to engage students morally, presidents also recognize the profound importance of the education that transpires in the interaction between teacher and student. Small liberal arts colleges like Amherst and Wellesley, to name just two, have the luxury of emphasizing the significance of this personal aspect of education. But even presidents at larger colleges and universities, including research institutions like Columbia, are equally strong in arguing for the innate moral value of the teaching and learning process.

The nature of the academy presumes an intimate and strong relationship between free speech and the life of the mind. Rupp provided a strong philosophical case for the unlimited value of free speech, even when it is hateful and destructive. He urged that the only antidote for such speech is more speech. Opposing voices have a responsibility to develop counterarguments based upon rationality and civility. Diana Walsh's and Thomas Gerety's experiences exemplify the inevitable difficulties resulting from free speech. The most important point, as these two leaders have shown, is that such occasions require wise and fair presidential leadership. As with the question often asked about values—whose values?—free speech must be maintained without taking the side of one individual or group against another. Colleges and universities and their fundamental values must form a platform transcending human disagreements and differences. Presidents are responsible for ensuring that this platform, often embodied in institutional saga, is sufficiently strong and visible to guide campus conversations and controversies. As an example, Walsh relied on Wellesley's saga and its tradition of free speech and fairness toward members of the campus community in navigating her position in the middle of the Martin affair.

Finally, presidents and their rhetoric play a crucial role in developing convictions and beliefs in the lives of students and shaping an environment for the education of the heart. Presidential exhortations for development of core personal principles as a cornerstone of education are a major element of the moral voice within the gates.

As seen in Duderstadt's sermon, the separation between the moral voice "at home" and the moral voice "abroad," like the separation between church and state, is less like a wall and more like points on a meandering line.[23] Issues in the collegiate context such as the moral development of students, freedom of speech, academic freedom, affirmative action, and racial justice are inevitably a part of a larger context in which colleges and universities exist. It is to the relationship of the moral voice with these broader issues and national and global concerns that we next turn our attention.

NOTES

1. George Rupp, inaugural address, President's Office, Columbia University, October 4, 1993, p. 5.

2. Ibid., pp. 5–6.

3. Ibid., p. 6.

4. George Rupp, remarks for Pulitzer Prize jurors, President's Office, Columbia University, March 1, 1994, p. 5.

5. Ibid., p 4.

6. Harold T. Shapiro, "Is Taking Sides a Good Idea for Universities?" *Science* 225, no. 4657 (July 6, 1984), p. 19.

7. Charles Sykes, *ProfScam: Professors and the Demise of Higher Education* (New York: St. Martin's Press, 1988).

8. Stephen Joel Trachtenberg, "Presidents Can Establish a Moral Tone on Campus," *Educational Record* 70, no. 2 (Spring 1989), p. 9.

9. Personal interview with President Thomas Gerety of Amherst College, July 27, 1994.

10. Personal interview with President Diana Chapman Walsh of Wellesley College, November 28, 1994. The account that follows is taken from Walsh's comments.

11. Diana Chapman Walsh, letter to alumnae, faculty, and friends of the college, December 15, 1993, p. 1.

12. Ibid., p. 1.

13. Ibid., pp. 1–2.

14. Personal interview with Walsh, November 28, 1994.

15. "College Row," *Amherst Graduates Quarterly* 46, no. 3 (Spring 1994), p. 8.

16. "Gerety Speech to Hartford County Bar Association," *Amherst Graduates Quarterly* 46, no. 3 (Spring 1994), p. 8.

17. Edward Malloy, C.S.C., address to the Faculty, President's Office, University of Notre Dame, October 3, 1990, p. 10.

18. James J. Duderstadt, "Freshman Convocation Address," September 6, 1988, Duderstadt Speeches, 1988/1989, Box 217, pp. 6–7.

19. *The Michigan Mandate: A Six Year Progress Report 1987–1993* (Ann Arbor: University of Michigan, 1994), p. 2.

20. James J. Duderstadt, "Michigan Mandate: The Hope, Promise, and Challenge of a Multicultural Society," President's Office, University of Michigan, June 24, 1990, p. 4. This opportunity to preach a sermon is a unique aspect of Duderstadt's record of public rhetoric. While Malloy, as a priest, has numerous opportunities to preach, to give homilies, and to provide active, liturgical leadership, the research evidence on the other current presidents and their immediate predecessors (again, with the exception of Hesburgh) does not reveal any sermons or speeches in other religious settings. Such opportunities were much more frequent for the turn-of-the-century presidents.

21. Ibid., p. 9.

22. Ibid., pp. 5–6.

23. For this description I am indebted to the thought of the American religious historian Sidney Mead, *The Nation with the Soul of a Church* (New York: Harper and Row, 1975), pp. 79–80.

PART THREE

BEYOND THE GATES

6

Hopes for Democracy

The history of the relationship between American higher education and democracy in America is a long one, traceable to the founding of the republic and of the colonial colleges. Despite their enormous variety, American colleges and universities, both private and public, have from colonial times enjoyed a close relationship to the democratic society and nation of which they are a part. Generally, this relationship has been one of mutual benefit and interest. However, there have also been warnings of the danger that higher education could easily become too strongly tied to government and its interests. These concerns have ranged from fear of intrusion and interference from governmental regulations to the priorities of institutions bending too willingly to follow the research agenda supported by national and state resources.[1] But government is less a malevolent force than a powerful influence for better and worse on colleges and universities. And the intentions of government, even if viewed as potentially harmful to higher education, should not be confused with the principles and values that undergird civic life in a democracy.

With remarkable consistency, presidents have nearly universally affirmed the important relationship of a college education to the fundamental demands of democracy. These presidential appeals have included the responsibility of colleges and their students to uphold the critical social and civic virtues associated with American society, and to address national and global concerns. Certainly, at times this has required firm criticism of and disagreement with national and state policies.

But in this role as critic and servant, presidents have been the leaders who have educated and challenged both college communities and the public about civic duty in a democracy. Presidents exert moral leadership and voice in this task of focusing the attention of their communities on life beyond the gates of the academy. The responsibilities for civic duty of those who are educated are rooted in expectations of what they should contribute to the nation and the world. In addition, presidents are the figures who lead their colleges and universities to contribute as institutions to the civic and ethical demands of society. It is in this realm that presidents make the case that a crucial connection always exists between the ivory tower and the world outside the gates.

The rhetoric of college and university presidents about democratic principles is substantially shaped by three elements. First is that the democratic heritage of the nation is imbued with fundamental moral, religious, and spiritual beliefs. Second is the notion that America's colleges have an incumbent duty to nurture the principles underlying democratic values and that the students' education should inspire the upholding of those values. Last is the Jeffersonian tradition that (these now) educated citizens are crucial to maintaining democracy. Presidential philosophy about the relationship of the academy to democracy nearly universally reflects these political and educational assumptions. The presidential voice, especially toward the end of the nineteenth century, was also largely shaped by democracy's survival of its true and ultimate test in the Civil War. Of equal importance are the influence of the Social Gospel movement (as a moral and religious response to Social Darwinianism) and America's emerging understanding of its responsibilities as a leading world nation and power.

In addition, four major themes emerge in the leadership of presidents as they urge the connection of the education at colleges and universities to the demands, issues, values, and needs of society and the world. Two of these themes reflect the aforementioned fundamental principles of the American nation: the importance of education to democracy and the significance of education in the development of the civic virtues and the commitments of citizenship. The other two themes concern the relationship of colleges and universities and the education they provide to social issues and to world events. The former themes are discussed in this and the latter in the next two chapters. Though each of these themes embodies unique and definitive qualities, all four are also closely connected and to a great degree overlap. Thus, the sections into which Part 3 is divided should be viewed as suggestive of broad and nearly seamless topics addressed by the moral leadership and voice of presidents rather than artificial distinctions in content and meaning.

NICHOLAS MURRAY BUTLER AND THE IMPERATIVES OF DEMOCRACY

One of the foremost presidential philosophers discussing the importance of education to democracy is Nicholas Murray Butler. Butler is considered as one of the giants of the university presidency, in part because of his lengthy tenure at Columbia (1901–1945), but also because of his high profile and weighty arguments in the public arena. Butler believed that America is founded on moral principles and should act toward moral ends. Early in his presidency, he acknowledged his Hegelian position that "morality is the ultimate end for which the state—that is, politically organized mankind—exists."[2]

Leading a major private university, Butler argued that public educational institutions did not possess a monopoly on the relationship, value, and service of higher education to the nation. He believed that the value of colleges and universities to the nation stemmed from their foundations as shaped by the nation's democratic principles, not from exclusive status conferred by governmental support and by public presumptions about the obligations they owed to society. Noting the unparalleled variety of higher education institutions in America and their unique relationship to the Republic, Butler made the important distinction that "whether a given institution is truly national or not depends . . . upon whether it is democratic in spirit, catholic in temper, and without political, theological or local limitations and trammels. It may be religious in tone and in purpose and yet be national, provided only that its doors be not closed to any qualified student because of his creed."[3] Butler's contention was that as long as Columbia and like independent universities were governed according to the democratic values and rights of the nation, they were as "national" as state-supported institutions.

As noted earlier, American democracy is closely tied to nonsectarian religious beliefs. Butler was a firm believer in the important role of religion in the university. But he was equally convinced that the presence of religious tone did not have to produce religious prejudice or discrimination. Quite on the contrary, he viewed religious values as instrumental in supporting democracy. Colleges and universities not only can, but must, embrace this religious and spiritual influence in order to fulfill their potential for contributing to democracy. He argued that "the constant application of these [religious] principles in educational debates and discussions would bring definiteness and clearness into many places that are now dark and uncertain, and would greatly promote the interest which we all have at heart—the conservation and upbuilding of our American democracy."[4]

The tension between the egalitarian principles of the nation and the enrollment selectivity of higher education is an aspect of the relationship of colleges to democracy that is difficult to resolve, and one with which Butler wrestled. Prior to becoming president of Columbia, he delivered a commencement address at the University of Michigan in which he addressed the issue. On one hand he acknowledged that "The political vitality and integrity of a modern state must rest, in the last instance, upon the character and clearness of the political opinions held by men who are without official station."[5] That the interests of society and the nation are best served by citizens, regardless of position or prestige, is the egalitarian dream. The issue for society and the consequent responsibility of education is the development of citizens with "character and clearness of . . . opinion." Butler was a realist and significantly Darwinian, believing that the division between equality and inequality in society was natural and immovable. Reflecting the meritocratic hope of Jefferson, Butler believed that "Least of all can a democracy hope to succeed without an *elite* of its own. Only we must see to it that this *elite* is recruited from talent or capacity for public service of whatever kin, and is not artificially limited by conditions of birth or of wealth." In an interesting twist on the Enlightenment and exhibiting the influence of Darwin, Butler described nature as knowing "no such thing as equality: it is a human invention thrown up as an artificial barrier against selfishness and tyranny. The law of life is the development of the heterogeneous, the dissimilar, the unequal: it tends away from the dull inefficiency of uniform equality toward the high effectiveness of well-organized differences. Destroy inequality of talent and capacity, and life as we know it stops. Democracy becomes unthinkable."[6]

This statement is the crux of Butler's position. Equality is a worthy aspiration of society. But for democracy to succeed, the goal of egalitarianism has to be predicated on merit and on constant efforts to expand equal opportunity. The Jeffersonian idea is to develop an elite class of educated citizens based on talent and skill rather than on birthright. Education, then, is critical to the success of democracy through creation of a meritocracy, rather than through perpetuation of an aristocracy. Butler clearly believed that education could not alter natural inequalities. Furthermore, any attempt to make the elimination of these inequalities a task and goal of education would be extreme folly. Butler's position would certainly not be viewed as "politically correct" in today's social and educational climate. But, beneath the surface of contemporary debates about the purpose of education and its relationship to a democratic state, the potential truth in Butler's views, though rarely acknowledged publicly, likely rests uneasily in the minds of many educational leaders.

The challenge of balancing merit and egalitarianism is not new, but rather is indigenous to the American experience. Butler's thoughts about merit and equality address fundamental concerns about the role of colleges in a democratic society. He urged that "The American college needs to turn its face to the front and to meet the problem of instructed and educated citizenship in men and women, to lead them to a knowledge of the principles upon which our institutions rest, and to give them a standard of judgment which will prevent their being swept away by the voice of passion, the shouts of the mob, or a desire for gain." The challenge faced by colleges and universities was to "train sane men and women; sane because their minds are informed, their passions tempered, and their wills disciplined by the liberal learning which has come to us through the ages. Such men and women, and they alone, can take the leadership in the era of American life which is about to open."[7]

In the final analysis, Butler is a strong advocate of the position that democracy requires an educated elite and that colleges and universities must assume responsibility for producing this elite class for social, civic, and professional leadership. His passionate rhetoric reflects the life of a young nation, barely a century old, advancing as a world power at the outset of the twentieth century. But his expectations of colleges and universities and the distinctive challenges they face in educating citizens in a democracy are equally timeless and contain elements of truth for today.

GEORGE HARRIS AND A THEOLOGY OF DEMOCRACY

A turn-of-the-century contemporary of Butler, George Harris brought to his presidency at Amherst years of training as a pastor, biblical scholar, and theologian. Harris had been a colleague of William Jewett Tucker on the faculty of Andover Seminary. When Tucker was offered the presidency at Dartmouth, he viewed it as a calling. A few years later, Harris was invited to become the president of Amherst and following Tucker's example interpreted the offer as a call to which he had a duty to respond.

Harris's theology and political and social philosophy were vintage Social Gospel. In his inaugural address at Amherst, Harris clearly stated a view of the relationship of education to democracy. In the address, "The Man of Letters in a Democracy," he affirmed education's mission as central to a democracy.

As did many of his contemporary clergy and theologians, Harris theologically linked Kingdom of God imagery to American democracy, contending that the nation and its political system are blessed by God. This is language of the Protestant and civil religious heritage, inspiring and undergirding the claim that America is a "city on a hill." Harris asserted that "Jesus came preaching and founding democracy. . . . He called it the kingdom of God, which is God's purpose for humanity, seen in the moral order of history as it has evolved. . . . Define the true democracy, then define the kingdom of God on earth; and you will find that you have simply given two titles to the same thing." Realistically noting the tasks challenging the nation and the college, Harris adds that "democracy has not yet in any State fully secured its object, but the social ideal of democracy is the divine order of humanity, and it is the duty of every one to promote that ideal." The Amherst student was to pursue this ideal by "acting his own part as the righteous citizen in the free State, making the most and the best of himself, making his pursuit contribute to the common weal and thus converting the actual into the ideal republic. Surely modern democracy, if this view of it is correct, is roomy enough even for the man of letters—especially for the man of letters."[8]

Harris believed that the state was responsible for educating citizens. But that belief served to raise the problem of egalitarianism, meritocracy, and aristocracy—who would have an opportunity for an education. For Harris, the resolution of this tension between egalitarian principles and the practical need for an elite was Jeffersonian. Harris's philosophy was that society invests in public and private education to produce a class who "may be fitted for highest service to the state, whether they hold political office or not. And this class is the real aristocracy. . . . For the aristocracy of birth it [democracy] has no great regard. . . . For the vulgar aristocracy of wealth it has supreme contempt. To the accident of

rank and title it is indifferent. But it recognizes the aristocracy of merit, knowledge, character." It was the crucial role of education to provide these qualities
for society. Offering such an education was Amherst's mission. Amherst would
produce the educated elite who could best further the principles of democracy.
In this regard "Democracy needs nothing so much as it needs such an aristocracy. . . . The very word 'aristocracy' means the rule of the best, the best men
in power. If the best men have guidance and control, progress is constantly
made. If they are set aside in favor of the incompetent, there is confusion and
every evil work. . . . Therefore in a democracy there must be higher education
for the few who are fit by nature and may become fitter by training for leadership."[9]

Harris's rationale is that the educational system, including both public and
private colleges and universities, will produce an aristocracy based on merit.
This is the practical, Jeffersonian conclusion: an educated class is a necessary
requirement for the success of democracy. Education's critical role is to produce
an educated citizenry, thereby countering an otherwise natural and likely development—a society shaped and led by lowest-common-denominator thinking.
A vital democracy cannot afford to allow an uneducated citizenry to dominate
the character of the body politic. Harris agrees with the longstanding Jeffersonian response to this danger: the development of an educated class. However,
as contemporary educational and political debates reveal, while producing an
educated class is a worthy goal, it fails to address economic, social, and political
circumstances that are inevitable and most difficult to alter. It is these forces
that create and perpetuate social inequality. In reality, status at birth produces a
situation in which some members of society are afforded the opportunity to
exhibit merit, while equally talented others never have a chance. In the final
analysis, the problem for educators and for democracy is that creating a society
that is truly indifferent to birthright and economic class is a most difficult task
in any earthly kingdom.

BLACK COLLEGE PRESIDENTS: BATTLING
DISCRIMINATION DESPITE DEMOCRACY

At the same moment that Butler and Harris were arguing for the education
of an elite to be the leaders of democracy, presidents of black colleges such as
Horace Bumstead at Atlanta University, William Crogman at Clark College, and
John Hope[10] at Morehouse College faced vastly different circumstances. By
comparison, and as previously mentioned, these presidents were forced into
positions of encouraging their graduates to overcome the discrimination and
racism looming beyond the gates of the academy. Their students gained an
education and as college graduates should have been the type of educated elite
whom a democracy should embrace. But discrimination was pervasive in American society, especially in the South, and to some extent even in the present
day, black college presidents have been required to prepare graduates to over-

come the rejection they would face because of race. Despite earning credentials and merit, these students would be prevented from full participation in democracy and society.

In many cases, blacks were so far excluded from democracy as to be unable to contribute to it at all. Certainly the black view of democracy was vastly different from that of the predominantly white culture. Because of the importance of the voice and the views of these leaders of black colleges on education's relationship to democracy, examples of their leadership are pertinent, though often tragically overlooked.

For example, in an 1884 speech to the National Education Association, Crogman commented on the unfortunate results of the prejudice faced by blacks. He noted that "above all and above every other, the greatest and most aggravating hindrance to the education of the negro in this country . . . is this counter education which is continually going on in society."[11] In a similar fashion, Bumstead addressed the problem of race and the responsibility of the nation to understand its duty to all its citizens. He decried "the danger which confronts the republic from an illiterate and degraded vote in the South," adding that this is a problem "which the North has had no small share in creating, and for which she is, consequently, responsible. It is the privilege, as well as the duty of the North, to further the work of Southern education." Bumstead could have appealed to the hope that this responsibility to educate the people of the South, black and white, would be borne out of the deepest national ideals. But realistically he knew that the North's yet-to-be affirmed commitment to this crucial national task did not need to be founded on anything other than pragmatic and utilitarian grounds. Bumstead's position was simply that "It is the dictate of self-interest that she should do so. A menace to the prosperity of the South is a menace to the prosperity of the whole country."[12] Compellingly, Bumstead urged the North to realize that supporting the expansion of educational opportunity in the South was essential to the Republic's democracy. Black college presidents at the last turn of the century simply knew that a central task was to assure that the opportunities provided by democracy would exist for all citizens.

John Hope's voice was nearly identical to his two colleagues. For example, in a report to the trustees of Atlanta University, Hope wrote that "There must be a deliberate effort on the part of schools to bring Negroes to see everything, to comprehend all, to be dismayed by nothing, but to continue the charted course to democracy."[13] A few years later, in a commencement address at Tuskegee, Hope noted to his black audience that "we have within ourselves the power and purpose to put our house in order, and to get our place in this great American commonwealth." Then, like Crogman, Hope made clear that this was not a "selfish" struggle, but a challenge that "all people without reference to race ought to have the opportunity to develop to the highest power that they can develop, and that all people ought to be interested in the welfare of every other person. There will never be real democracy until there is a disposition and a purpose on the part of all citizens that all citizens should be free."[14]

Nearly a century later and decades after the civil-rights struggles of the 1950s and 1960s, Elias Blake, a successor of Crogman as president of Clark College, highlighted the continuing national problem created by the fact that the racial experience of African Americans alters their moral perspective on the nation and democracy. This divergence between the black and white experience of democracy poses interesting difficulties for educators. In the mind of Blake and other black educators of the latter twentieth century, this problem was complicated by the understandable and necessary expectation that black students should possess awareness of their own history and be committed to change the imperfections in the nation's democracy. A starting point in that process, Blake believed, is to confront black students continually with the question of how they will apply their learning in the world, especially on behalf of those who are oppressed. Blake argued that at black colleges, educators must "*ask the question* in the context of unfinished social change . . . and deep racial discrimination still embedded in our national life. . . . [I]f a black institution does not now and in the future force its students to confront the choice of meeting their obligations to our historic struggle, it will lose its way. It will become a mirror image in black face of all other American institutions of higher education."[15]

Blake joined his voice to that of his predecessors, Bumstead and Crogman, in calling attention to the need for social change and justice. This is a position shared by many black higher education leaders. These black college presidents uniquely address an understanding of democracy and democratic values significantly affected by the realities of race. They speak in the tradition of voices such as W.E.B. DuBois, Booker T. Washington, Howard Thurman, and Martin Luther King, Jr., a tradition that calls on the promise of democracy to deliver justice to black people. It is a tradition that urges that the political and social marginalization of blacks must be brought to an end for the good of the nation and for the sake of democracy itself. Black college presidential leadership has sought to instill this promise and this challenge in the lives of their students.

DEMOCRATIC VALUES IN THE CONTEMPORARY ERA

As previously observed, Theodore Hesburgh's religious beliefs and identity as a priest significantly shaped his educational philosophy. Hesburgh also knew well the importance of the common religious and spiritual framework undergirding both the founding of the nation and the goals of education. His strong belief in the role of religion and spirituality in education produce the importance he attached to religious values in the nation's future. As a major figure in American higher education in the latter portion of the twentieth century, Hesburgh contributed significantly to our understanding of the relationship of education to democracy.

Early in his presidency, Hesburgh voiced thoughts about the link between education, especially when grounded in religion, and the Republic. In remarks to religious educators, Hesburgh observed that "an ever-increasing number of educators in America are becoming more concerned with the place and adequacy of religious education in our times." His assessment was that "This concern for religious education stems from the growing conviction that the spiritual values that highlighted the stirring documents of our Founding Fathers are even more important today if young Americans are to be prepared to carry to the world the God-given heritage of human dignity and freedom which our Founding Fathers brought to the birth of this nation. Indeed, our cherished American way of life is unintelligible apart from God and spiritual values."[16] For Hesburgh education possessed an almost missionary quality, revealed in the capacity of education to encourage students to carry into the world the "American way."

The American way had become a prevalent description of American society in the 1950s. The notion that the life of the nation could be called "the American way" was linked to another critical issue that developed in that decade and the decades after World War II: the Cold War. Hesburgh spoke often, especially in the 1950s, about this emerging clash between democracy and communism. He believed that this international conflict was at its core ideological. Therefore, it was a battle to be contested in the arena of ideas, in which "truth . . . will gain or lose in this struggle for the souls of men."[17] In this sermon at the beginning of an academic year, Hesburgh suggested to students that they had an important role to play in securing the spiritual values of American democracy. Hesburgh encouraged students to think about their spiritual values and the ideas underlying democracy. Warning of the grave possibility of corrosion of society from within, Hesburgh asserted that "death comes to a culture or a civilization, not solely from external pressures, but, even more often, from the inner withering of a vital principle, from a loss of faith, from moral anemia, and from the abdication of a basic commitment to truth and integrity." Lest his audience believe that Communism was the only force which should motivate them, Hesburgh added that even in the absence of this threat "we would still be obliged to revitalize our faith, to revivify basic respect for our philosophical roots, not because they are useful or helpful to us in this conflict, but because they are true."[18] Though made in the context of the fears about communism in the 1950s, Hesburgh's appeal for education to assume its responsibility in support of democracy is timeless.

Among other contemporary presidents offering perspectives on the relationship of education to democracy are Harold Shapiro and Nannerl Keohane. In presenting a charge to the first graduating class of his Michigan presidency, Shapiro described the connection between students' obligations to society and to democracy. He asserted that "it is now your responsibility, indeed obligation, to respond thoughtfully and intelligently to local and national issues of concern—whether in politics or science—and to assist your communities in clarifying and understanding these issues so that we may all deal more effectively with the challenges before us. The underlying premise of democracy is the active participation of a broad group of enlightened and thoughtful citizens. It is important that all of you now take up your place in this process."[19] Using the familiar rhetoric of obligation and responsibility, Shapiro employs the traditional Jeffersonian assumption that citizens become "enlightened," that their "discretion can be informed" through education. Simply put, students must be prepared to realize the expectations society holds for them and to use their educations in acting as responsible citizens.

This Jeffersonian thread not surprisingly runs through the philosophical thinking of many college presidents. In an address to the National Association of Independent Schools, Keohane, then president of Wellesley College, hearkened directly to the early years of the Republic. Commenting about the needs of democracy in contemporary public life, she focused on the contemporary dilemma of ethical behavior in public service, a problem magnified in recent times by political scandals. Invoking "Jefferson and his contemporaries," she noted that they "could take for granted that the moral standards of the time, rooted in large part in religion, would lead conscientious citizens to deplore such behavior, and penalize politicians who were found guilty of it." In contrast, she claimed that "in our own time, the diffusion of ethical consensus means that we can no longer take for granted that citizens will hold and enforce such norms. It is up to us, their teachers, to make sure that they understand the importance of honesty and integrity in public life, and hold political leaders accountable for their behavior."[20]

Keohane's comments are noteworthy for two reasons. First, she acknowledged the impact of a diminishment of moral and ethical consensus in American society. These social and cultural changes, and an increasing lack of public consensus, have also affected the moral voice and leadership of college presidents as well as other leaders in America. We will concentrate more fully on this issue later. However, it is clear that this change in the morality and ethics in our culture has had an impact on leadership on campus and in society. This change simply cannot be underestimated. Second, Keohane underscored the essential role of education in sustaining democracy. She specifically highlighted the role of teachers in addressing the ethical basis of public leadership. This task of teaching and learning is also complicated by the erosion of moral consensus in the Republic. Commentary by presidents about the importance of education to democracy serves as a context for examining more specifically their expressions of the moral voice addressing the responsibilities of citizenship. To this aspect of presidential leadership we turn now in more detail.

THE INSPIRATION OF SOCIAL AND CIVIC VIRTUES

As corollaries to admonitions about democracy, college and university presidents use their leadership to promote social and civic values and the responsibilities of citizenship. In an address to the Phi Beta Kappa Society at Vassar College shortly after assuming his presidency, Nicholas Murray Butler addressed the significance of the core values underlying the civil order. As one of his "five evidences of education" he mentions "those refined and gentle manners which are the expression of fixed habits of thought and of action." He then raised the interesting point that "the Latin language has but a single word (*mores*) both for usages, habits, manners, and for morals." These manners "of a truly educated man or woman, are an outward expression of intellectual and moral conviction. . . . Manners have a moral significance, and find their basis in that true and deepest self-respect which is built upon respect for others."[21] In the contemporary campus climate, there is a great deal of concern about decency and the need for civil behavior. Butler's belief, certainly no less valid today, was that mutual respect in human relationships could be enhanced, if not produced, by education. This respect in human and civic affairs was an essential and basic tenet of a university's life. Butler shows that the fundamental human value of manners and respect for self and others is a product of education's influence on individual moral character.

Like many presidents from his and other eras, Harris believed that college graduates must play a role in civic affairs. Harris spoke from personal involvement in civic life, especially during his many years in Andover while on the seminary faculty. One of his biographers commented that Harris's departure "made the regret of Andover town an echo of the regret of the Seminary when he decided to come to Amherst."[22] As he began his presidency, Harris was forced to address concerns raised at Amherst about the reduction in the number of their graduates pursuing careers in the ministry. Building on the Pauline notion of many parts and one body, and echoing his belief in the connection between the Kingdom of God and democracy, he asserted that "the religious man has manly character, is sound, sane, moral, social, simple, real. He trusts God and serves his fellow men with his talents and culture and strength in the kingdom of God, which is the Christian democracy." A liberal arts education such as that offered at Amherst is sufficiently broad to create a climate in which it is "understood that all men of letters have a place and a work in the Christian State, and adjustments of function—preaching, teaching, healing, manufacturing, legislating, governing—will be rightly made."[23]

Harris argued adroitly and creatively that any student's chosen vocation is not necessarily the most important result of their education. Rather, it is critical that students, as educated citizens, meet the important social and civic functions of American democracy. (Not surprisingly, this was the way in which the students would thereby build the Kingdom of God.) In the final analysis in both Harris's time and our own, the crucial issue is that colleges such as Amherst provide the educational and moral foundation that will inspire students to contribute to society.

Another extraordinarily prolific president in addressing matters of civic duty and responsibility was James Angell at the University of Michigan. Nearly all Angell's rhetoric about civic values and virtue is based on a strong belief in the value of moral capital. He believed that students' contributions to society were significant. As alumni, they and their work in the world cast meaningful reflection on the institution. Many of his ideas are a direct reflection of the public university context from which he spoke. But it is interesting that much of his thought resembles that of his contemporaries who were leading private colleges and universities.

In a baccalaureate address, Angell dwelt on the need for graduates to consider their debt to society. Angell knew that a special and justifiable burden was created by the public support of the university. To illustrate this burden, he related the personal and engaging story of a doctor trained at the university, going out in the night to save the child of a poor couple. Rhetorically, Angell asked "who is reaping the greatest benefit from the education he has gained here, the physician, with or without his scanty fee, or the anxious parents to whom he has restored the child from the jaws of death?"[24] Angell used this tale to convey his message clearly and convincingly to various constituencies. The university contributed to the world through the lives and professions of its graduates, often in such practical and easily ignored, but nonetheless important, ways. The value of public support of the university should therefore be beyond question.

Angell devoted much of his final baccalaureate address to the theme of civic responsibility. Here as elsewhere, he focused on the state's reasonable expectations of students who were being educated at state expense. Directly addressing students, Angell affirmed that "we have a right to ask, and we do ask, the University asks, the state asks of every one of you that your life be shaped on a larger and fairer pattern because you have been here." With a profound sense about the importance and the meaning of its graduates to the university (and a little sense of humor), Angell noted that "we are told that it was once the proud declaration in the days of the Roman Republic, 'Wherever is a Roman citizen, there is Rome,' '*Ubi Romanus, ibi Roma.*' So we shall allow ourselves to say with pride, 'Wherever a graduate is doing noble deeds, there is the University of Michigan,' '*Ubi alumnus, ibi Universitas.*' "[25] Whether in public or private institutions, presidents have a public responsibility to affirm that the college experience does indeed shape the lives of students and that they in turn offer lifelong salutary service to the world.

In another baccalaureate address, Angell spoke about the theme that students need to think and act beyond self-centered desires. A major purpose of the university's education was to lead students to consider their need to serve others and the public good. Angell reminded the students of their relationship to God and of the importance of living by ideals. The profession of the graduates, in addition to earning a living, should more importantly "render . . . some valuable service to . . . fellow man. . . . [E]very one of you, whatever his calling, should regard himself as called by the very fact of his education to cherish this large and humane purpose to render ministrations to society."[26] Service is the basis of the contribution graduates must make to the commonweal. Coupled with that service was the need to recognize the role of personal sacrifice.

According to Angell, students should be prepared to work toward "securing good government . . . [and] be willing to subject themselves to some inconvenience in bearing their share of civil burdens. . . . When called by your fellow citizens to such work, which is commonly unrequited in money, be ready to do your full part in the spirit not of personal aggrandizement, but of devotion to the public good."[27] Angell's argument, like that of contemporaries such as Harris and Butler, was that sustaining the democratic state requires students to be active participants in ways that support civic values and contribute to the public good.

Thus far in this address, Angell's rhetoric conforms to the mainstream of what was no doubt expected by citizens of any leader at a public university. However, as Angell continued, he made specific reference to Jesus' example of Christian service to underscore the value of public service. He advocated the importance of Christian principles in the mission and educational philosophy of the university by claiming that service to humanity should be carried out in the context of a relationship with God. As an example of the importance of balance between worldly and otherworldly commitment, Angell criticized the previous generation, which he believed had focussed on relationship with God and Jesus Christ to the neglect of concerns for fellow citizens. He further encouraged his generation of students not to "make the mistake which is the opposite . . . and quite as grave. . . . Let not the absorbing cares and duties of life, let not even our human sympathies, put far away from us the idea of God."[28]

Angell's exhortation concluded with a plea that students adhere to personal ideals in all their involvements in the world. Reminiscent of warnings in numerous other addresses, Angell noted the temptation of abandoning standards and principles. He then advised students that they would "be called to compete with men who have few scruples about the means to accomplish their ends. You will be advised, and perhaps tempted, to fight fire with fire. You will be told that ideals are for dreamers, but ambitions are for men of sense." Preparing students for what they would find in the world, Angell warned that "When you are surrounded and pressed on all sides by men with these low ambitions, you may find it harder than you now imagine, to remain true to your better self, to scorn victories won with unworthy weapons, to follow the example of Him, who when offered by the evil one all the kingdoms of the earth said, 'Get thee hence, Satan.' "[29]

During Angell's presidency there was a unique connection between Wellesley College and the University of Michigan. Angell had recommended Alice Freeman Palmer, a member of the Michigan faculty and a university alumna, to be president of Wellesley. Her subsequent presidency of Wellesley overlapped with Angell's. Given his likely familiarity with the Wellesley motto and probably with it in mind, Angell concluded this final baccalaureate address by adding "that in such lives of devotion to the good of others you will all be most closely following the example of the Great Master, who came to minister to others rather than to be ministered unto."[30]

Angell's rhetoric reflected and was supported by the religious and cultural context of his time. His primary social arguments about the role of the university and student commitment to serve society could be reiterated by the presidents of the University of Michigan, or of any other public (as well as most private) universities today. By contrast it would be difficult to imagine similar public rhetoric about such specific (read: Christian) religious affections by a president of a public university today.

Another turn-of-the-century president, Caroline Hazard (and also a successor of Freeman Palmer's) also cast students' civic and social responsibilities as citizens in strongly moral terms. Like Harris, she invokes an understanding of the Kingdom of God in describing the students' responsibilities. Late in her presidency, Hazard made a sabbatical trip to the Holy Land. This experience shaped her sense of the world that she encouraged students to build. Upon returning, Hazard gave a series of chapel talks about her experiences.[31] In these short addresses, in the form of brief sermons or homilies, Hazard offered commentary on biblical stories and how these stories came alive when she visited the actual sites where the events took place.

For example, Hazard used the experience of seeing and touching the Dead Sea to comment on society and the challenge it presents to students. Beginning with the assertion that "Society has its Dead Seas," Hazard contended that "too often public opinion is indifferent as to great evils, too often men are treated with contempt and neglect. Whole classes of people—and shame to us that there should be classes—are oppressed. Life becomes sordid, crushing poverty blights, and men live in desert places of the soul and body."[32] Finding solutions to these inequities, social injustices, and class distinctions was the responsibility of educated men and women. It was these students "who go out from places of learning, where they have been nourished not on the dry bones of knowledge, but on the very bread of life, that they too may spread life."[33] Like other presidents, Hazard advocated collapsing the distinction between the college and the world. The task of the collegiate experience was to establish the pursuit of knowledge as a lifelong exercise. This would then result in the development of meaning in the lives of students and in greater benefits to society.

Like some of her presidential contemporaries, Hazard possessed the piety and fervor of the late nineteenth century Social Gospel. She thus concluded this talk with a challenge about building the Kingdom: "It is the new Jerusalem we seek—the new heaven and the new earth; heaven here and now on earth is our special business. If we can be part of that blessed river flowing from the sanctuary of God, if we can be included in that life-giving stream, and do its renewing work in a waiting world, then we indeed shall be blessed."[34]

Previously we noted Bumstead's warning to the black students at Atlanta University that education would not guarantee them acceptance in the communities in which they would live. In a fashion similar to some of his contemporaries, he used the hope of the Kingdom of God to inspire students to overcome discrimination against them and thereby to be Christ's witnesses. He believed that these aspirations encouraged students to transcend the limitations of prejudice—real and imagined—in their personal lives. This would allow them more freely to shape an understanding of their role and the expectations of them in the world.

Bumstead placed these civic values in a religious frame, asking students "are you still troubled about the restoration of the kingdom to yourself, your kindred, you own peculiar Israel?" In scriptural terms and with biblical admonitions in mind, Bumstead warned that "The times and the seasons of that restoration you cannot know, but this you do know, that they will be just as much shorter, and the restoration just as much nearer, as your own faithful witnessing to Christ tends to bring about that result. Do you wish a kingdom placed in your own hands? The surest way to get it is to give it no thought whatever, but just to be a witness-bearer for Christ."[35]

In a baccalaureate address, Crogman also highlighted the specific moral contributions expected of students. For a variety of social and cultural reasons, many graduates of Clark and of other southern colleges and universities at the time studied to become teachers. Speaking about the teaching profession and encouraging students to revere it, Crogman advised that "no more important or sacred work was ever committed to the hands of men or angels. . . . Someone has beautifully said that the teacher is like a candle which consumes itself while lighting others. Happy will it be for you, if at the end it may be written on your tombstone: 'Here lies one who consumed his own life enlightening the lives of others.' "[36] Regardless of the treatment of his black graduates by society, Crogman was convinced of, and conveyed to students, the belief that their lives would be ennobled by the blessing of God as a result of electing the esteemed and important profession of teaching.

As we have observed, many of these turn-of-the-century presidents were strongly affected by the Social Gospel emphasis on corporate as opposed to individual faith and responsibility. They forthrightly proposed that the principles of democracy, readily synonymous with ideals of the Kingdom, created an imperative for students to be civically responsible. The ends of education were not the fulfillment of individual desires and needs and the pursuit of selfish gain. Rather, endowed by education it was the responsibility of students to make civic and social contributions. These actions by the educated held the promise of perfecting the imperfections in democracy and thus were conveyed as a hope and inspiration for all citizens.

This tradition of presidential leadership affirming the relationship of education to democracy and challenging students about their responsibilities in the world continues well into the middle of the twentieth century and beyond. Theodore Hesburgh is a most noted and profound voice of this tradition that ultimate values are at stake in the choices students make about commitments to social and civic life. He claimed that students' influence on the world "will be for good or for evil. There is no in between unless you cease to live. Indeed, when your lives are finished, this will be the judgment upon your life, that the world will have been better or worse for your having lived in it."[37] Reminiscent of the warning of his predecessor, Cavanaugh, about being tested and tempted, Hesburgh confronted students with their clear choices in exercising responsibilities in the world.

Hesburgh reiterated this theme in a 1962 address at the Massachusetts Institute of Technology. The early 1960s were a time in America when the postwar domestic economy appeared to have no limits in increasing prosperity and security. At the same time the economic gap between rich and poor nations was becoming increasingly visible. Against this backdrop, Hesburgh attempted to provoke the social conscience of this audience of aspiring scientists and engineers. He wanted them to consider the needs of the world, not only the parochial interests of America. Hesburgh's belief was that they should contribute technical expertise to solve problems and improve living conditions.

After posing questions about the role of science and technology, he rhetorically asked whether the world needs more or less science. His answer is "more." However, Hesburgh quickly qualified his response. Using a classic critique of advances in science and his pastoral commitment to social justice, he added that "when I say more science and technology, I am not thinking of more luxurious living conditions for Americans. . . . I am thinking of the broader context of the world in which never before have so many millions of people been more poorly housed, or fed, or clothed. Never before have there been more illiterates, more infant deaths, or more people with frustrated hopes for a better life." In the preaching style often associated with Hesburgh's public rhetoric, he challenged these future scientists, engineers, and researchers: "More science and technology does indeed have an answer for all of these very real human problems, but the answers will only come if scientists and engineers put their science and technology to work in the true service of mankind everywhere, to respond to real human needs rather than pampering imagined wants, piling luxury upon luxury, and convenience upon convenience."[38]

Though students are free to choose their futures, Hesburgh made clear that the choices about what they will do with their lives are never free of the burden of conscience. His voice would simply not allow these students, supposedly the best and brightest of scientific learning and knowledge, to relax into comfortable detachment from the civic and social values that society demanded of them.

Another president, Nannerl Keohane of Wellesley, also expressed thoughts about the civic duty expected of students. The first major source that Keohane used was Wellesley's motto and its founder's claim that the purpose of a Wellesley education was to lead students to live "lives of noblest usefulness." Responding to the motto's charge "not to be ministered unto, but to minister," Keohane noted that students come to their decisions about service to others "with diverse gifts." A Wellesley education "multiplies them and gives them room. We leave to minister to the world and one another in a great variety of ways. So Wellesley women talk, *and* philosophize, *and* pray, *and* read, *and* certainly they do act and make a difference in the world."[39] Given the contemporary context in which religious references are increasingly less used in well-defined secular settings, it is interesting that Keohane included prayer as an activity of Wellesley undergraduates and alumni. But Keohane wished to contend that there is both a spiritual aspect and moral significance to a Wellesley education.

Granted, she uttered these words before an alumni group, clearly a "safe" audience. They may well have been highly sympathetic and romantically inclined in recalling the place of religion in their lives as undergraduates. Nevertheless, including prayer in a list of the educational, social, and civic activities of Wellesley alumni and students is unique for the president of a nonsectarian college in the latter twentieth century.

Second, Keohane shared concern with other presidents about the moral tension between elitism and egalitarianism, especially as related to the matter of service in the world. Her sense was that, interpreted in certain ways, the challenge of the Wellesley motto could be viewed as elitist. As she described it "even this wonderful motto—not to be ministered unto but to minister—has its own dangerous deformation. It can, in the wrong mood, become paternalistic (or maternalistic) and condescending." The problem was that "if one sees ministering as an act of a strong and noble person, it is easy to assume that people who are 'ministered unto' are somehow less worthy, less noble." In an effort to reinterpret the motto for contemporary society, Keohane suggested that "all of us need ministering unto sometimes in our lives; and in our ministering phases, we should occasionally remind ourselves of this rather than assuming that the world is permanently divided into the strong and fortunate, who do the ministering, and the rest, who need our attention."[40] Keohane developed a more contemporary (and it could be argued feminist) interpretation of the Welleseley motto.[41] She urged reflection about the attitude required by those who serve when they engage in service to others. For Keohane the often missing ingredient in those who serve is the degree to which they do so with humility. Keohane's point was that this aspect of service—that everyone at one time or another may be the person who is served—needed to be understood. Thus, teaching humility about service was the critical part of the education of the social elite.

Third, Keohane offered an interpretation about women's education and about the evolution of women's role in society. No doubt in response to critics, she admitted the danger that at a women's college feminism and education can be contrived and can serve to isolate the individual. In defense, Keohane asserted that "[F]eminism is not a selfish movement, but one that wants us to look at the whole picture, and not subordinate the talents and needs of women artificially, but rather to work towards a society in which both women and men . . . can flourish as individuals and as family units."[42] With this statement, she simultaneously addressed two sets of sometimes overlapping critics of the education of women. The first group are those who categorize education at women's colleges as only in the interest of women and not the whole of society. The second group are those who assume that increasing professional opportunities for educated women threaten the social fabric.

Keohane's responsibility as the president of a women's college to advocate for the view that women are contributors to the whole of society is remarkably similar to the battles waged by presidents of black colleges for black education. Following the Civil War and into the early twentieth century, Bumstead and

Crogman stressed the importance of educated blacks to the future of the South and about the need for blacks to view themselves as serving all of society, not merely the needs of black communities. Like Keohane, their plea was for society to view black education, not as isolating, but as a critical path in educating blacks who would in turn serve society. In the 1970s, Elias Blake, a contemporary of Keohane's as President of Clark College, used his office to affirm Clark's mission. Responding to prejudicial criticism about social and civic contributions of the institution and its students, Blake noted that "we must be clear in our own minds of our continued right to exist as well as be prepared for an intensification of questions about our role. Racially biased views of diversity always suggest that majority black schools are expendable."[43]

Keohane and Blake, and many if not all of their predecessors and successors, faced the imperative of using their moral voices as presidents to defend institutional existence and to justify the important role played by their students in the world beyond the gates of the campus. This task, dictated and guided by institutional mission, contrasts with the more overtly inclusive purpose and nature of a public university. For example, in an interview Duderstadt commented that "if there is a particular phrase that captures the spirit of the University of Michigan, it would [be] that the University was created to provide an uncommon education for the common man. That is the public character of the institution, its Jeffersonian character [as] an institution created by society, that is obligated to serve that society, to serve all of that society. So in that sense throughout our history we have been somewhat more inclusive than most institutions."[44] Duderstadt contended that external political forces make the leadership of a public university much more complicated than that of a private university.[45] However, because of its "'Jeffersonian character," public universities are in many ways less vulnerable than private colleges and universities to charges of exclusivity, elitism, and isolationism from society.

As observed here and in earlier chapters, presidential leadership integrally influences institutional mission. This connection becomes even more apparent and persuasive at colleges, such as historically women's and black colleges, with clear purposes, missions, and reputations, and concomitantly well-defined primary constituencies. Presidents of colleges dedicated to educating specific groups—in this case women and blacks—play an extraordinarily crucial role in defending their institutions against charges of exclusivity and isolationism by underscoring the contribution of their institutions and their students to the common good.

We have observed in this chapter the concerns, exhortations, and articulations of presidents regarding the foundations of democracy. These presidents are notable for inspiring their students and campus communities to pursue the time-honored imperatives of democracy and the social and civic virtues of American society. In the next chapter we continue the story of presidential moral leadership and courage beyond the gates as presidents address major national social and political issues. What national concerns do presidents believe bear directly on the campus and await college and university graduates as they move beyond the gates? How are these issues to be understood and evaluated? What moral imperatives demand the attention of students and anyone looking to the world beyond the ivory tower? In this context, the hopes for democracy and the ideals it inspires face the realities and problems of the nation and the world.

NOTES

1. For treatment of this topic, see Robert Nisbet, *The Degradation of the Academic Dogma* (London: Heinemann, 1971); Charles Sykes, *ProfScam: Professors and the Demise of Higher Education* (New York: St. Martin's Press, 1988); Bill Readings, *The University in Ruins* (Cambridge, Mass.: Harvard University Press, 1996); and Thorstein B. Veblen, *The Higher Learning in America* (New York: Hill and Wang, 1962).

2. Nicholas Murray Butler, "Some Fundamental Principles of American Education," university convocation, Albany, N.Y., June 30, 1902, Misc. Butler Addresses, vol. 1, no. 39, p. 4.

3. Ibid., p. 8. Butler summarizes this point by saying "it is my contention that none of these institutions are properly described as 'private'; they are all public, but not all governmental" (p. 9).

4. Ibid., p. 16.

5. Nicholas Murray Butler, "The Education of Public Opinion," June 22, 1899, Butler Speeches, vol. 1, p. 3.

6. Ibid., Address at Inauguration of President Swain, p. 10. He makes the same argument in an address at Swarthmore College at the installation of President Joseph Swain, November 15, 1902. Addressing the relationship of liberty to equality, Butler suggests that "liberty cannot exist with equality, and equality cannot exist except by the destruction of liberty. . . . The Creator has so made the human race that if we were all made equal today in capacity and equal in possessions, we should be far apart before the setting of the sun. There is no possible way to secure equality—except equality before the law which is a part of liberty—except by putting weights upon those who are strong, or by applying artificial stimuli to those who lag behind. If society attempts to put all of us on an equality with the least energetic and the least capable, it will utterly annihilate and destroy itself." Misc. Butler Addresses, vol. 1, no. 45, p. 3.

7. Ibid., p. 4.

8. George Harris, "The Man of Letters in a Democracy," *Amherst Student* 33, no. 3 (October 11, 1899), pp. 20–21.

9. Ibid., p. 21.

10. For a complete and insightful biography of John Hope's career and his presidency at Morehouse and Atlanta University, see Torrence Ridgely, *The Story of John Hope* (New York: Macmillan, 1948).

11. William H. Crogman, "Negro Education: Its Helps and Hindrances," National Education Association, July 16, 1884, p. 10.

12. *Atlanta University Bulletin* no. 21 (October 1890), p. 6a.

13. Torrence Ridgely, *The Story of John Hope* (New York: Macmillan, 1948), p. 343.

14. Ibid., pp. 343–44.

15. Elias Blake, Jr., Founders Day address, From Personal Papers of Elias Blake, Jr., February 19, 1980, p. 16.

16. Theodore Hesburgh, document addressed to the Religious Education Association of the United States and Canada, August 12, 1953, UND Archives, 1947–1967, Box 141/4, p. 1. It is unclear whether this document was a letter or brief speech to this group.

17. Theodore Hesburgh, sermon opening the school year, September 25, 1955, UND Archives, 1947–1967, Box 141/7, pp. 4–5.

18. Ibid., p. 10.

19. Harold T. Shapiro, graduation address, May 3, 1980, Shapiro Collection, Box 177, pp. 3–4.

20. Nannerl O. Keohane, "Educating Citizens for a Modern Democracy," February 26, 1987, Keohane Speeches, 1986–1990, p. 4.

21. Nicholas Murray Butler, "Five Evidences of an Education," *Educational Review*, November 1901, p. 329.

22. Herman Humphrey Neill, "President George Harris," from the 1901 Olio, George Harris Biographical File (AC 1866), p. 6, Archives and Special Collections, Amherst College Library.

23. "Man of Letters in a Democracy," *Amherst Student*, Oct. 11, 1899, p. 24.

24. James Burrill Angell, "The Debt of the University Graduate," *Michigan Alumnus* 5, no. 46 (July 1899), p. 409. This emphasis on the way alumni represent the University of Michigan is noted specifically by two other presidents. In this apparent tradition at the University of Michigan, Duderstadt mentions the significance to the university of the fact that the clinical trials for the polio vaccine were carried out there by an alumnus, Jonas Salk. (Personal interview with President James J. Duderstadt of the University of Michigan, March 6, 1995.) Second, as previously mentioned, Walsh notes how the moral voice of Wellesley College is embodied in its alumnae in the world. (Personal interview with President Diana Chapman Walsh of Wellesley College, November 28, 1994.)

25. James Burrill Angell, "The State and the Student," *Michigan Alumnus* 15, no. 146 (July 1909), p. 437.

26. James Burrill Angell, "Ambitions and Ideals," *Michigan Alumnus* 3, no. 27 (July 1897), pp. 245–46.

27. Ibid., p. 247.

28. Ibid., p. 249.

29. Ibid., p. 250.

30. Angell, "The State and the Student," p. 437.

31. Caroline Hazard, *A Brief Pilgrimmage in the Holy Land* (Boston: Houghton Mifflin, 1909).

32. Ibid., p. 101.

33. Ibid., pp. 101–2.

34. Ibid., p. 103.

35. *Atlanta University Bulletin* 1, no. 11 (June 1889), p. 4b.

36. William H. Crogman, "Life's Deeper Meaning," *Talks for the Times* (Cincinnati: Jennings and Pye, 1896), p. 44.

37. Theodore Hesburgh, commencement address, Trinity College, Washington, D.C., May 31, 1954, UND Archives, 1947–1967, Box 141/5, p. 3.

38. Theodore Hesburgh, "Science and Technology in Modern Perspective," June 8, 1962, UND Archives, 1947–1967, Box 141/18, p. 5.

39. Nannerl O. Keohane, Alumni Association talk, June 7, 1981, Keohane Speeches, 1981–1985, unpaginated.

40. Nannerl O. Keohane, "What Counts As a Life of Noblest Usefulness," Washington, D.C., Alumni Club, October 28, 1988, Keohane Speeches, 1986–1990, p. 8.

41. Keohane's comment may also presage the concerns Walsh mentions about alumni reporting the motto as presenting such a high ideal that the inability to attain it becomes burdensome for their lives.

42. Nannerl O. Keohane, "The Liberal Arts Today," Rotary Club of Boston, March 2, 1983, Keohane Speeches, 1981–1985, p. 4.

43. Elias Blake, Jr., inaugural address, October 27, 1978, p. 2.

44. Personal interview with President James J. Duderstadt of the University of Michigan, President's Office, University of Michigan, March 6, 1995.

45. Ibid.

7

The Milieu of Social and
Political Issues

ADVOCACY FOR CIVIL RIGHTS

Beyond the gates of the campus, presidents and the colleges they lead confront an array of political issues and social problems. Their magnitude is frequently of significant interest and legitimate concern to a variety of the college's or university's constituencies that they cannot be ignored. Presidents will elect to use their leadership on these public and civic concerns for a number of reasons. Sometimes issues become compelling because the public perceives them to be significant and applies pressure for a response. In some cases, presidents become involved because their conscience and sense of commitment leads them to speak and act. At times pressure from internal and external university constituencies is exerted on presidents to respond on behalf of the institution.

Since the Civil War, and probably earlier, one of the major public issues that presidents have addressed is civil and human rights, especially regarding the struggles of black Americans. Long before it was fashionable to do so, well in advance of the civil-rights revolution of the 1950s and 1960s, college presidents repeatedly claimed this territory as morally important.

While examples abound, we begin with Nicholas Murray Butler's willingness in the early twentieth century to take public stands and to act on behalf of civil rights. On the occasion of the 1924 national meeting of the Negro National Educational Congress, Butler wrote a letter to the organization's president, J. Silas Harris. In the letter Butler stated that "civilized human beings can live together in orderly society while permitting the honest and sincere manifestations of every possible difference of opinion. Those who would advance civilization must labor in season and out of season to resist and to check that persecuting tendency which is a mark of barbarism and which manifests itself now in lynching, now in prohibition, and now in the cowardly and unpatriotic activities of the Ku Klux Klan." With a faith in education typical of presidents and educators, Butler added that "Every liberal will wage war on this spirit of persecution until a sound and truly liberal education drives it from the human heart."[1]

Butler rarely shrank from exercising his voice beyond the gates of Columbia. Not willing to rest his argument on moral rhetoric alone, later that year, Butler put words into action by drafting an Anti–Ku Klux Klan plank for the New York Republican State Convention.[2] During his presidency, Butler maintained an active role and affiliation with the Republican party. This public political connection provided him a national platform for addressing issues such as civil rights.

Another example is Nannerl Keohane's address at a United Nations Day celebration. In this setting, she raised the worldwide problem of racism. In a vein similar to Butler she highlighted the tragic products of human depravity and damage caused by racial hatred. Keohane acknowledged realistically that eliminating racial prejudice was a large task because "The causes are deep seated and the effects are ugly, frightening, and pervasive." Then she noted the true importance of the effort because dealing with racial discrimination and animosity "is inextricably connected with the cause of peace since racial hatred and misunderstanding are historically a potent source of war and conflict."[3]

Theodore Hesburgh's tenure in the 1950s and 1960s provides an example of presidential moral leadership in relation to the civil-rights issues of that time. Like Butler, Hesburgh's stature and long tenure as president created an enormous public presence and respect. Hesburgh served on the first Civil Rights Commission as an appointee of U.S. President Dwight D. Eisenhower. This provided him a visible pulpit from which to speak about racial justice and the right to vote, the latter one of the major civil-rights issues of that day.

As the decade of the 1960s dawned, the civil-rights movement continued to develop from its roots in the 1950s. In an address at the University of Rhode Island in the spring of 1960, Hesburgh joined the emerging national debate about race.

Hesburgh knew that the social challenge inherent in America's race problem was enormous. Always willing to confront an audience, he asserted that "We are still fighting that battle, and none of you can disengage yourselves from taking a stand on this national blight that makes one-tenth of the American people second-class citizens, without truly equal opportunity in voting, education, housing, employment, or even in the administration of justice." In language appropriate to the forceful black civil-rights leaders of his day, Hesburgh recalled the exemplary power of the moral convictions seeded in the American soul. And aware of the historic ground on which he stood, Hesburgh concluded that "We have had enough of compromise, of gentlemen's agreements, of restrictive covenants, of the myth of white superiority, of white citizens' councils. Roger Williams said: 'I have not hid within my breast my soul's belief.' In a world whose uncommitted peoples, one-third of all humanity, are almost entirely colored, let us who believe in freedom and justice for all not hide that belief within our breasts or deny it by our practices here at home. The cost of following Roger Williams' lead today is not exile, just courage."[4] Earlier than was fashionable and with great moral courage, Hesburgh advocated racial justice and the emerging agenda of the civil-rights movement.

THE BLACK COLLEGE TRADITION

As we have previously observed, the presidents of black colleges have continually been at the nexus where black education and the racial concerns of African Americans meet. During his presidency, Horace Bumstead traveled frequently to the North to raise money and rally support for black education in the South. In one of his stump talks for these trips, "Education in the South," Bumstead attacked the matter of the debilitating effects of the slave heritage inherited by blacks. He observed that "the negro fails to be a wealth producer partly because of his history and partly because of his environment. Heathenism and slavery in the past have brought him a legacy of evil. The wretchedness or inadequacy of his training in home, school and church together with the spirit of caste which denies him the legitimate reward of his attainment when he had risen from a lower condition, combine to discourage him and retard his progress." With the optimism of an educator, Bumstead believed that education was a key to righting these wrongs. Bumstead concluded noting that it was Atlanta University's purpose to undertake "to put within the negro the power to make the most of himself and to claim the reward of his progress."[5]

Another important issue for blacks after the Civil War and during Reconstruction was their self-image and the concomitant manner in which they were portrayed by society. Addressing the Mohonk Negro Conference, Bumstead discussed the frequently constructed and unfair characterizations of black people in the culture. One outrage he noted was the "tendency to make too much of the comical and grotesque side of Negro life and character. . . . We do not make much fun of the Chinese or the Indian or other races that are inferior in their present condition to ours. We go at their elevations with a seriousness of speech that we do not find enough of in our dealings with the colored people." From his years working with black people and in the ringing tones of the preacher he was trained to be, Bumstead concluded, "Let us rise to a higher plane. Let us learn to treat these people more as human beings. Let us rid our minds of the picture of the Negro as he is burlesqued in the comic papers and on the cover of the shoe-blackingbox, and get a higher conception for him; for the higher conception is much nearer the truth."[6] Bumstead was committed to undermining one of the recurring major stumbling blocks to the advancement of blacks, one that unfortunately continues in many quarters of American society to this day—

the perpetration and perpetuation of racial stereotypes designed to demean and disparage.

Bumstead was not beyond using humor in highlighting the ironies of racial prejudice and the serious concern about the place of blacks in American society. Urging a change in the perception of blacks in a talk at Old South Church in Boston on April 21, 1898, he remarked that "the American Negro of to-day is not the same as the American Negro at the close of the Civil War. It is necessary, I think, to make that statement. There are a great many people in our country who do not seem to be aware of the fact. We hear much about '*the* Negro,' as if there were just one kind of Negro in this country. Only two or three years ago, a prominent gentleman made this statement at a sociological conference: 'The kind of education that is needed by the boys at Harvard and Yale is not suited to the average American Negro.' Why, of course not; nor is that education to the *average* white boy of this country."[7] The statement speaks eloquently for itself. Society's decisions about access to education, then as now, could not be allowed to be made on the basis of false assumptions rooted in prejudicial thinking.

As previously observed, Bumstead was a master at making the practical moral argument that blacks who become more productive individuals will then be greater contributors economically and in other ways beneficial to society. His speeches and trips north were opportunities to highlight Atlanta University's crucial mission in reaching this goal. Bumstead refused to be distracted by the inability of some citizens in both the North and South to be persuaded about justice and equity purely on the basis of democratic principles and moral ideals. He knew that the body politic needed only to understand and change behavior on the basis of a utilitarian concern for the improvement of the whole society.

William Crogman was a close colleague of Bumstead's as a fellow president in Atlanta and in his moral advocacy about racial problems. While still a professor and well before becoming president, Crogman spoke to the Freedmen's Aid Society on the occasion of its eighteenth anniversary, August 13, 1883. Invoking language similar to Bumstead's, Crogman pleaded for racial harmony and understanding. He urged, "let us rise above low, narrow, absurd, wicked discrimination against men on account of their race, their color, or their nationality. Let us endeavor to repair the wrongs of the past. Let us be just and let us be humane." Reminding his predominantly white audience of the important economic role of blacks in the development of the South, Crogman remarked: "Let us see to it that in the future fair play is given to that six and a half millions of people in your midst who felled your forests, tilled your fields, developed the resources of a section of your country, received insult and injury untold and unspeakable, yet, in the midst of it all, have beautifully illustrated

How sublime a thing it is
To suffer and be strong"[8]

A few years later, in August 1885, at Chautauqua, Crogman gave another speech, "The Negro Problem." In it he spoke about racial prejudice and civil rights as major issues of public concern. His assessment was that at its heart the race problem was a moral problem. He argued that "there is involved somewhere in this problem a moral element, an element of right, the ignoring or evading of which must keep it a problem for all time, no man of sound mind and honest heart for a moment doubts."[9] Like Butler in his call for liberal education, Crogman too desired an educated and rational discussion that he believed would lead to ultimate moral truth about race.

Nearly one hundred years later, Elias Blake spoke as a successor of Crogman to the graduating class of Clark College about their relationship to the history of blacks in America. He wanted the students to remember their past, their heritage, and the path that got them to a college education. Blake reminded their parents that "your children must know that there were legions of quiet heroes, many of whom through their strength and courage, brought you to this college graduation. . . . Your children must not forget that the diploma which buys their ease was bought with hundreds of years of snarled fingers from gripping shovels and picks in ditches, miles too long and in ground too rocky and hard." Creating this point of passage in the lives of the students came with a price: "your diplomas have been earned with back troubles from lifting loads too heavy for men but not heavy enough for beasts of burden; from working two bad jobs to earn the wages of one good job."[10] Blake and his rhetoric stand firmly in a long tradition at Clark of ensuring that students comprehend the sufferings and sacrifices of those who have gone before. This commitment continues today as Blake's successor, Thomas Cole, has made a commitment that black history, in particular the civil-rights movement of the 1960s, is emphasized in each year's orientation of new students at Clark Atlanta. Spanning decades and over a century, these leaders of predominantly black colleges share the concern that knowledge of the past is critical to inspiring students to lives of moral commitment to the unfinished agenda of civil and human rights. These presidents and the institutions they lead stand to ensure that this tradition continues.

THE DILEMMAS OF MULTICULTURALISM AND RACIAL JUSTICE

We have seen that James Duderstadt was a president who possessed strong commitments to diversity. He thought and spoke at length about race and racial problems. His reflections on these difficult and often divisive issues form a philosophy of the relationship of the university and what has come to be called multiculturalism. Immediately prior to his inauguration, Duderstadt gave his first State of the University Address. His career had been spent almost entirely at the University of Michigan, and before becoming president he had served as a dean and provost and vice president for academic affairs. He knew the institution well and now had the opportunity to present his concerns and expectations of what the university ought to do about the matter of race.

Duderstadt's statement of personal and presidential commitment called on the university to become a model in higher education. In this address, he defined the commitments necessary for the university to become a truly multicultural institution.[11] Reflecting the demands on everyone in a position of leadership, Duderstadt urged that "all of us—faculty, staff, and students—must recognize that the challenge of diversity and pluralism is our personal challenge and responsibility." Leaving little doubt about where he stood, he continued: "let me clearly state now, at this, the beginning of my presidency, that my personal commitment to meeting this challenge is both intense and unwavering. I am determined that the University of Michigan achieve leadership in higher education by developing a model of what a pluralistic, multicultural university must be to serve America of the 21st Century—and I urge each of you to join me in responding to this mandate!"[12]

Duderstadt viewed the university as an institution in society that had an important role to play in the development of multicultural communities. The university's leadership on this matter transcended the confines of its boundaries to include all higher education and society. Underscoring this assertion in a student inauguration luncheon address the following day, Duderstadt discussed further the challenges of racial justice and diversity to the university community and the nation. He contended that "in this future, full participation of currently underrepresented minorities will continue to be of central concern for reasons of equity and social justice. But, in addition, this objective will be the key to the future strength and prosperity of America, since our nation cannot afford to waste the human talent represented by its minority populations." As other presidents, Duderstadt appealed not only to high moral impulses, but also to the practical benefits of a more respectful and integrated society. He concluded by reminding the students that "full participation of underrepresented minorities is not just a matter of equity and social justice. America cannot afford the loss of this human potential, cultural richness, and social leadership."[13]

For any college president, or any leader in society, publicly addressing issues of race is a difficult and sensitive matter. Harold Shapiro, Duderstadt's predecessor at Michigan and subsequently president of Princeton, provides a pointed example of this problem. Problems of race and race relations were matters that he, like most college presidents, addressed throughout his presidency. On occasions, racial matters become unavoidable for presidents. Often these episodes have been the ironic by-product of efforts to diversify the composition of university communities.

Shapiro's response to a series of racial incidents on campus displayed his deep concern about matters of justice. He said, in part, to the university community: "Several troubling incidents of racism and other forms of bigotry have surfaced on our campus over the past months. These have included offensive graffiti, abusive language, and personal insensitivity of various kinds on the part of members of the University community. This is matter of profound concern to me and, I believe, to most other members of the University of Michigan community." He then noted the connection of educational values to simple justice and respect: "Every incident of racism or bigotry—whether blatant or otherwise—undermines our aspirations and diminishes the ideals of our community. Each such incident is a cause of grief and dismay for us all. The values upon which this academy rests are tarnished by capricious actions that demean the worth and integrity of any one of us."[14] Shapiro did not shrink from making this strong statement to his campus community.

A year later, in 1987, Shapiro had developed his thoughts about this highly sensitive and often equally highly charged subject of racism on campus and in society into a draft paper, "Confronting Reality While Building the Future— Beyond the Rhetoric of Racism to a Changed World." He circulated this draft confidentially to a small group of major college and university presidential colleagues for their comments and response.[15] Because of sensitivities about the issue of race and the potential political ramifications of what he had written, Shapiro sought consultation with these other presidents about the ideas he had developed and the conclusions he had drawn. The paper was Shapiro's attempt to fashion a middle ground between the ideologues on the left and the right. In the cover letters to his colleagues, hoping to elicit their candid opinions and thoughts, Shapiro acknowledged the difficulty, if not impossibility, of publicly addressing race relations. Their advice was that he should be extremely careful, that while he had valid and probably truthful positions, there was great risk for negative backlash.

Shapiro stayed the course and reworked the paper, eventually publishing it as "Confronting Reality and Building the Future: Race Relations and the Future of Liberal Democracy" in a book of essays and speeches.[16] It provides one president's view on an issue permeating much of contemporary university life.

After discussing assumptions about how both whites and blacks view race relations, Shapiro suggested that "if *both* Blacks and whites are perceived as helpless victims of racism, it seems futile to consider new initiatives. In short, the rhetoric of racism may have fixated us on only part of the truth. It may be serving less to illuminate the present than to confuse our potential future with certain aspects of our history and to deflect our attention from what we need most: community-wide initiatives that can create a better future for us all."[17]

In an attempt to resolve this dilemma, like many other presidents, Shapiro turned to the liberal hope of pluralism, contrasting it with what he labeled the "cultural utopia" of various forms of fundamentalism. It is at this point that the concern of his fellow presidents about Shapiro's vulnerability becomes clear. But this argument is also evidence of Shapiro's moral courage and his unflinching concern about the corrosive effects of ideologies in the academy.

Aware of the worldwide reach of fundamentalist thinking in religion, politics, and other ideologies, he suggested that "the opposite of pluralism, fundamentalism (in its various guises), proclaims the superiority of one particular culture, often citing a special source for its revelation. Rather than celebrate the free play of ideas, fundamentalism—like other extreme ideologies—deplores dissent as a barrier to the achievement of some cultural utopia." Especially in a democracy and most importantly if that democratic vision is to be maintained, "the great challenge for a liberal/pluralistic culture is to sustain a morally energizing vision of its prospects while foregoing utopian tactics. Realizing this goal will require responsibility, self-discipline, and, above all, a commitment to human reciprocity and community needs." Then capturing one of the great dilemmas of the academy—the need to rely on traditions while being prepared to embrace change—Shapiro noted that "while we must certainly stand for something (or we will fall for anything), we must also constantly encourage critical evaluation of new alternatives. We attempt this delicate balancing act in the name of a truly equitable, just, and inspiring future."[18] In spite of these clear and grave anxieties, Shapiro still affirmed that "cultural diversity is an inherently valuable and probably enduring characteristic of our society. Since we are unlikely to arrive at a common idea of what is just, beautiful, right, holy, or worthy, our moral worth depends on a toleration of diversity."[19]

Shapiro was deeply concerned that reasoned dialogue about and satisfactory solutions to race problems were so often elusive. His analysis of the significant dilemmas posed by racial issues in the university is both interesting and convincing. Shapiro exposes the difficulty of engaging rational discussion and of developing some common ground for solutions as a result of the resistance of competing political ideologies to the traditional and generally accepted principles of liberal education. In the tradition of Kenneth Minogue, Shapiro believed that these ideologies are antithetical to the core values for which universities must stand. His analysis describes a dangerous prospect for the contemporary university: that it has become a battleground of competing and self-interested ideologies.[20] Though aware of the potential for resistance, Shapiro urged rational and educational discourse—the basis of liberal learning—as a way to counter the dangers of ideological conflicts. He did not naively believe that ideologies could be eliminated from the debate, but rather their exponents should be challenged to engage debate in a spirit of commitment to rational inquiry.

FEMINISM AND THE EDUCATION OF WOMEN

Advocacy of women's education, like that of education for blacks, is grounded in part on the need to remove barriers and improve access for the formerly disenfranchised. This educational philosophy also assumes that expanding opportunity to these groups has positive effects on society. Women's colleges were founded to broaden educational opportunities for women in order to open previously closed doors. Championing the cause of women's education, presidents of institutions such as Wellesley make principled and practical proposals designed to advance the status of women. They have argued for the changes required in society for women—and the same may be said for any minority group—to find rightful places in the academy and in the world.

In her turn-of-the-century inaugural address at Wellesley, Caroline Hazard discussed the importance of the feminine and the value of women to the whole of humankind.[21] She knew and believed that women must be permitted to play a full role in the affairs of society. The threat to women and their educational advancement was that they would be marginalized as only feminine and thus be prevented from making contributions to society. In a comment no doubt directed at educators throughout higher education as well as her Wellesley constituency, she asserted that "sentimentality and mannishness like Scylla and Charybdis stand on either side. The intellect must be trained to its full capacity or there will be an uneven balance. Heart and hand in happy union must rule the conduct. And so we believe in what is called Higher Education. Ideal justice is not a common virtue and the powers of the mind must be trained to regulate the emotions."[22]

Nannerl Keohane commented on the place of women in society in a similar vein, but with noticeable changes reflective of her distance of almost a hundred years from her predecessor. The two presidents were joined in their concern about the need for society to provide equal opportunities for men and women. Keohane argued that "democracy will only work as it is supposed to work if women and men, as full and active citizens, educated in a truly liberal version of the liberal arts, across classes and colors, all take their political lives seriously. Women and citizenship no longer need to be at odds, if women seize and use their powers and responsibilities as citizens." Education was clearly a most important part of this social goal: "We can only do this if we are empowered by a truly liberal education in which the virtues traditionally ascribed to males and those ascribed to females are both understood and valued. And women citizens will only be taken seriously if their men folk have enjoyed an equally liberating education."[23]

For Keohane, the prospects of social change were founded on the fundamental values of a liberal education. Only rational discourse and liberal learning could improve the position and thereby the contribution of women in society. Keohane expressed similar sentiments in addressing the more practical issue of women's power in society. Again, she fully understood that opposition to the advancement of women, much of it rooted in the fears of men, was a reality to be confronted. Like so many presidents, she remained ever the educator, remarking that "*this is where education comes in*: in order to make a dent in the 'glass ceiling' for bright and ambitious young women, we must educate both young women and their prospective partners to understand the obstacles to their success and to see themselves as powerful enough to change them."[24]

But women educators and college presidents have not been alone in advocating women's education and rights. James Angell was a frequent supporter of the education of women. This included an extensive argument in his inaugural

in favor of the admission of women to the University of Michigan. He believed
that support for this position was gathering and that the university's example in
taking this bold step would likely be imitated by eastern schools.[25] A product
of the East, educated at Brown and serving as president of the University of
Vermont before coming to Michigan, Angell advocated a healthy competition
between the West and the East. At times he imitated eastern colleges, as seen
in his support for Michigan to embody religious principles and to educate students for the ministry as had the eastern colleges. But Angell also wanted to be
a trendsetter and thus he pushed for the admission of women at Michigan ahead
of its eastern counterparts.

Angell subsequently wrote an an essay about the education of women, developing the theme used in the inaugural.[26] In it he challenged the higher education community, and especially the New England colleges, on the question of
women's education. Angell posed arguments supporting gender-equal admissions and attacked arguments against the movement for accepting women at
formerly all-male educational institutions. The historical record interestingly
shows that it took many more decades—and in the cases of some institutions,
such as Amherst, Dartmouth, and Yale, which Angell no doubt had in mind,
nearly a century—for his urgings to reach fruition.

NATIONAL ILLS: POVERTY, CITIES, AND VIOLENCE

Two contemporary presidents—Edward Malloy of Notre Dame and Thomas
Gerety of Amherst—exhibit leadership from within the ivory tower about pressing ills in society. Malloy regularly used the presidency to show the relationship
of the university to social issues beyond the boundaries of the campus. Whether
making reference to local concerns in the community of South Bend or to social
issues facing the nation, Malloy constantly spoke about the importance of building the common good. His educational philosophy joined the values of the
university, what it teaches students, and how these values are part of their education, to the imperative for an ethical response to needs of the world. Malloy's
social concerns have their genesis in personal interests and in his background
as a Christian ethicist. A number of examples illustrate this.

A distinguishing feature of Malloy's philosophy, and that of his Notre Dame
presidential colleagues, is its grounding and expression in Christian principles.
Notre Dame's presidents have unapologetically used the rhetoric of faith and
belief when urging active involvement by the university's constituencies in solving social problems. In Malloy's words "Notre Dame can never grow content
or complacent with its response to the needs of this sometimes troubled world.
Service always must be an integral part of the education we provide and the
witness we give."[27]

Malloy encouraged service to the world but framed the importance of service
in the context of bearing witness to Catholic and Christian faith by those who
serve. His theological understanding of service is found in a message to grad-

uating seniors about service and the expectations of the world: "Love without justice is cheap. It comes too easily. We boast that our media dominate the airwaves and the movie screens of the world, but who could claim that what we present to the world is of real quality or cultural value?" To this rhetorical question Malloy answered that "wherever we look, in the professions, in the leadership of businesses, in civic organizations, in government service, in the academy, we see opportunities to take the love that we have inherited from our families and tested during our time here, and to express that love in action in the concrete circumstances of the world."[28]

This position is rooted in his personal experience of service. In the summer of 1962 while a Notre Dame undergraduate, Malloy went to Mexico as a student volunteer. Working among the poor in a setting he described as "inexplicable and wondrous," Malloy first felt his call to join the priesthood.[29] His sentiments about service are a variation on Dietrich Bonhoeffer's concept of the costliness of discipleship and of the impossibility of "cheap grace." To Malloy, service is the action inspired by an education rooted in the context of Christian belief.

Malloy was also passionate about the future of America's cities and related matters of domestic violence and gun control. In an address at Catholic University, he connected an array of social ills and forces he believed could not be ignored. Malloy challenged the graduates and others attending the ceremony to look just outside the gates of the campus: "How many people in this city, in this neighborhood are terrorized by violence in the streets? . . . what has happened in this city [Washington] in recent years is enough to embarrass all of us, that we have not exercised proper responsibility: drugs, gangs, inadequate medical care, housing that is not appropriate to our citizens." The response he supplied was that "we need to find new ways of leadership, a new agenda for this city. We need to find a way to repair the divisions that we have seen manifest in our country in recent weeks: the reality of race and ethnicity and gender. We need to find a way to speak a language that we can hold in common. We need to find ways that will allow us to recognize the perspective of everyone in this city and this land."[30] Again, Malloy reflected deeply held beliefs based on his experience of working and empathizing with the poor and on his assessment of the needs of society. Malloy also applied Roman Catholic "just war" theory to his extensive knowledge of law enforcement and criminal justice to emphasize moral concerns about domestic policing and law enforcement.[31]

In closing an annual address to the faculty, Malloy described the role of the university as both a servant and a critic of society. Malloy claimed that Notre Dame "should always be a resource for critical reflection on values, for the search for steps of amelioration relative to social, economic and political problems, and for the education of informed citizens who will support policies that seek the common good." Addressing the ancient tension and presumed separation between the ivory tower and the "real" world, Malloy noted that "our activity as a University may keep us one step removed from the fray, but we should never allow ourselves to betray the common trust either by indifference to the great issues of the day or by a failure in courage to take on the demons that divide and destroy."[32] Bringing this idea to the relationship between Notre Dame and the South Bend community, Malloy added that "the relationship of these [the university's] programs and the problems they address cannot be over-estimated. Our future well-being as a University cannot be separated from the community of which we are an integral part."[33]

Gerety shared Malloy's personal concern for the ills of urban America. He connected these social and political problems to the ideals of democracy. Gerety believed education could instill civic and social virtue in students. Commenting on urban America, Gerety remarked that "the difficulties—and the joys . . . of America's cities are an especially important subject for reflection and study in the liberal arts. If our political and constitutional system is . . . one of America's great achievements, then its failure to integrate city and suburb, rich and poor, black and white, stands as a great contradiction of the astonishingly durable virtues of our constitutional order." The reality is that "at a time when the world as a whole seems passionately to desire free markets and free politics, America's failings in its cities sober our enthusiasm and test both our resolve and our wisdom."[34] Gerety highlighted social concern about the dire situation of cities and urged that citizens must contemplate their civic responsibility for remedying urban problems. This task is not something beyond, but rather integral to, the study and action that can be inspired by the liberal arts tradition.

Both Gerety and Malloy believe that universities and colleges can and should be both servants and critics of society. This conception of the university as both servant and critic reflects the complexity of its tasks. Simultaneously, it also explains at least a portion of the recurring criticisms that befall the academy. But understanding the university as critic and servant is a major theme in the leadership of presidents. Malloy offered the caveat that the university should maintain a degree of detachment, be "removed from the fray," regarding social issues. Though wishing the university to be prepared to oppose evil in the world, he knew that the university must avoid domination by solely politically moti-vated forces. Navigating these challenges is neither simple or easy. As an ideal, Malloy sought a university that would be in but not of the world. ·Malloy's caution is well founded and wise. But even here, critics such as Kenneth Minogue, while viewing this posture as admirable, would nonetheless argue that it is sufficiently risky to the real purposes of the academy as to be avoided.

In the final analysis there is a distinctive yet flexible line—fashioned by pres-idential courage and judgment—between the aspiration for purity of purpose in letting the university be the university (Minogue's position) on one hand, and the unavoidable milieu of social and political issues that the university must continually confront and in which it must selectively elect to become involved on the other. The critical determining counsel for presidential leadership of col-leges and universities may be John Kemeny's advice that while institutions "cannot effectively take stands on controversial issues, individuals must take stands."[35] Though this principle is not an infallible guide, Kemeny's assessment highlights the importance of presidential moral leadership and of debate based in free inquiry about the crucial issues to be addressed by the academy. The absolutist position that would resist and avoid debate on campus altogether about often contentious social issues is dangerous itself, for it risks robbing the university of the very intellectual and scholarly vitality upon which it is fundamentally founded.

During the last century and a half (and probably for much of the preceding history of American higher education) college and university presidents have placed major emphasis on civil and human rights. In addition, we have observed numerous expressions of moral leadership encouraging students to be active participants in other matters critical to civic and national life. We turn next to the response of presidents to global issues and the commitments suggested by their moral voice to these aspects of life beyond the gates of the academy.

NOTES

1. Nicholas Murray Butler, letter to J. Silas Harris, June 13, 1924, Butler Speeches, vol. 6, no. 82, p. 2.

2. Butler Speeches, vol. 6, no. 91, pp. 1–2.

3. Nannerl O. Keohane, U.N. Day celebration, Boston, Mass., October 24, 1983, Keohane Speeches, 1981–1985, p. 4.

4. Theodore Hesburgh, commencement address, University of Rhode Island, June 13, 1960, UND Archives, 1947–1967, Box 141/15, p. 9.

5. Horace Bumstead, "Education in the South," *Atlanta University Bulletin* no. 23 (December 1890) p. 7. The portion of his talk cited here is part of the full address as it appeared in the *Boston Post* covering Bumstead's appearance in Boston before the New England Women's Club, November 25, 1890.

6. *Atlanta University Bulletin* no. 31 (November 1891), p. 6a–b.

7. *Atlanta University Bulletin* no. 92 (May 1898), p. 2b.

8. Longfellow, Henry Wadsworth, "Thy Light of Stars," in William H. Crogman, "The Eighteenth Anniversary of the Freedman's Aid Society," *Talks for the Times* (Cincinnati: Jennings and Pye, 1896), pp. 120–21.

9. Ibid., "The Negro Problem," August 1885, pp. 242–43. For additional reflections by Crogman on the moral issues confronting blacks and the moral dimensions of the race problem, see an evening talk at Henry Ward Beecher's church in Plymouth, Mass., on October 14, 1883 (p. 192), and the previously cited talk to the Freedmen's Aid Society, pp. 116–17.

10. Elias Blake, Jr., talk to graduates, from the personal papers of Elias Blake, Jr., undated, p. 16.

11. James J. Duderstadt, "State of the University Address," October 3, 1988, Duderstadt Speeches, 1988–1989, Box 217, pp. 4–5. It should be noted that Edward Malloy is another president who uses the moral voice to bring the national social agenda for affirmative action into the affairs of the university. Examples are found in Malloy's Address to the faculty, President's Office, University of Notre Dame, October 2, 1989, pp. 2 and 11. Here he argues for both a continuing commitment to faculty recruitment and student admissions of minorities and women. In addition, he notes that the resulting

changes "will require that all of us be sensitive in our use of language and examples and even more respectful in our ways of dealing with students and colleagues alike" (p. 11).

12. Ibid., p. 6. In this same address he cites as important "other sets of values which we must not ignore: Values of moral character such as: honesty, integrity, courage, compassion. Values of a civilized society: tolerance and mutual respect, collegiality, civility, and community" (p. 17). These values are the elements commonly associated with moral character, as Duderstadt points out, and also have been observed as major themes and constituting parts of the moral voice.

13. James J. Duderstadt, student inauguration luncheon address, October 4, 1988, JJD Speeches, 1988–1989, Box 217, p. 5.

14. Harold T. Shapiro. "A Personal Message," *University Record* 41, no. 15 (January 13, 1986), p. 1, Shapiro Collection, Box 177.

15. Harold T. Shapiro, Racism draft, Shapiro Collection, Box 206. Original copies of Shapiro's correspondence to his colleagues and of the drafts returned by the presidents to whom it was circulated with their commentary and letters are located in this file.

16. Harold T. Shapiro, *Tradition and Change: Perspectives on Education and Public Policy* (Ann Arbor: University of Michigan Press, 1987), pp. 63–71. Comparisons between the original draft as circulated to other presidents and the final version as published are most interesting. In both the original and final versions Shapiro states that "we cannot allow our disappointing progress to sink us into a crippling pessimism. We must instead remain dedicated to the idea of eventual deliverance from suffering and oppression which is one of the great themes of Western political thought" (p. 63). This was followed in the original but not in the final version by "Insistence on ideological purity and the failure to accept partial movement towards a goal often generate inaction when at least some progressive action is possible. In the extreme, failure to compromise can generate great evil" (racism draft, p. 3). This change appears to have been made in the interest of minimizing the polemics of his argument and reducing the possibility of negative reaction to his reasoning.

17. Ibid., p. 65.

18. Ibid., p. 67–68. This passage was followed in the original draft by "Freedom without vision is a waste, and a vision without values is never quite compelling" (racism draft, p. 6), which in the published version became "Without a compelling vision, freedom to choose is almost a waste" (p. 68). The revision of this sentence appears to reflect interest in avoiding arguments over what type of values Shapiro would suggest should guide vision and to modify the nature of what he considers wasteful.

19. Ibid., p. 70.

20. For his additional thoughts on this subject, see Harold T. Shapiro, "Are Schools for Learning?" *Innovation* 15, no. 1 (August 1983), p. 5.

21. Caroline Hazard, *From College Gates* (Boston: Houghton Mifflin, 1925), pp. 228–29.

22. Ibid., p. 229.

23. Nannerl O. Keohane, "Women, the Liberal Arts, and a Democratic Society," March 4, 1989, Keohane Speeches, 1986–1990, p. 24. This address was given as the founding Dora Anne Little Lecture at Duke University, where Keohane subsequently became president in 1993.

24. Nannerl O. Keohane, "Educating Women for Leadership" City Club of Cleveland, April 26, 1991, Keohane Speeches, 1991–1993, p. 4.

25. *Exercises at the Inauguration of President Angell* (Ann Arbor: Courier Stearn, 1871), p. 12.

26. James B. Angell, "Shall the American Colleges Be Open to Both Sexes?" *Rhode Island Schoolmaster* 17, no. 8, pp. 265–69.

27. Edward Malloy, C.S.C., Sesquicentennial opening Mass homily, President's Office, University of Notre Dame, September 15, 1991, p. 8. Italics mine. For another example of Malloy's Christian expression of the moral voice regarding the importance of service see his baccalaureate Mass homily, May 14, 1994.

28. Edward Malloy, C.S.C., baccalaureate Mass homily, President's Office, University of Notre Dame, May 16, 1992, p. 10–11.

29. Edward Malloy, C.S.C., *Notre Dame: The Unfolding Vision* (New York: Newcomen Society of the United States, 1993), p. 5.

30. Edward Malloy, C.S.C., commencement address, Catholic University, Washington, D.C., President's Office, University of Notre Dame, May 9, 1992, unpaginated.

31. Edward Malloy, C.S.C., "The Control of Violence, Foreign and Domestic: Some Ethical Lessons from Law Enforcement," United States Air Force Academy, President's Office, University of Notre Dame, September 6, 1990. In the interview Malloy also cites guns and violence as issues to which he has applied the moral voice beyond the campus. Personal interview with President Edward Malloy, C.S.C., of Notre Dame University, September 20, 1994.

32. Edward Malloy, C.S.C., address to the faculty, President's Office, University of Notre Dame, October 12, 1993, p. 25.

33. Edward Malloy, C.S.C., address to the faculty, President's Office, University of Notre Dame, October 1, 1991, p. 18. Also see address to the trustees, Spring 1990, p. 11.

34. Thomas Gerety, "Work Hard, Play Hard: Rigor and Joy in the Liberal Arts," Trinity College, Hartford, Conn., President's Office, University of Notre Dame, p. 6.

35. Jean Kemeny, *It's Different at Dartmouth* (Brattleboro, Vt.: Stephen Greene Press, 1979), p. 22.

8

The University and the World

LESSONS FROM THE EXPERIENCE OF WAR

College and university presidents lead communities that exist in the context not only of local and national, but also of global and international concerns and affairs. Thus, the moral leadership of presidents is critical in connecting colleges and universities, and students and their education, to world issues. Because America's role in the world, especially as an increasingly powerful and influential player among nations in the last century, presidential moral leadership has been increasingly called upon to address global problems.

Nicholas Murray Butler is one of the great presidential thinkers in developing this connection between education and the concerns of nations and people beyond the boundaries of America. Beginning in the early decades of his presidency, Butler was engaged in global politics, especially through his involvement as World War I loomed in the debate about isolationism. And after the war, Butler spoke and wrote at length about the lessons to be learned from confronting Germany as an adversary.

As a leading and influential Republican throughout his career, Butler spoke strongly against isolationists in debates about American entry and participation in the war. Resigned to what was taking place, he believed the fighting, while unfortunate, was necessary. When the country was finally forced into warfare, Butler realistically recognized the commitment required to subdue the enemy forces and thus encouraged members of Columbia University to fulfill their duty to their country. He did so despite the realization that as his community heeded his advice, there would be a substantial decrease in the university's enrollment and shrinkage in the faculty ranks. Many members of the university community, like others around the country, would go to war and never again return to campus either to complete their educations or resume their careers.

At the time the First World War was viewed as the war to end all wars. The world community had not previously witnessed an armed struggle of such magnitude in terms of the numbers of nations involved and the toll of death and destruction. Many Americans viewed the war apocalyptically and believed it to be a second major test—the Civil War being the first—of national resolve, now on the global stage.

In a commencement address during the war, Butler described for the graduates a "Kingdom of Light," what he argued was "an invisible commonwealth which outlives the storms of the ages. It is a state whose armaments are thoughts, whose weapons are ideas, and whose trophies are the pages of the world's great masters."[1] For these graduates "every activity of life has its material aspect and its spiritual aspect. It has its result in visible accomplishment, and it also has its result in invisible mind-building, will-building and intellectual enjoyment."[2] Though the war raged, the students needed to keep their minds focused on the highest values inspired by their education. Butler enjoined graduates to enter into a kingdom of ideas and a world of philosophy in action. Reflecting the impact of the war on his thinking, he described an ideal educational vision through a mixture of theological language and militaristic images.[3] This vision is of a kingdom marked by the enlightenment that results from gaining knowledge and by its contribution to the development of character. One of the most important purposes of education was to prepare students to continue applying and enjoying its results throughout their lives. Even the reality of war was not to intervene in or distract Columbia students from that purpose.

The war concluded a few weeks before Butler's annual Thanksgiving Eve address to the Columbia community in 1919. He normally used these talks to underscore the blessings of the nation. He always noted the importance of being thankful and of feeling the sense of family within the university. For years prior to the outbreak of hostilities, Butler viewed America's entry into the war as a necessity. Now with the conflict at an end he was just as convinced and quick to urge that the task that loomed was to rebuild what had been destroyed. For Butler, the university and its members as part of the educational community and the nation had no choice but to undertake that challenge.

On this occasion his comments show the effect of the war as he sought to bring a message home to the Columbia campus. Butler used an analogy between human beings and discoveries being made about atoms to suggest lessons from the war. He urged students to begin thinking about the need to rebuild the world from the war's destruction, asking "are not we, too, each one of us storehouses and reservoirs of yet undiscovered and unrevealed power for the mental, the moral, and the spiritual health of mankind? . . . If each atom of the material universe is the centre of unmeasured force, what must be true of each atom of the mental, moral and spiritual universe?" Imploring his audience to comprehend the task at hand, he added "if we could only realize the full meaning of the words opportunity and responsibility! The opportunity is not someone else's, it is OURS; the responsibility is not another's, it is OURS. It is the timid waiting for someone else to bring back health to the world that keeps it ill so long." What was demanded then of the university and its talent? Butler answered unswervingly that "The world needs not cautious, timid and shrinking calculators of reconstruction, but brave, courageous volunteers, who will carry forward to the very front line of action every ounce of power they possess—mental, moral, spiritual—and put it into the service of this broken and tired world."[4]

In another address he underscored similar sentiments about the challenge facing those who were among the educated. He asserted that "this is a troubled and difficult world of ours, and nobody is going to improve it except the people who are in it. By waiting for some mysterious, providential interposition we shall only make matters worse." Reflecting the values he believed to be embodied in education, Butler noted that "It is the people of the world who will have to provide the intelligence, the controlled emotion, and the disciplined will that will deal with these complicated questions of human nature and human ambition and human association, and that will deal with them in a spirit of justice, a spirit of progress, and a spirit of genuine human feeling and human sympathy."[5]

Like Peter Pouncey's assumption about moral responsibility in the "Abraham and Isaac" address, Butler believed people must assume responsibility for the needs of the world and not await action by someone else. His comments are exemplary of his use of the presidential pulpit. Here he encouraged students and other members of the Columbia community to realize the moral and spiritual dimension of what the world required and to use their talents in meeting those needs. In one of his commencement addresses during the war, with the ranks of Columbia's faculty, administration, and students depleted by service to the nation, Butler stated that "the heart of man has made an articulate cry and the world has heard it! It is a cry for those fundamental things that lie at the very foundation of a reasonable and moral life. It is a cry for the protection of the weak against the strong. It is a cry for the enforcement of human law and for the establishment of human justice."[6]

Butler's continual reflections about the meaning of the war led to an important development in his thinking. One of Butler's interesting contributions to thoughts about the value of education resulted from what he believed to be the lessons learned from the war experience. As though on a mission, he undertook publicly to describe and convey the realities and meanings of his conclusions.

In Butler's world of the early twentieth century, the industrial revolution had produced substantial material gains. This in turn generated a societal optimism about the even better world that would be created through industrial growth and emerging technology. But Butler also knew that there were sobering lessons to be learned from the course of the German nation and its people as a result of these same forces. But beyond those characteristics, Germany's rise as a war power was significantly supported by education and research, hallmarks of the university. The major conclusion he drew was that Germany succeeded in perpetuating the war effort for as long as it did because the educational, research, and industrial sectors of the United States and its allies were vastly less efficient than those of Germany.

Butler wanted the nation to be certain that such an inferiority would not happen again. However, Butler also believed that efficiency was far from the most important quality a nation could possess. In fact, striving for efficiency as an end in itself was purely seductive. Drawing a classic distinction, he noted that "the war has taught the lesson that the proper place of efficiency is as the servant of a moral ideal, and that efficiency apart from a moral ideal is an evil and a wicked instrument which in the end can accomplish only disaster."[7] The impact of Butler's analysis on his moral thinking about education is clear. Efficiency in the absence of moral capacity led inexorably to moral downfall as manifest in the forces that brought about the war. Butler sought to illuminate the question—which was to be further exacerbated by Germany in World War II—of how the pursuit of educational excellence in Germany had resulted in evil and destruction.

Based upon these lessons of war, Butler forged an educational philosophy diametrically in opposition to that embraced by the Germans. He classically defended the liberal arts and passionately embraced the need for the triumph of good over evil. He contended that "we should do better to insist that education is a process of body-building, spirit-building and institution-building, in which process skillful and well-interpreted use is made of the recorded experience of the human race, of the capacities, tastes and ambitions of the individual, and of the problems and circumstances of the world in which he at the moment lives." Understanding and heeding the lessons of history was important, but education did not end by merely accomplishing those goals, however noble. Butler concluded that "The purpose of this body-building, spirit-building and institution-building is not simply to strengthen and perpetuate what others have found to be useful and good, but rather by building upon that to carry both the individual and the race farther forward in their progress toward fuller self-expression and more complete self-realization." His lasting warning to all educators, to the university, and to the nation, was that "To attempt to turn education into a merely mechanical process, with a purely gainful end, is nothing short of treason to the highest, most uplifting, and most enduring human interests."[8]

Butler's offered this advice in the hope that the country and the world would avoid a repetition of the disaster the war represented. In his opinion, the German concept of education, especially as a servant of a nation's pursuit of evil intentions, had debased the very purposes of education. Butler's view was that an important end of education was to represent and establish a higher civilization and culture. As an educator and leader, Butler believed that colleges and universities had to deepen their understanding of their highest and best purposes. Only such a step would help them to learn the necessary lesson presented by the destructiveness of war. Butler's attempt to shape an educational perspective from the lessons of a world at war and to urge serious reflection by educators and the nation is a unique and powerful example of the moral seriousness of his leadership.

ADDRESSING THE CONCERNS OF THE CONTEMPORARY WORLD

Like his Columbia predecessor, Michael Sovern made frequent public references to world problems during his presidential tenure in the 1980s and early 1990s.[9] He did so because of a belief that the alleviation of these problems was a challenge that the university must confront. In a commencement address, he asked rhetorically "what are we to do? What will be the response of your generation to the almost overwhelming odds that seem to favor the forces that tyrannize, corrupt and kill?" Rejecting one possibility, Sovern noted that " 'Despair,' Elie Wiesel reminds us, 'is not the solution. Despair is the question.' Choices must be made. You cannot cure all the ills of the world, but you can do far more than you may yet realize." Providing encouragement in the face of the scope of these problems, Sovern advised his audience of students, families, and faculty that "the moral test of your life will not be what the world is like when you leave it, but whether you did your part, as best you could, to make this small and fragile planet a better place."[10] Sovern's moral leadership combined this mixture of challenge and confidence: the challenge of what the world demanded and the confidence that students were capable of making positive contributions. He viewed these challenges as nothing less than a "moral test" for undergraduates as they prepared to enter the world and applied their learning, skill, and knowledge.

At another commencement Sovern discussed the need for moral response to two major issues for which he laid blame on the Reagan administration. The first were budget reductions that had been made in student aid support and the resulting constriction of access to education for students of lesser economic means. The second was the international fear and danger created by a renewed nuclear arms race.[11] But these concerns served only as a prelude to his comments about South African bishop Desmond Tutu. The university had intended to give Tutu an honorary degree. But he was not permitted by his government to travel out of his country to the United States. Sovern indicated that the chair in which Tutu would have sat at the commencement exercises was vacant and would remain so until the time when he would be free to travel and receive the degree. This practice had been initiated at many colleges and universities during the 1980s as a way to honor Tutu in absentia and to criticize his nation's policies. Sovern used the moment to decry the forces of apartheid in South Africa and the fight for justice in which Tutu was involved in his homeland.

Sovern revealed that "the Trustees' decision to award an honorary degree to Bishop Tutu is more than a re-emphasis of our University's deep repugnance for apartheid, of our revulsion at a government's sustained effort to degrade its citizens through the most systematic abuse of law to outlaw a people since Hitler's Nuremberg Laws. The resolve to recognize Bishop Tutu is all of that, but much more." In taking this stand, Sovern claimed that Columbia was recognizing Tutu as "a beacon of hope and decency in a dark land, and we want to help keep that light burning. We want him to know that we care. We want the government of South Africa to know that the world is watching. And we want to reaffirm our own humanity by presuming to claim that he and we are brothers."[12] Sovern spoke both personally and institutionally—as a reflection of the stand taken by the board. His moral claim about Tutu and condemnation of the South African regime served to highlight the gravity of this world situation for those gathered at Columbia.

George Rupp followed his Columbia predecessors' tradition of using the presidential pulpit to address world issues. Offering an analogy between recent changes in world affairs and the lives of graduates, Rupp asserted that "a new world is indeed struggling to be born. At times the labor pains seem excruciating and almost unbearably prolonged. But then there are glimpses of the new world as it bursts forth with historic drama. This year we have witnessed tentative but hopeful steps toward peace in the Middle East. Even more dramatic have been the culmination of decades of struggle for a democratic South Africa." Despite this optimistic review of recent world events, Rupp quickly noted that "We rightly join in exultation at each and every movement toward this new world that is struggling to be born. By all means, we should cheer, even as we cheer for you on this occasion of your commencement. But as with every birth, what is needed is labor along with the celebration."[13] Rupp's presidential voice, like that of many of his colleagues, urged students to respond to the demands of what will be required of them. However, Rupp's self-professed Calvinism tempered his analysis of recent world events. The moral message for students and others in attendance was quite clear: while inspirationally remarkable events are occurring in the world, much work would always remain to be done by educated and committed people.

THE RISK OF NUCLEAR WAR

Immediately following the use of the atomic bomb ending World War II, the threat of nuclear war became a decades-long national and international issue. As World War I was a defining moment for Butler and his generation in the early decades of the twentieth century, nuclear arms and the prospect of their use captured the attention of presidents in the latter twentieth century. Early in his presidency, Theodore Hesburgh publicly began to express concern over the advent of nuclear weapons. Once again, as was the case with his concerns about civil rights, Hesburgh was well ahead of his time on this grave issue regarding the survival of the human race. Stressing the importance of liberal education, Hesburgh stated that "the very crisis of our times is heralded by the holocaust of Hiroshima and Nagasaki, where the first worldwide demonstration of the most startling scientific discovery of our age was applied to the destruction, rather than the enoblement of mankind." He joined other scientific and intellectual thinkers of his generation, including some of those responsible for the development of this new weaponry, in criticizing the use of knowledge to produce destructive outcomes. The question was whether human technological capability now exceeded human ethical capacity and judgment. In Hesburgh's mind this fear was captured by the prospect that "The symbol of this new age might be the Greek statue of winged victory in the Louvre, a breath-taking sense of form and power, without a head and, therefore, without intelligent meaning and direction."[14] His hope was that education would rise to the challenge of providing the intelligence and, most important, wisdom to cope with this dramatic change in human capacity and in the power to do harm.

Throughout his presidency Hesburgh continued to speak about the arms race. In the early 1980s he was a participant in international discussions about ways to reduce the armaments and the dangers of nuclear war. In the summer of 1983 this involvement included a trip to the Soviet Union, where Hesburgh met academic and scholarly counterparts, including scientists. The trip stimulated and heightened his concern.

Shortly after he returned to the campus, Hesburgh was scheduled to make the annual presidential address to the faculty. In an otherwise quite normal talk, but without warning or foreshadowing, Hesburgh inserted a powerful and extended coda about nuclear warfare as the ultimate moral problem facing humanity. He believed that the faculty needed to view this as a crucial moral problem that they should feel compelled to address as educators. He urged the faculty to consider "how we might face the greatest moral problem confronting humanity today or ever. Weak tea will not do here. I speak of the nuclear threat to humanity."[15] Hesburgh discussed in detail the magnitude of the problem. His primary suggestion was that the university could contribute to solutions in two ways. One would be by bringing scientific and religious leaders together for strategic discussions. The other was to engage students and faculty in grassroots political movements and in academic study. In the remaining years of his presidency, Hesburgh put words into action, leading Notre Dame to involvement in international dialogue and campus discussions about the arms issue.

Peter Pouncey of Amherst, a contemporary of Hesburgh's in the 1980s, likewise placed the matter of the nuclear threat before his campus community. In his convocation address at the beginning of the 1986 academic year, Pouncey drew upon the image of Edward Hicks's classic Peaceable Kingdom paintings depicting the biblically inspired day when "the lion will lie down with the lamb." Discussing the relationship of humankind to nature and the natural world, he asserted that "if we define culture very loosely as a complex of human works and systems, then we must be aware that from the beginning, men and women with or without a sense of biblical entitlement, whether with greed or with taste, have sought to impose their culture on nature." But it was Pouncey's view that the stakes in the contemporary world may indeed be higher for "the only difference is that now, with swollen populations and developed technology, the mark we make on our landscape is wider, more permanent and more lethal potentially."[16]

Following a litany of an array of contemporary disasters ranging from environmental destruction to nuclear warfare, Pouncey concluded that "We admonish ourselves that as a species we are the most predatory of species—the only one that can destroy all others, the one that plays most resolutely with the hazard of destroying itself."[17] Reiterating the theme of the Peaceable Kingdom, Pouncey cited the contemporary prophets who "foretell the dark and final freeze of the nuclear winter that awaits us all at the end."[18]

The threat of nuclear war may not have focused attention on the campus and in the nation to the same magnitude and with the same immediacy as the two major world wars, the Vietnam War, or even some of the lesser wars and conflicts of the century. However, in many respects the prospect of the use of nuclear weapons and the fear of destruction in a nuclear holocaust raised concerns similar to those of world wars. These concerns, shared by a number of presidents, were about the future of the human race and about the role, if any, that education was able to play in influencing the course of events. Finally, these world issues are also of concern to educators because they are about fundamental issues of right and wrong.

Hesburgh and Pouncey, to name just two presidents who spoke about the threats of the nuclear age, knew that the ivory tower could not be a refuge from global concerns. This is especially true in the face of the proliferation of nuclear armaments and the risks of their use, whether intentional or accidental. Theirs are voices of hope that the academy can be involved in these issues and has the potential to ameliorate even the gravest threats to the world beyond the gates.

The same might be said of many issues about which presidents speak. However, a major question raised by these national and world problems is the degree of severity and visibility they must reach before gaining sufficient presidential attention. Some issues—the environment, the plight of the cities, and the need for racial justice—can viewed as "avoidable" because they impinge (with the possible exception of urban universities) less directly on the campus. These issues often become moral concerns only because of special and personal presidential interest. Other matters—war, the arms race, and campus unrest—may generate greater and more immediate attention from the impact of their more imminent, sometimes dramatic, qualities on both the leadership of presidents and the stability of the institutions they lead. The campus unrest of the 1960s and early 1970s primarily related to the Vietnam War and clashes over civil rights between white and black America, which created an ethos in which presidents of varying political persuasions did feel compelled to comment. Hesburgh acknowledged the tensions and difficulties of those times, times when national and international issues became nearly unavoidable on America's campuses and presented severe challenges to college and university leaders.

Presidents regularly face choices about speaking publicly on issues of significant concern to the academy and to those beyond its gates. Especially in the
arenas of national and international affairs, presidents cannot control the issues
that arise. However, in their response to events, presidents possess the potential
to exert influence on their campus and with other constituencies. In asserting
moral leadership and voice in the face of campus, national, and international
concerns presidents must use the broad reach of their leadership. There indeed
is a public who are watching and looking for the cues given by college and
university presidents.

In the chapters of part 3 we have seen examples of the moral leadership of
presidents in a number of important settings. These have included their rhetoric
about the relationship of education to democracy and its civic virtues and commitments of citizenship. These presidents have also spoken about local and national political and social issues and about global problems and world events.
In the next chapter we will examine presidential reflections on the use of the
moral voice and its importance to presidential leadership.

NOTES

1. Nicholas Murray Butler, "The Kingdom of Light," June 7, 1916, Butler Speeches,
vol. 3, no. 8, p. 1.

2. Ibid., p. 2.

3. The impact of the war on Butler's thought and leadership is a primary example
of the effect on the moral voice of external events and issues.

4. Nicholas Murray Butler, Thanksgiving Eve address, November 25, 1919, Butler
Speeches, vol. 4, no. 48, pp. 6–7.

5. Nicholas Murray Butler, Columbia Teachers College alumni address, Butler
Speeches, vol. 6, no. 6, p. 3.

6. Nicholas Murray Butler, "New Values," June 5, 1918, Butler Speeches, vol. 3,
no. 69, pp. 2–3. Other examples of this aspect of Butler's moral voice are (from Butler
Speeches, with volume and item number cited): inaugural address, "Scholarship and
Service," April 19, 1902 (vol. 2; reprint in *Educational Review*, June 1902, p. 3); and
Christmas Eve letter to Columbia students (vol. 3, no. 1a, p. 2); a February 6, 1917,
address (vol. 3, no. 18, p. 2).

7. Nicholas Murray Butler, "Education After the War," November 29, 1918, Butler
Speeches, vol. 3, no. 94, reprint from the *Educational Review* 57, no. 1 (January 1919),
p. 67.

8. Ibid., p. 68.

9. In addition to the citations that follow, Sovern's moral voice on world issues can
be found in his discussion of nuclear armaments and war in his commencement address,
May 17, 1983 (p. 8); similar concerns in the commencement address of May 16, 1984
(p. 8); and an address to the Illinois Humanities Council, October 22, 1984, in which he
discusses international issues in Central America (pp. 6–15) (Sovern Addresses).

10. Michael Sovern, commencement address, May 18, 1988, Sovern Addresses, p. 7.

11. Michael Sovern, commencement address, May 19, 1982, Sovern Addresses, pp.
3–6.

12. Ibid., p. 8

13. George Rupp, "When the Cheering Stops," May 19, 1994, handwritten insert to typed copy, pp. 3a(1)–3a(2).

14. Theodore Hesburgh, "Liberal Education in the World Today," Association of American Colleges, January 12, 1955, UND Archives, 1947–1967, Box 141/71a, pp. 8–9.

15. Theodore Hesburgh, address to the general faculty, October 4, 1983, UND Archives, 1968–1987, Box 142/20, p. 13. Hesburgh continues, "after total nuclear conflagration, all other human problems are moot" (p. 14).

16. Peter Pouncey, convocation address, September 1986, p. 6, in Peter Pouncey Biographical File (N/A), Archives and Special Collections, Amherst College Library.

17. Idem.

18. Ibid., p. 6.

9

Ideological Battles and the Soul of the Academy: The Burdens of the Presidential Pulpit

ORTHODOXY AND THE SEARCH FOR KNOWLEDGE: DILEMMAS FOR THE MORAL VOICE

An ideological battleground exists at colleges and universities. It is a battleground simultaneously impinging and yet demanding expression of the moral voice of presidents. This battleground mirrors that in society. But ideological conflict is more intensified on campuses because the academy embraces the principle of discourse. Ideas should be openly discussed, differences made known, and disagreement permitted. Recent disputes about the character of American college and university education were intensified in the mid-1980s, heralded in part by Allan Bloom's critique, *The Closing of the American Mind.* His subtitle reminds us of his thesis: *How Higher Education Has Failed Democracy and Impoverished the Souls of Today's Students.*

This battle is deeply rooted in history.[1] Today, on one side are advocates of what is called "political correctness." On the other side are upholders of the true purposes of the university. The shape of the contemporary debate was established earlier in the social and political movements on campuses such as Berkeley in the 1960s. Bloom, William Bennett, and fellow commentators react to that era and declare its reforms as causing the failings of the modern university. And who is viewed as more responsible for these failures than its leaders: college and university presidents?

In the contemporary climate the challenge of this debate creates a demanding imperative for presidents. They will battle ideologies on both the left and right of the political divide. Both sides use political ideologies and agendas to argue, often ironically and disingenuously, that the opposition controls the agenda on campuses. Both sides want their values to determine the future of the academy. Beyond all the rhetoric lies the true issue: a battle for the soul of the university.

Colleges and universities are expected simultaneously to engage the pursuit of values and the pursuit of knowledge. They are to provide a superior education while ensuring the development of moral principles and character. The fundamental task is twofold: to maintain enduring values and principles *and* to search for new knowledge. But each of these goals has advocates who form opposing sides. They tend to coexist uneasily, if not unwillingly. The implicit freedom of the academy challenges the orthodoxies of both sides. The resulting conflicts between competing values and ways of knowing pose dilemmas for the moral voice of presidents.

Division between those contending that the purpose of education is to establish values and those contending that its purpose is to search for knowledge existed in the colonial colleges of New England. Their heritage was not to nurture new ideas, but rather to buttress "the various cultural traditions which they served."[2] The preservation and promotion of morality was the *raison dêtre* of the colonial colleges. The Enlightenment coupled with expansion of knowledge created by eighteenth century advances in science and technology forced a change in that singlemindedness. The educational philosophy of American colleges and universities that emerged called into question previously held orthodoxies founded exclusively on morality and centuries-old knowledge.

However, the tension between tradition and change continued and remains fundamentally unresolved. Even as new ideas were accommodated and the sense of purpose of many colleges reevaluated, the old orthodoxies and their moral foundation maintained an influence. Elias Blake unambiguously claimed that black colleges, and the same could be said of all, are "obligated to . . . tie together intellectual and moral authority."[3] As a result, the task of education and of presidential leadership has become more complex.

The expectation of integrating knowledge and conscience does not tell the whole story. A more complicated characterization is that the modern university as it has developed in the twentieth century faces a complex and multiple role "dedicated to selective preservation and change."[4] The assumption is that modern colleges and universities can simultaneously preserve proven values and engage new knowledge to produce change. For the better part of the last century or more this has been the assumed mission of colleges and universities. But in recent years competing ideologies and values have produced strident and contentious debates about what will and what will not be preserved in the academy.

Disparate critics such as Pat Robertson, Stephen Carter, Robert Bellah, Arthur Schlessinger, Bennett, Bloom, and others characterize the present cultural crisis as a search for values in a society perceived to lack core mores and principles. In the university are those on one side who believe values have no place, a purist contention usually marked more by rhetoric than practice. Claims that the academy should be value-neutral are unsustainable in practice. However, advocates of this position often succeed on one or both of two fronts. Values are pushed to the periphery and their importance is diminished to a level of inconsequence. Or all values are assumed to be of equal weight, but of no effect in shaping society. On the other side are those who believe that values must be embedded in the university and that they are the ones who will dictate the code of values for the academy. In either case, when values are at stake the question inevitably becomes a debate about "'whose values?'"

Presidents are able to use the authority of their office to stress the need for agreement on common values in social and civic life. Values are instrumental in shaping societies and communities, and colleges and universities are no exception. The problem is the "possibility that the age of tolerance ushered in by the ideals of the Enlightenment could yield a bitter harvest if we succumb to the idea that all values are equally acceptable and, thus, deny the existence of any absolute values."[5]

Presidents have the responsibility to lead campus communities in discussion of shared values and principles. The goal is to develop the common understanding necessary for the body politic to function with reason and civility despite inevitable individual differences and social diversity. One guidepost, not without its own fragility, is to rely on a civil religion.[6] In an environment combining beliefs that all values are equally valid with wariness of external moral authority, presidents must begin by creating the language and ethos for moral discussion.

This simple formula for developing the commonweal is rarely an equally simple reality. The American national experience reflects the difficulty of holding together the center of its religion of the republic. It should not be surprising that corresponding ideological debates are inevitably amplified in the scholarly, intellectually critical college and university ethos.

Thus, the task facing presidents is not easy. The contemporary problems of the academy are exacerbated by what Shapiro labels "radical ideologies." These ideologies are "unable to compromise on any issue, are fundamentally hostile to a social order such as ours and to the role of integrative institutions. Such groups do not include in their agendas that critical toleration of others—the hallmark of Western civilizations—that creates the foundation for social and political reconciliation and compromise." By contrast, Shapiro suggests that while the institutions of society, including colleges and universities, do "not proclaim any ultimate truths, they nonetheless provide the 'working hypotheses' which broadly govern our social behavior at any point in time."[7]

These "working hypotheses" are at the core of a civil religion. Common agreement, however, is often stymied by ideological differences. Their influence in the academy tests the leadership of presidents. They must deal with these radical ideologies, which are at the same time easy targets of external critics such as Bennett and Bloom. The danger is that capitulation by colleges and universities to "radical ideologies" stifles the open debate fundamental to the search for truth in the academy. This problem is complicated by the reduced influence of social institutions, including education, traditionally important for maintaining the social fabric, and by the increased leverage of special interests.

This understandable yet lamentable situation confronts leaders of academic institutions today. But the influence of ideologies and pressures on the university from the political right and left heighten the need for moral leadership. Many latter twentieth century presidents were not silent as moral leaders. Their perspectives provide a unique view of the demands of the presidency and of the colleges and universities they led.

The moral leadership of today's presidents is crucial in developing the common agreement essential for guiding and governing campus communities. This quest requires delicate balance. Presidents must avoid the creation of a new moralism, the imposition of values, and the adoption of moralistic positions. Shaping working hypotheses demands a different style than merely exerting authoritarian power, but presidents at times, must use their moral voice, in uncompromising ways.

A number of contemporary examples are instructive. Following the release of Diana Chapman Walsh's letter to the community about the publication of Tony Martin's book, *The Jewish Onslaught: Despatches from the Wellesley Battlefront*, minority students requested a meeting with her. They took exception to her use of the corporate "we"—speaking as president for the entire community—to condemn Martin.

Though using a consultative approach in preparing the letter, Walsh is responsible as president to speak for the community. Disagreement is the right of any individual or group and some may feel excluded by a presidential statement. But differences of opinion should not restrict the imperatives of leadership.

This episode exemplifies the battle over "whose values?" and over "whose moral voice?" Ideally, conflicts about values should be discussed openly in communities. Noting the close and delicate relationship between values and communities, Walsh warns of exercising "the moral voice without destroying the possibility of community."[8] However, when the president as the leader of the community argues a moral position, unanimity is not the only goal and is not guaranteed.

Community participation in the delineation of its moral norms presents intriguing challenges for presidential leadership. At smaller colleges discourse about ethics and values is possible and can be valuable. However, at larger universities engaging the entire community in discussion about ethical standards, while not impossible, is vastly more difficult.

There are also legitimate questions about the lasting quality of norms determined by communities in the absence of at least some preexisting, possibly transcendent, moral basis. Communally determined moral consensus can be fragile and elusive. Certainly, campus communities can create a portion of the platform for presidential moral leadership. But it is only a part of the foundation. The relationship of presidential moral leadership to the moral wisdom of the community is a two-way street. The presidential voice cannot exclusively rely on community consensus about morals and values. Lack of agreement on common moral principles and rejection of categories of right and wrong create a vacuum in which presidents are instrumental in providing a foundation for discourse. In many cases presidents must risk speaking forcefully on issues without broad community support. Failure to do so jeopardizes the influence of their moral voice.

Though the establishment of ethical norms need not be reduced to choice between the morality of the community and the moral vision of the leader, the dangers in the contemporary campus climate are inescapable. Allowing institutions to be dominated by radical ideologies rooted more in particular agendas than in the common good makes agreement on moral principles more difficult, if not impossible. The result will be to limit presidential leadership, especially in areas of moral concern.

In the final analysis, the moral voice is grounded in each president's personal beliefs and philosophy. Presidents must avoid basing moral leadership on transient moral claims of communities, rather than on personal moral convictions. Their moral leadership requires more than simply gauging and then reflecting moral norms determined by the community, no matter how inspirational or noble.

INSTITUTIONAL PRESSURE AND POLITICS

Presidents have always had to deal with institutional and political pressures. The extent of these pressures has become amplified since the advent of the multiversity or what James Duderstadt describes as both an "international conglomerate" and an "entrepreneurial" university. Especially in these large public institutions presidents encounter increased stridency and contentiousness.

Duderstadt's tenure at the University of Michigan provides a forceful glimpse of the political and institutional dynamics facing presidents. Contending that the difficulties and dangers, particularly for public university presidents, are greater than at any time in history, Duderstadt notes that this political environment can cause presidents to hesitate in exercising the moral voice.[9] At private and public institutions this climate heightens the importance of making deliberate choices on sensitive issues. For example, Duderstadt proposed the addition of sexual orientation to the university's affirmative-action and employee-benefits policies. Though approved by the board of regents, he surmises that the same initiative would have led to his termination if it had been suggested to another board of different political composition.[10]

Presidents have also always had to judge carefully what should be said and done in the context of politics and expediency. Expressing hope that presidents normally know what is right and that they will follow those instincts, Duderstadt adds that on any issue presidents are able to "decide that this is not the ditch that they choose to die in."[11] Duderstadt spoke these words less than a year before he made a choice that led to his resignation as president. His story is a reminder of the inherent fragility of presidential tenure, especially in the contemporary era. And though Duderstadt is a profile in courage, the end of his term in office is an equal reminder of the price of courage.

As result of a broad swing of the national political pendulum in the 1994 elections, Michigan's board of regents became significantly more conservative. For some time Duderstadt had been concerned with the increasingly political nature of a publicly elected board. He concluded that the electoral process produced board members who were not as appreciative or supportive of the university as most private and many other public institutions enjoyed. Board decisions were increasingly based on the litmus tests of the election process. Open and unprejudiced discussion of issues was dramatically reduced. Ideologies were forming the foundation of university governance.

Duderstadt's conviction about what was transpiring led to his attempt to change the board's selection from popular election to gubernatorial appointment. When the Board learned of this intention, his resignation became a *fait accompli*. In response to this turn of events, Michigan's governor John Engler accused the regents of ending the tenure of "one of the nation's finest university presidents."

Other presidents have faced comparable pressures and choices. These moments for leaders occur regardless of institutional size and complexity. In fact, smaller colleges are frequently more vulnerable to political and social pressure. This is due to the inherent fragility of their more specific missions compared to larger, more established public institutions. Presidents of small institutions often wield more influence when they take moral stands than do their counterparts at large ones. But at small colleges substantial criticism of presidents can result in notable risks for themselves and their institutions.

Regardless of the institutional context, internal and external pressures on college presidents are real and, more often than not, beyond their immediate control. Moral leadership in campus communities and in society often stimulates opposition. To use Duderstadt's metaphor, presidents may regularly have to choose whether to die in a given ditch or to continue down the road to battle the same or another cause in the future. This choice, unpleasant as it is, is integral to the presidency. Presidents inevitably face difficult decisions when they guard the foundations of the university from precipitous change and ensure that the fundamental educational principles of free inquiry, open debate, and individual choice and responsibility are maintained.

PRESIDENTIAL IDENTITY AND RESPONSIBILITY

The responsibilities of the office and presidents' personal identities circumscribe the demands of leadership. Two major themes emerge. The first is the freedom of presidents to take moral stands on issues of consequence and conscience. The second is the role of the personal beliefs of presidents in their rhetoric and action.

Institutional aspirations are critically related to the freedom of presidents to exert moral vision. A major impact is the recent shift in the qualifications expected by colleges and universities of candidates for presidencies. Presidents have evolved from scholars and academicians to managers and executives.

This change in qualifications produces some presidents who avoid becoming publicly involved in moral issues because they lack interest or inclination.[12] Presidents at some major institutions are not expected to take moral stands on issues. However, presidents at universities such as Notre Dame have bully pulpits and these institutions happily anticipate its use.

The personal background of presidents is a second feature important to the development of moral voice. There is an intimate connection between the personal commitments of presidents and their moral leadership. Though rarely discussed, the personal qualities of those who aspire to presidencies shape the creation of moral voice. Rhetoric and action are often rooted in a president's own liberal education and personal beliefs determined by religion, philosophy, the search for meaning, or a combination. This foundation creates the capacity of presidents for moral suasion.

The personal qualities of candidates for the office should not be overlooked. Moral capacity should at the very least be weighed equally with other credentials necessary for the office. In selecting leadership, colleges and universities will get what they seek.

Though some presidents shun opportunities to exert moral leadership, critics who opine about the lack of moral vision among today's presidents compared to that of their predecessors present an incomplete picture of the presidency.[13] These critics base conclusions on a selection of a few, highly visible presidents of preceding generations. Using these "giants" to contend that today's presidents are shallow imitations is historically inaccurate.

Contemporary presidents and their reflections about leadership counter impressions that there are no longer any "giants" in presidencies. Malloy has personally and repeatedly exerted moral influence on national and international issues as well as on the campus scene. Asked whether being a priest is a curse or a blessing for a president, he suggests that Notre Dame is "a place that espouses a certain set of values and is very public about it" and that he embraces the bully pulpit of the presidency.[14]

In similar fashion, George Rupp's self-professed Calvinism defines a portion of his identity as he responds to the demands and needs of his university. Columbia did not seek Rupp because he was trained in religion and was an ordained minister. However, they selected a leader with highly refined personal beliefs derived from a Calvinist Presbyterian background. Rupp's Calvinist view judges all actions against an enormously high standard: if he is not doing the good that needs to be done in the world, by definition he sides with evil.[15] His commitments, borne primarily of personal theological beliefs, underscore the importance of stewardship, the need to care for the present in order to provide for the future. Regarding the moral aspects of education, Rupp echoes John

Dickey's insistence that education is more than the attainment of competence. Rupp believes that the moral aspect of education should not be viewed as an appendage. Education, including the gaining of competence, is moral and develops the "moral imagination" of students.[16] This philosophy opposes the frequently assumed dichotomy between the in- and out-of-the-classroom undergraduate experience.

Rupp prefers to exercise moral leadership rather than merely seeking refuge in rhetoric. His voice in action is witnessed in his efforts during the first year of his presidency to improve connections between Harlem and Columbia. The university's history has been marked, and at times marred, by the stark contrast between its wealth and the poverty of the local community. When Rupp undertook this major initiative to build bridges with Harlem, staff urged capitalizing on his stand for its public-relations value. Reflecting assumptions about both leadership and the doing of good works, Rupp shunned this advice. His personal style and his Calvinist beliefs led to his conclusion that "in the long run it works better not to talk too much on the front end. [I]t is a lot better if the words trail after the fact rather than lead it. Based on experience it is better to talk less and do more."[17]

In an intriguing sequel, Rupp has been criticized by one of his mentors. This fellow clergyman and urban social activist publicly expressed concern about what he views as Rupp's minimal commitment to involve Columbia in the social justice needs of the local community. Like the challenge to Walsh's presidential letter, this episode confirms the difficulties for presidents created by the confrontation with radical ideologies.

Historically, the personal presence of college and university presidents in their campus communities was an important part of their role. Though the era of the president as "Mr. Chips" may be over, the personal leadership of presidents remains significant in campus life. This is even the case at an institution the size of the University of Michigan. Duderstadt is convinced that "to change an institution in a fundamental way, the president has to get out on the front line."[18]

For example, Duderstadt challenged fraternity leadership to address incidents of sexual harassment and degrading behavior directed toward women. The consequence of their inaction would be steps taken unilaterally by the president. He also hosted "town meetings" of staff, faculty, and students to discuss issues of employment and equity for women and minorities. At these gatherings Duderstadt would, in the manner of a talk-show host, moderate conversations with university employees and senior administrators about the impact of affirmative action and other university personnel policies on their work.

Visible presidential engagement with their communities is a requirement of moral leadership. Personal involvement is also a reminder of the tradition of presidents as mentors to students. Fulfilling this responsibility is not easy in an era when many presidents, including those at smaller colleges, are expected to dedicate extensive time to external affairs, relationships, and development. But the power of the office and the embodiment of the institution in the presidency combine to maintain the importance of an on-campus role.

THE BURDENS OF BLACK PRESIDENTIAL LEADERSHIP

Black leaders in society bear unique burdens of race. The same is true of the expectations and responsibilities of black educational leaders. Thomas Cole grew up during the civil-rights movement of the 1950s and 1960s. He believes that a deeper appreciation of this history is critical to the formation of values in today's students. At Cole's insistence Clark Atlanta University annually incorporates the recent history of the civil-rights struggle into new student orientation. He also believes that greater awareness of this racial struggle and their own roots stimulates students to give of their talents to the community.

Encouragement of character formation remains essential to the presidential role. To gain receptivity from students, presidents must choose their moments and words wisely. But there are occasions when presidents have little choice about addressing moral issues in the lives of students. Regardless of the potential for success in seizing these moments, failure to do so is a failure of leadership.

Concern about the image often portrayed of black college students led Cole to comment on the annual spring event in Atlanta known as Freaknik. Begun as a black student alternative to the predominantly white major spring weekends at southern colleges, Freaknik draws large crowds of black college students to Atlanta. As with many such mass events involving college students, there are often negative consequences for the city community.

In a commencement address, Cole challenged his students not to succumb to the worst aspects of Freaknik. He warned of the negative reputation students bring upon themselves by investing a great amount of time and money so exclusively on fun and entertainment. He contrasted their frivolity with the pressing needs of the local community, many of whose members must tolerate the students' behavioral problems. He suggested that students transform the event into something that would creatively combine camaraderie and service to the community.[19] Presidents who assert moral concerns do not always find their views embraced. Cole notes that you could hear a pin drop in the audience, but he received little or no positive response from students. One faculty member did support Cole's statement of displeasure with student conduct. Unfortunately, the challenge went unheeded.

In addition to concerns on his own campus, Cole's leadership must also address the special concerns of black higher education. One of his interests is emphasizing student involvement with the African-American community. Cole believes black students have a greater obligation than their predecessors to help solve the problems of their minority communities because the needs of African Americans are now so profound. The responsibility of black students includes returning after college to work in minority communities. Cole's sadly accurate assumption is that black students must make this commitment because no one else will.

Cole joins black educational leaders to defend the importance of black higher education, connecting the future of black leadership to the quality of education for African Americans. This mission is paramount and is linked to the problem of racism in the country. Ensuring the quality and prestige of black colleges and universities is not a simple or easy task. It is made more difficult because of the assumption that difference, in this case all-black education, automatically implies inferiority, and thus the conclusion in the minds of many that black colleges are by definition inferior.

College presidents are normally expected to invest much of their time on "external" affairs, cultivating support directly to benefit their campuses. Cole and black college colleagues must work beyond their own gates to secure the future of black colleges. Cole passionately defends the critical role of black colleges in creating the environment that will prevent the loss of a generation of black young people.[20] The leadership burden of black college educators is even more crucial because of the increasing recruitment competition from prestige colleges for qualified black students.

Historically, the presidents of Clark Atlanta, like black college and university leaders nationwide, experience the effects of racism on black education. They are not naive about the implications of racism's tragic legacy for their institutions and students. However, these presidents do not blame racism or use it as an excuse for the difficulties faced by African Americans and by black colleges. They do acknowledge race as a cause of some difficulties and, more important, view black education as the best way to defeat racist attitudes. The burden and challenge of the moral leadership of these presidents is to continue the rich tradition of their colleges in helping to solve the nation's racial problems.

THE HESBURGH YEARS: LESSONS FOR THE PRESIDENCY

Throughout his presidency, Theodore Hesburgh was likewise enmeshed in major public issues and encountered political pressures on and off the campus. He took principled, if not popular, positions on social issues such as civil rights, the arms race, and the Vietnam War. In the latter case, he was accused of being a "hawk" for supporting government policy being protested at campuses across the country, including Notre Dame. During this time when colleagues and students publicly questioned his position, Hesburgh privately agonized about the war and the student disruptions on his and other campuses.

Hesburgh's key for survival was religious faith. He believes religion was the bond that held the campus community together. Only a select few colleges possess the religious characteristics capable of producing institutional cohesion in the face of divisive controversy. Reflecting the loneliness of a leader in time of crisis, Hesburgh concludes that the Mass and other liturgical moments were the "one bright light in the pervading darkness."[21] While particular to the ethos of Notre Dame, Hesburgh's experience underscores the value of common vision to a college community. Presidential leadership is crucial to developing the common bonds—the fabric of institutional saga—that sustain campuses in turmoil and difficulty.

During the 1980s, Hesburgh faced similar opposition for siding with "the establishment" concerning divestment of university financial holdings in corporations with business dealings in South Africa. Hesburgh rarely, if ever, feared saying what he believed to be the truth even when unpopular.

Presidencies are not popularity contests. However, decisions and institutional positions must at least have rationales that can be publicly acknowledged. Understanding must be sought even when agreement is lacking or impossible. At a student convocation on apartheid filled with opponents of his and the university's position, Hesburgh defended his stand. Claiming that the easy and readily satisfactory position would be to divest, Hesburgh countered that he "learned long ago that there is no real virtue in doing what is easy, or popular, or cheap in its cost, unless one is convinced that it is also morally justified as an effective move against injustice."[22]

Nearing the conclusion of his tenure in his last address to the faculty, Hesburgh reflected about his voice and leadership. As a "dean" of American higher education, Hesburgh defined moral leadership as "the embodiment of personal values that exists pre-eminently in the lives that we all live." On the matter of teaching values, he notes that it is of primary importance for students to see "personal lives convincingly speaking to them of dedicated intelligence, justice, honesty, integrity, fidelity, generosity, especially love and magnanimity" in their faculty and mentors.[23]

These traits are high-sounding and, it might be argued, are beyond the grasp of mere mortals. However, they do represent the ideals of the moral voice and are the qualities of character that should be expected of those who lead and guide colleges and universities. Regardless of the contemporary demands on presidents, these characteristics form the foundation of moral leadership.

THE PRESIDENCY IN AN ERA OF CHANGE

Critics, academicians, scholars, and casual observers have opinions about the current state and future of the college presidency. The thoughts of contemporary presidents are a valuable ingredient for understanding the presidency and assessing its future. Their observations provide insights about crucial issues: Does the presidency any longer allow latitude to devote time to moral issues? Are presidential responsibilities destined to focus nearly exclusively on fundraising and political management? And what is the role of presidents in articulating the moral components of a college education?

A central theme in discussions of the state of higher education is the change in the moral foundation of today's colleges and universities. Duderstadt and Cole trace the major changes to events of the 1960s and 1970s. Duderstadt also cites significant developments in the immediate post–World War II years. During this period the university's coherence began to erode as a result of massive increases in support from both the public and the private sectors. Concomitantly there developed "an incentive, reward system for faculty that stimulated entrepreneurial activity."[24]

These changes radically altered the ethos of colleges and universities, especially large research institutions. Institutions began seeking multiple sources of funding for an array of initiatives from research to building projects to student financial aid. In the process, loyalty and attachment to universities lessened as faculty (pressured by universities themselves) became less dependent on campus support for research. Duderstadt's characterization of the implications and results of this change is that when "the university becomes rather than a community of scholars, a holding company for entrepreneurs, [i]t changes your appetite."[25]

This shift disturbed the fabric of the university and established a context in which other changes occurred more readily than otherwise would have been the case. Developed from his experience at Michigan (where prior to his presidency he served as faculty member, dean, and vice president), Duderstadt's theory is that multidimensional missions conceived by independent, entrepreneurial faculty produce an incoherent institutional mission. This context, in which university constituents have increasingly less institutional loyalty and more institutional autonomy, poses enormous difficulties for the presidential moral voice.

In the 1960s and 1970s, developments at Michigan were similar to those at many colleges and universities across the country. The role of the moral voice of presidents was in many cases diminished when institutions departed from the doctrine of *in loco parentis* and were less able to dictate student behavior. Both student and institutional cultures changed. Like many colleges and universities, Michigan assumed less moral responsibility for the lives of its students. Its educational life increasingly emphasized the development of knowledge over concern about values. The result was that events of the 1960s and 1970s severed the university "from any tie to our tradition, our heritage and our sense of values."[26]

Duderstadt believes that these changes in fundamental moral aspects of institutional life are unfortunate, and may well be wrong. This problem is amplified by faculty, themselves products of reaction against traditional values in the 1960s and 1970s, who are less interested and eager than students "to discuss values, [to] guide their lives according to some higher sense of meaning."[27] One way in which Michigan and other universities attempt to bridge this gap is through increased encouragement of participation in community and volunteer service to inspire ethical reflection in students. Presidential leadership can fill some of the gap created by faculty reluctance to discuss moral values with students. But this is indeed a large task.

The effect of student protests and rebellion against authority in the 1960s and 1970s was amplified at black colleges. Due to changes brought about by the civil-rights movement, Cole believes that fewer black students came to college from exclusively segregated communities. Traditionally, these communities insulated black young people from changes in society. The new breed of students was more influenced by the assault on authority and values. They were less of a "captive audience" for black college presidents than had been the case for their predecessors such as Benjamin Mays, Rufus Clement, Bill Dent, and Samuel Proctor in the 1950s and earlier.[28] As incoming students became more skeptical of conventional values, the moral guidance of black college presidents was less readily heeded.

Two other important and provocative observations emerge about the 1960s and early 1970s. First, Cole believes that because of increasing social and professional mobility, many outstanding potential candidates for black college presidencies chose professions other than higher education. The reduction in the quality of leaders for black colleges contributed to a diminished moral authority in their presidencies. Though this problem is presently reversing itself, a generation of leadership may have been lost.[29]

Second, Cole claims that colleges "backed away from some principles that should have been maintained. We essentially lost control over the environment, over the ethos of the campus."[30] He specifically cites the loss of required chapel. Ending required and voluntary chapel contributed symbolically and practically to a reduction in moral dialogue on the campus.

For many years chapel represented an emphasis on moral discourse and reflection in the academy. It was critical to the character formation of many students. In its absence many presidents have searched for replacements: community reflections gatherings, special convocations, presidential lecture series and symposia. Though designed to stimulate reflection on values and morals, these events lack the regularity and transcendent focus of required or even voluntary chapel. Cole acknowledges that his peers disliked, even hated, chapel as undergraduates, but that without chapel they would not have been exposed to influential black leaders such as Mays and Martin Luther King, Jr. The power of chapel is captured by Cole's conclusion that hearing "these giants and what they have to say and influenced my life beyond just what I learned in the classroom." Chapel "put a stamp on the students. We lost that."[31]

Chapel is a recognizable symbol of the numerous changes altering the ethos of colleges and universities. Since the 1960s, these changes, including greater faculty autonomy from institutional life, expanded student freedom, increased secularity, and the rise of radical ideologies, have profoundly influenced the moral leadership of presidents.

Lastly, we turn to the question of whether the consuming responsibilities of the job diminish the ability of presidents to make time for moral issues. Though there is no clear consensus among the current presidents, two broad types emerge. First are presidents who experience little or no time for moral reflection and action. Second are those who integrate these activities into their presidential responsibilities. Reflections representative of both types aid our understanding of the modern presidency, especially the role in it of moral thought, leadership, and action.

Having sufficient time to think about issues of consequence is a difficulty and frustration for presidents. Presidents counsel each other, even though not always heeding their own advice, that it is critical to preserve time for thinking. Soon after becoming president, Diana Chapman Walsh realized that her former level of investment in professional work was simply no longer possible.[32] The presidency afforded little time for intellectual projects, writing, and thinking.

Thomas Gerety notes a certain irony in this problem. The inability of presidents to maintain a personal regimen of reading and reflecting places at risk their very reputation as thinkers, which initially makes individuals seem attractive as presidential candidates in the first place.

This reality is brought home by Duderstadt, who notes that the demands of leading a $2.5-billion-a-year multinational corporation leave few moments for thinking and reflection.[33] The era of the "perpetual capital campaign" compels presidents to invest extensive time in institutional development. Paul Gray's joking definition of the modern university president as someone who lives in a large house and begs for a living is an apt description of the demands on a president's time.

Duderstadt found opportunities for moral action even in the context of leading an "international conglomerate." He applied moral leadership to the responsibility for the welfare of tens of thousands of employees, to the management and ethical conduct of a massive health-care system, and to the implementation of the Michigan Mandate, his major affirmative-action initiative. Presidents of multiversities, as well as those leading smaller but in their own ways equally complex institutions, can fashion a moral voice in leadership despite time constraints on intellectual reflection.

The predominant view today that college presidents are chief executive officers makes them in the eyes of many no different from their corporate counterparts. The late nineteenth and early twentieth century was another time when college and university presidents were very much like the corporate barons of the day.

Even in that era, life for presidents was still somehow different. James Freedman notes the luxury enjoyed by Nicholas Murray Butler, who traveled to Europe for the entire summer each year.[34] There Butler would read, write, and relax, returning to the Columbia in September for the beginning of the academic year. Reconceptualizing the presidency to provide more time for personal reflection and renewal will require support from boards and other university constituencies. A worthwhile innovation would be for boards of trustees to mandate that presidents take a consecutive month of vacation each year and a sabbatical year once every seven.

Presidents who incorporate the moral voice into their responsibilities are exemplary of an integrative model of presidential leadership. Since the end of the era when presidents taught capstone seminars in applied ethics to seniors, the daily activities of the presidency have changed dramatically.[35] These "old style" presidents were more directly involved in moral education than presidents today. Rupp counters that leadership is not divisible into separate compartments. His presidential leadership treats *all* university activities as essentially moral. Specifically, Rupp claims that "moral leadership is tend[ing] to those managerial responsibilities, that if done appropriately and well, make an enormous difference in how effective, how *morally* effective, as well as effective in other ways, the institution can be, and if neglected in order to exercise [the] moral voice, will be done very badly because no one else can do them."[36]

Another integrative president, Malloy, affirms that his priestly vocation including "preaching, teaching, pastoring, occasionally giving retreats, participating in ethics-oriented conferences, and writing" forms the core of his presidency. Acknowledging changes since becoming president, Malloy is still able to tend to all aspects of institutional life without neglecting the presidential role in advising, teaching and counseling, and exhibiting moral leadership in public rhetoric and decisions. This treatment of the presidency is highly reminiscent of the "old style." Even with this holistic approach, Malloy feels the pressure of time, indicating that he would devote more time to moral issues and personal study if the presidency afforded more leisure.[37]

Today Hesburgh's and Malloy's model of the minister-president is not a mere artifact of a previous time. They are just two contemporary examples of how such presidencies function and how individuals in such positions view their role and identity. The integration of moral leadership in the Notre Dame presidency is a living reminder of the historic tradition of commitment by ministers and religious institutions to the development of colleges in America. It is a heritage that need not be completely lost in today's presidency and colleges.

The pressures on presidents are not new. The presidents of old also experienced the extraordinary burdens of the office and wished for more time for personal reflection, study, and thinking about moral issues. College and university presidencies have always been positions of leadership on which great expectations and hopes have rested. The job has always been one with, in the words of Harvard's Charles Eliot, "no equal in the world."[38]

Regardless of whether today's presidents have the same amount of time for intellectual and scholarly pursuits—the more professorial life—as their predecessors, their role as teachers remains. Presidents need to embrace a relationship to students as teachers. They need to reclaim the importance of making the time to teach. Teaching offers presidents direct contact with students and reduces the distance between administrative duties and the classroom. In addition to these benefits, Thomas Gerety notes that teaching provides intellectual refreshment and requires the discipline of reading and writing.[39]

Classroom teaching is only one aspect of the president's role as teacher. Equally, if not more, important is the ability to use the office of the presidency itself to teach. Gerety contends that "the moral core at colleges like Amherst is teaching as conversation—a certain kind of conversation about ideas." The presidency should engage this conversation, a conversation that can be provocative because "the liberal arts means the most radical ideas, even ideas that are inimical to the liberal arts, that the tradition is oppressive, should be embraced with joy." It is the president's responsibility to maintain "the morality of conversation."[40]

This conversation about education is integral to the soul of a college and belongs at the heart of the academy. Relying on educational dialogue, presidents can shift the ground of debate concerning morality and values today so frequently rooted in political correctness. Just as more speech is the best antidote and defense against hate speech, the free exchange of ideas counters the trend toward narrowing what is deemed acceptable in the academy. This position staunchly affirms that the moral good will prevail in open debate. Presidential leadership must defend freedom of thought and speech as fundamental values.

Prospects for the future of the moral voice are characterized by signs of both concern and hope. One concern is the continuing trend toward professional administrators assuming college presidencies. This emphasis on management over academic background began in the 1950s. Though the management strengths of presidential candidates are important, the desirability of academic preparation remains an important, often irrefutable, consideration. Presidents appointed from the ranks of academic administrators almost always begin their academic careers as faculty members. Many of these potential candidates for presidencies continue to teach while assuming administrative duties. These presidents are not trained solely as professional administrators. However, there are a breed of prospective presidential candidates who, following graduate work, spend their entire careers exclusively as academic administrators.

Some campuses have experimented with selecting presidents with professional executive experience exclusively in the business and political sectors. In the current environment, political and public-relations skills are valued as much as if not more than sheer management expertise and fundraising ability. Though some of these presidents have been less than successful, the potential continues for colleges and universities to lean more than at present on professional—as opposed to academic and scholarly—administrators.

From experience in the health-care field, Walsh sees an ominous sign in the hospital industry, which until recently had doctors as head administrators. These experienced medical practitioners often brought a moral perspective to health care in their leadership. Now hospitals are tending to appoint professional administrator-presidents who often do not speak in ways that frame moral issues.[41]

Should higher education follows a course similar to that which Walsh believes to be taking place in the health-care industry, colleges and universities could find themselves led by presidents with strong management orientation, but vastly less concern for the moral aspects of the presidency and of education. Such an evolution would not bode well for America's colleges and universities and for influential moral leadership from presidents.

A second concern for the future of presidential moral leadership is the difficulty of maintaining coherent institutional missions, especially though not exclusively in universities. The size and complexity of research universities makes it difficult for a single, unified voice to produce a sense of common purpose and mission. Duderstadt acknowledges that whether these institutions maintain themselves centrally as mega-universities, or experiment with breaking into smaller colleges within universities, the prospect for the moral voice is not hopeful.[42] In either case, the likely result is that common agreement on values and mores will be reduced and that as a result the moral voice will be weakened. Certainly movement toward greater internal autonomy in colleges or universities, no matter how large or small, will further complicate the ability of presidents to identify a common mission and to establish an integrated institutional moral voice.

A third potentially negative impact on the contemporary presidency is the increasingly short tenures of presidents. One of the reasons why the giants of previous eras and even leaders such as Hesburgh in our own appear so large is directly related to their length of service. Reasonably long presidential tenures are critical for the establishment of the credibility necessary to exercise a moral voice.

Cole is hopeful that if he can remain long enough in the Clark Atlanta presidency he will be able to infuse moral authority into the culture of the university and beyond its gates as well.[43] He feels that black college presidents with longer-standing reputations can play a larger role in education. If he is right, these presidents may recapture in the future the historical tradition of moral advocacy in black education.

Extending the average tenure of college and university presidents would likely create more leaders who would appear as giants. Their moral voice would then be able to mature to a point of greater impact on campus and in society.

There are also hopeful signs of rejuvenated moral leadership. First, society is yearning for examples of moral leadership especially in the face of problems requiring responses rooted in a moral framework. Malloy uses the image of a fabric with "motheaten bits of cloth that nobody controls" to describe contemporary American society.[44] The gravity of this situation leads to the prospect of a return to the tradition of looking to educators for guidance and solutions to these problems of which society is well aware, but in the face of which it also feels paralyzed. This view serves as a reminder to the academy of its traditional role as a place of wisdom. Recapturing this vital moral ground will enable college presidents to regain prominence in society. In the process the university can come to be viewed as an esteemed source of ethical thought and action.

Second, the moral voice is strongly rooted in a unique American tradition combining democratic principles and liberal education. A starting point for reemphasizing this alliance is for presidents to ground their voice in the educational values of the college. These values represent an enduring ideal of the American democratic experiment, an experiment at the heart and soul of the nation's colleges and universities.

Though an unrealized ideal, this partnership is crucial for developing meaning in people's lives, for recreating the foundations of civility in society, and for establishing the shared ethos essential for the commonweal. This ideal is a counterpoint to the tyranny of political correctness and to the influence of radical ideologies on campus and in society. A degree of hope is at the basis of Gerety's contention that educators "speak for a certain utopia, a very important utopia we all recognize. We speak in that sense for democracy and for the democracy that education can be."[45] College presidents can take the lead in stressing the importance of this utopian vision for educators, students, and America's educational institutions.

The optimistic view is that democratic principles and liberal education—an education that seeks to liberate and inspire the mind—will continue to be the foundation of colleges and universities and of the presidents' moral voice. The ideals of this core of education provide a crucial, certainly the only reasonable, response to the legitimate threat posed by ideologies to the purposes of the college and university. The educational and democratic principles of the Republic are the best and only antidote to the longstanding presence of ideologies in the university, a presence magnified and intensified in the contemporary era.

The moral voice was once grounded in more easily developed common agreements. The diminished influence of integrative social institutions, frameworks, and leadership increases the difficulty for presidents to exercise their moral voice. Presidents can draw upon the inspiration of predecessors in developing expression of a moral voice and arguing for this voice to retain its role in the college presidency. Only with a renewal of moral authority will presidents be able to wage successfully the battle for the soul of the university.

NOTES

1. A seminal work on the role of ideology and its impact on the university is Kenneth Minogue, *The Concept of a University* (Berkeley: University of California Press, 1973).

2. Harold T. Shapiro, "American Higher Education: A Special Tradition Faces a Special Challenge," Academy for Educational Development, May 22, 1986, Shapiro Collection, Box 178, p. 23.

3. Elias Blake, Jr., Founder's Day address. From the personal papers of Elias Blake, Jr., February 19, 1980, p. 16.

4. Shapiro, "American Higher Education," p. 35.

5. Idem.

6. The term *civil religion* is traceable to Jean-Jacques Rousseau, but it was popularized by Robert N. Bellah in his seminal article "Civil Religion in America," *Daedalus*, Winter 1967, and which later appeared in William G. McLoughlin and Robert Bellah (eds.), *Religion in America* (Boston: Beacon Press, 1968). Shapiro suggests that the nation's founders developed a working compromise between absolute values—"moral certainties"—and the demands of new knowledge: "a secular regime buttressed in important ways by a civil religion." See Harold T. Shapiro, "Ethics in America—Who Is Responsible?" *New York Times* Presidential Forum, December 1, 1987, Shapiro Collection, Box 178, p. 4.

7. Shapiro, "Ethics in America," p. 5.

8. Personal interview with President Diana Chapman Walsh of Wellesley College, November 28, 1994.

9. Personal interview with President James J. Duderstadt of the University of Michigan, March 6, 1995.

10. Ibid. As noted, the constantly changing commitments of board of regents' members is due to the political process by which they are elected.

11. Ibid. He makes the concluding comment with gallows-humor laughter.

12. Personal interview with President Edward Malloy, C.S.C., of Notre Dame University, September 20, 1994. In this context, Malloy cites the historical tendency of presidents to speak publicly on the major generational issues of their time noted by another president, Joseph Crowley, in *No Equal in the World: An Interpretation of the Academic Presidency* (Reno: University of Nevada Press, 1994).

13. As an example, see William H. Honan, "At the Top of the Ivory Tower the Watchword Is Silence," *New York Times*, July 24, 1994.

14. Personal interview with Edward Malloy, C.S.C.

15. Personal interview with President George Rupp of Columbia University, November 16, 1994.

16. Personal interview with George Rupp. He makes this point numerous times in the interview. His point is that morals and ethics in education must not be viewed as "icing on the cake."

17. Personal interview with George Rupp.

18. Personal interview with James J. Duderstadt.

19. Personal interview with President Thomas Cole of Clark Atlanta University, February 16, 1995.

20. Personal interview with Thomas Cole.

21. Theodore Hesburgh, "Reflections on a Church-Related University," June 21, 1979, UND Archives, Theodore Hesburgh Speeches, 1968–1987, Box 142/14, p. 11.

22. Theodore Hesburgh, convocation on apartheid, October 1985, UND Archives, 1968–1987, Box 142/22, pp. 13–14. At the time of this speech, Hesburgh and Notre Dame, along with many other colleges and universities, were adhering to the "Sullivan Principles" as guidelines for the behavior of corporations doing business in South Africa.

23. Theodore Hesburgh, address to the faculty, October 13, 1986, UND Archives, 1968–1987, Box 142/23, p. 14. This address contains a magnificent history of the university's founding by Father Eduard Sorin. Hesburgh's account captures Notre Dame's saga.

24. Personal interview with James J. Duderstadt. Duderstadt's position is supported by the work of Thorstein B. Veblen, *The Higher Learning in America* (New York: Hill and Wang, 1962), and Robert Nisbet, *The Degradation of the Academic Dogma* (London: Heinemann, 1971).

25. Personal interview with James J. Duderstadt.

26. Ibid. He notes further that the university had no publicized standards of student behavior during the late 1960s and 1970s.

27. Ibid. He adds that the faculty who were educated in the 1960s and 1970s bring "a certain rebellion against values and traditional structures," which may also affect their response to the role of morals and values in education.

28. Personal interview with President Thomas Cole of Clark Atlanta University, February 16, 1995.

29. Ibid.

30. Ibid.

31. Ibid.

32. Personal interview with President Diana Chapman Walsh of Wellesley College, November 28, 1994.

33. Personal interview with President James J. Duderstadt of the University of Michigan, March 6, 1995.

34. James O. Freedman, "Our Work Should Not Silence Our Wisdom," *Boston Globe*, January 19, 1997.

35. Personal interview with President George Rupp of Columbia University, November 16, 1994.

36. Ibid. Italics indicate Rupp's emphasis.

37. Personal interview with Edward Malloy, C.S.C.

38. Eliot's characterization of the presidency is used by Joseph Crowley in the title of *No Equal in the World: An Interpretation of the Academic Presidency.* Crowley provides an excellent historical review indicating that presidents early in this century, if not before, ofttimes found the demands of the office oppressive in terms of expectations, media criticism, and burdensome personal schedules.

39. Personal interview with President Thomas Gerety of Amherst College, July 27, 1994.

40. Ibid.

41. Personal interview with Diana Chapman Walsh.

42. Personal interview with James J. Duderstadt.

43. Personal interview with Thomas Cole.

44. Personal interview with Edward Malloy, C.S.C.

45. Personal interview with Thomas Gerety.

10

The Presidency in the Crucible

WHAT IS THE CONTEMPORARY STATE OF THE PRESIDENCY?

Where does this story of the historic and contemporary moral voice of presidents lead both casual and seasoned observers of the state of American college and university leadership? Does this profile of leaders in the ivory tower suggest greater optimism or increased pessimism about the future of the presidency? Are the men and women serving as presidents capable of being the moral leaders we ideally wish them to be? Are they capable, given the pressures and distractions of their positions, of influencing the mores of the campus and society? Is there any longer a foundation—or if not can one be fashioned—to support presidents in exercising moral leadership and voice from the ivory tower? And finally, are the changes that have occurred in the presidency of such magnitude and consequence as to render the moral voice of presidents already an artifact of the office?

What is the current state of moral leadership from college presidents? It is not surprising, cynics notwithstanding, that the answer varies in large measure because the presidency itself is in a state of flux. Context is critical. Thus, judgments about where the presidency is and where it may be headed must begin with an assessment of changes in the presidency and of the forces that impinged on it during the course of the twentieth century.

The first major change, one with significant implications and its own set of problems and difficulties for the presidency, is the change in where moral language fits in our society. Greater pluralism and secularity have increased skepticism and suspicion about the religious values that underlie such large portion of moral thinking. The assumption is that there is a fine line between moral commentary and moralizing. And moral thinking can easily slip into proselytizing. So leaders can have an understandable reluctance about using moral language in their voice and leadership. Also, dangers lurk in entering the values debate (read: the dreaded discussion of whose values?). Those who do enter this fray frequently risk accusations of moralizing. The position of those who would disconnect moral leadership with the college and university presidency is itself symptomatic of higher education's difficulties and dilemmas.

Certainly, today's presidents usually, if not exclusively, use language differently—in some cases dramatically so—from their distant predecessors in expressing moral concerns. Language rooted in Judeo-Christian religious values and social and cultural ideals has been modified, though certainly not eliminated entirely from contemporary public discourse. For example, George Harris's argument in his inaugural address that Amherst students were being educated to prepare them purposefully for building the Kingdom of God, a kingdom synonymous with democracy, is a historical relic. Such a frame of reference would simply not appear today at Amherst or at most other schools. The only exceptions might be at specifically Christian, and likely extremely fundamentalist, colleges such as Liberty Baptist. Overall, Harris's message would be viewed as too sectarian, too parochial, and too narrow for use today.

Thus, the more unified set of beliefs of previous centuries, even earlier in our own, has given way to a vastly more pluralistic diversity of beliefs (and lack thereof) today. This is a major reality faced not only by college presidents, but by other leaders of society as well. Examples are abundant and clear. James Angell used religious language to describe the value of education at Michigan and its interest in matching traditional New England colleges in preparing students for Christian ministry. By contrast, Harold Shapiro and James Duderstadt provide leadership to Michigan as a vastly more complex major research university in which the beliefs of Angell's day no longer predominate at the institution or in society.

The moral language of early twenty-first century presidents simply is not the same as that of earlier eras. Today's acceptable public moral language generally carries less of a sense for depth of the religious foundations, principles, and heritage at the heart of many colleges and universities. The same could be said about diminishment of the religious legacy in the social fabric of the nation. As a result, contemporary presidents are forced to develop language adequate to the task of articulating the moral importance of education, but which will not prove offensive to some sectors of society. Finding this necessarily more pluralistic common ground upon which political and social, let alone religious, moral concepts can be expressed is an increasingly complex and difficult task in our intensely secular and diverse cultural climate.

The moral voice of the college and university presidency has a rich history. But this voice is not merely an artifact of the past. Asserting this fundamental characteristic of moral leadership and voice as vital to the presidency requires overcoming resistance to having moral leadership associated with the office and its responsibilities. The contemporary embrace of presidential moral leadership will determine much about the future of the presidency.

A second observable change in the presidency has been the development of greater tentativeness in the expression of moral concerns on the part of contemporary office-holders compared to their nineteenth and early twentieth-century predecessors. Presidents indeed confront numerous obstacles and difficulties to expressing moral stances on issues. For presidents of both public and private institutions there are constituents, including those with the power of presidential appointment, who directly and indirectly urge presidents to avoid moral expression in public settings. For example, commenting about the fear of negatively affecting fundraising endeavors should some group or constituency be alienated, former Brown University president Vartan Gregorian noted: " 'It's not natural for me, but I must speak with tact and diplomacy. . . . I have come to agree with Lord Chesterfield that wisdom is like carrying a watch. Unless asked, you don't have to tell everybody what time it is.' "[1] Gregorian expressed the very real pressures that can lead presidents to operate with extreme care in their expression of potentially unpopular moral stands.

There are numerous other examples of this problem of tentativeness for presidents. Before publishing his previously mentioned paper on racism, Harold Shapiro circulated a draft to colleagues for their counsel on whether its contents might be viewed as inflammatory. They agreed that his thinking needed to be shared with a wide audience. However, based undoubtedly on extensive experience, Shapiro's colleagues expressed fear that his ideas would be subjected to misinterpretation and unwarranted, but likely, backlash. Thus, they urged him to be deliberate in making his paper public. As discussed earlier, Diana Chapman Walsh received almost identical advice from her presidential colleagues on the handling of the Martin affair at Wellesley. From his perspective of the presidency, Duderstadt believed this tendency to be hesitant about public pronouncements resulted directly from the dangerous political environment in which presidents, and all leaders, must lead. To one extent or another this is the situation at most colleges and universities, but it is quite pronounced in the governance of major public institutions such as Michigan. Given the end of his tenure as a result of an exercise of political power by the board of regents, Duderstadt's own case confirms his point and proves instructive.

A variation on this theme is that in the contemporary climate, the legal and politically damaging implications of misjudgments and missteps in handling sensitive matters are amplified. The cautionary advice offered to Shapiro and Walsh reveals the presidential assessment that in a polarized and politicized environment extreme care must be exercised when taking moral positions. The presidents who counseled Shapiro and Walsh were not suggesting that moral stands be avoided altogether. But they were highly suspicious and savvy about the contemporary climate and the great potential for negative repercussions in response to presidential action. In addition, these leaders were well aware of the ease and speed with which opposition to a public position can engulf a president. In general, presidents in previous eras, while not completely safe from a similar fate, were freer to speak about moral issues. A major factor insulating them was the greater sense of commonly held beliefs about values and ethics that they enjoyed in the campus communities and society of the day.

The extent of changes in the responsibilities and demands of the presidency and in the texture of society in the last one hundred years or more will no doubt always be a subject of debate. A definitive answer to the question of how much change may have occurred remains elusive. However, there are some informed insights into what may have taken place in the changing role of the president. For example, both Tom Gerety and George Rupp agree that the nature of the presidency has changed, that the "old-style"[2] presidency is certainly no longer predominant, if it exists at all. Their daily experience in the job leads to an assessment that there is a stark contrast between themselves and the professorial, academician presidents of previous eras. While not alleging to speak for others, their conclusion no doubt reflects that of many, if not most, college presidents.

However, among contemporaries an exception to this change in the presidency presents itself in the persons of Theodore Hesburgh and Edward Malloy of Notre Dame. Not surprisingly, given their vocation as priests and their presidencies of a religious university, these two closely fit the more classical description of the presidency. Theirs is an integrative model nearly identical to that of the colonial college presidents. Their presidencies feature teaching, counseling, preaching, and living in student residences, as well as tending to administrative, managerial, development, and long-range planning responsibilities. Their presidential manner is similar to "old-style" presidents who, whatever their daily schedules, maintained all these responsibilities, including tending to the details of the physical well-being of their institutions. All the while they were and were expected to be moral leaders of their campuses.

In most cases these presidents "of old" led the generally much smaller institutions of previous eras. But they also did so without the significant levels of staff support found at contemporary colleges and universities. Though current presidential tasks are characterized as significant and complex, they are also handled by numerous specialized administrators who provide support for a diversity of tasks. Joseph Crowley dispels another frequently assumed difference between today's presidents and their predecessors. Presidents have historically faced remarkably similar difficulties. Like many of their contemporary counterparts, earlier presidents were frustrated by crowded schedules and what they believed to be unfair treatment by the media.[3] Thus, even these complaints, often thought to be new burdens borne by contemporary presidents, actually have significantly longer histories.

CHANGES IN THE PRESIDENCY

Overall, the responsibilities of presidents have remained substantially the same over the last one hundred years and probably longer. But have some elements of the job and its expectations changed, and which are therefore keys to the perception that today's presidents are more burdened and busier than their predecessors?

One logical, but rarely mentioned, answer is that presidents today are more distracted by certain responsibilities and tend to concentrate less on others than their predecessors. The number and even the scope of presidential responsibilities have changed little, if at all, since the beginning of the presidency in the colonial colleges. What has changed is the manner in which presidents allocate their time to these different, now viewed as competing, tasks. The distraction results in large measure from the accepted expectation that presidents must, or at least feel compelled to, tend to the fundraising and administrative tasks at the expense of attention to the moral voice. And this expectation of their presidents is shared by trustees, governing boards, influential alumni, and faculty. After all, even professors want their institutions run well, and they certainly want financial stability and development growth.

A second element altering the job of college presidents is that various constituents and the public frequently misunderstand the nature of the presidency. Those not involved in the day-to-day affairs of a campus, including many alumni, simply lack a comprehension of the diverse and competing tasks that presidents must perform. These observers' lack of clarity about the job in turn complicates the exercise of the office by presidents. Another factor often attached to these misperceptions and creating its own set of difficulties is the rise of cynicism about leadership in higher education and elsewhere in society.

A third problem is the increasing lack of a common core of social agreement. James McGregor Burns, a scholar and student of leadership, believed that moral leadership is based upon a leader who "looks for potential motives in followers, seeks to satisfy higher needs, and engages the full person of the follower."[4] But he suggested that this leadership of college and university presidents has become increasingly difficult in the contemporary era. Changes in social perceptions were the culprit. Leadership in this environment is more demanding and complicated because "without a powerful modern philosophical tradition, without theoretical and empirical cumulation, without guiding concepts, and without considered practical experiences, we lack the very foundation for knowledge of a phenomenon—leadership in the arts, the academy, science, politics, the professions, war—that touches and shapes our lives."[5]

Burns highlighted this crucial question of what becomes of leadership, especially moral leadership, when there no longer exists a central, common core of beliefs and principles—the problem highlighted by Shapiro—about which leader and follower can agree. In the context of the life of colleges and universities, this situation makes the presidency and the expression of moral leadership and voice vastly more difficult in the modern than in earlier eras. The ramifications of this change are of significant consequence for the academy and American society.

So today's president must overcome the greater distractions created in some measure by the heightened expectations of college and university constituencies. Simultaneously, presidents face the need to define and communicate what they are doing and the responsibilities they bear to many who simply do not understand the role and demands of the office. And finally, a much less well defined common core of principles and values, diminished even further by a more politicized climate on campuses and in society, further complicates the leadership of presidents.

UNCHANGED ATTRIBUTES IN THE PRESIDENCY

While during recent decades some increased complexities have evolved in the nature of the office of the president, there are also some characteristic elements of the presidency that have changed little, if at all. Of special interest are a number of them that focus on the presidency's relationship to the moral issues and vision integral to education.

The first is the role of the presidential voice in fostering character formation. Certainly many of the traditional settings in which presidents reached students directly have changed substantially, if not completely. These moments included speaking at required and voluntary chapel, teaching the senior seminar on applied ethics, and delivering baccalaureate addresses. However, there remain important occasions when presidents can address the values of education, the moral imperatives of learning, and their expectations about campus life. These settings include annual ceremonies such as convocations and commencements and periodic moments such as inaugural addresses, symposia, campus meetings, and discussions with students individually and in groups. These are opportunities when presidents can still stress that education is more than the pursuit of knowledge and the attainment of competence. They can still extol the virtues of liberal education and the importance of the search for meaning and the value of learning throughout life.

Closely related to these presidential moments is the characteristic capacity of presidents to emphasize the moral aspects of education, expressed in positions and philosophies that education is at its heart moral.[6] These comments characterize education both throughout the curriculum and in campus life as having a moral component and frequently include exhortations about the formation of character.

A second continuing aspect of the presidential moral voice is its extolling the link between education and democracy. With great consistency and frequency, presidents discuss the moral and educational imperatives of democracy. Many demonstrate a strong tendency to support democratic ideals even when criticism of the nation's leadership and of governmental policies becomes necessary. We observed this in the example of John Kemeny, among others. Regardless of political affections and the actions of political leaders, college presidents understand the need to underscore the ideals of the nation. They also advocate the important responsibility of college graduates for building democracy and serving the country. There is a clear thread in the tradition of presidents indicating that the nation, whether judged right or wrong on specific matters, requires contributions by its citizens. The task of higher education is to prepare those who will provide the leadership essential to support the principles and values of the nation. These are the citizens who are also critical participants in correcting the flaws in civic life.

Closely linked to encouraging an embrace of the responsibilities of democracy is the consistent emphasis of presidents on the expectation of social service in the education and the lives of students. This expectation is usually conveyed through encouragement of students to commit themselves to improving society through both their professions and as citizens and volunteers. These admonitions for action in social service is a theme also frequently joined to the promotion of democratic and civic values.

A third constant feature of the office is the propensity for presidents to address the major generational issues of their times. Our story about the presidency attests to their urging an expansion of access to education for all citizens. They have consistently appealed for commitment to civil rights and equal opportunity for African Americans and other minority members of society. This has included advocating women's education and professional opportunity and expressing concerns about the plight of urban America. Presidents have also regularly involved themselves in the issues of patriotism, world events, international conflicts, and the endangerment of the environment.

Certainly not all presidents elect public engagement in moral and ethical issues. Many do not have the inclination. Others feel that their constituencies would not tolerate their speaking out on moral issues. In an interview, President Edward Malloy commented about presidents of other major universities who have confided envy that the expectation of his job at Notre Dame demanded that he speak publicly on moral concerns. Meanwhile, to protect their positions, they feel confined by boards and other powerful constituents to do the opposite: avoid moral problems and controversies. While not discounting the reluctance, for whatever reasons, of some presidents to speak publicly, there is clear evidence of presidents who are committed to matters of consequence in the public square. The profiles of presidents we have observed contradict claims that compared to predecessors, today's presidents are largely silent on public issues.

If the moral voice is alive and if it is to continue vigorously in the future, an obvious question is: What sources will inform and shape the moral aspects of contemporary presidential rhetoric? Certainly, the religious norms and values that provided a substantial foundation for the rhetoric of the colonial college presidents have been radically altered during the last two centuries. Enlightenment thought, the scientific revolution, subsequent technological change, greater pluralism, and assaults from religious critics are merely a few of the forces that have combined to change the landscape of religious and moral language and discourse. Despite these battles that have resulted in the creation of the modern era, religion remains a critical component of American culture and thus will remain an element of the voice of presidents. These religious foundations of American society, though changing, are not disappearing and will continue to inform public life. This will be the case for the foreseeable future.

In addition, these prevailing religious foundations will continue to broaden their influence by selectively incorporating the more pluralistic strands of belief apparent in society. Added to this is the fact that America's religion of the republic, what is more commonly referred to as our civil religion, will prevail as highly influential cultural foundation. Though not without its own set of challenges, including those from the multicultural extremes and radical ideologies that Harold Shapiro reasonably fears, civil religion will remain constituted of moral principles and norms derived from generally agreed upon civic values and beliefs. These sources readily provide a strong and available basis from which presidents can fashion moral utterances.

In shaping moral rhetoric, presidents are also likely in the future to rely to a greater degree than in the past on the values reflected in the consensus of their college communities. The times dictate that leaders everywhere must be more responsive to the values of their constituents and utilize them. This is a way of ensuring that followers will follow leaders. However, whether in the national arena or on a college campus, this process is not without dilemmas and difficulties. While the counsel that leaders not get too far ahead of those whom they lead is well founded, at the same time there is a problem for leaders when they do nothing more than reflect the thinking of their followers: to do so at the least produces a lowest-common-denominator thinking. At its worst, it represents the dumbing down of the communal, in this case campus, culture and intellect.

Major social and political issues will unavoidably continue to prompt, at times compel, moral responses from presidents. John Kemeny's response to the events at Kent State in 1970 is a noteworthy but by no means isolated example. Presidents will be expected, possibly with increasing frequency, to seize such occasions as opportunities for moral expression. There is a gathering concern in society about the erosion of moral and ethical principles. This creates a heightened expectation of college leaders to take moral stands.

The moral leadership of presidents is finally contingent on the thinking and action of the men and women who hold the office. Their moral compass must complement rather than be directed by the values held by members of college and university communities. In shaping moral leadership, current and future college presidents will rely on the ethical principles and core beliefs derived from their religious faith, personal philosophy, and social and cultural assumptions. In this regard, contemporary presidents and their successors will be remarkably similar to their predecessors.

MORAL VOICE AND THE FOUNDATIONS OF THE ACADEMY

An understanding of the presidency and of the role played by the moral voice is not complete without noting important connections to three elements that contribute significantly to the fundamental and distinctive shape of colleges and universities in America. These are, first, the relationship of presidential leadership to the formation of institutional and organizational saga. Second is the social and educational philosophy resulting from presidential debate about the tension between egalitarianism and meritocracy in a democratic state. And third is the responsibility of presidents to encourage and engage the great educational conversation.

The moral voice of presidents is intrinsically involved in the affirmation and reaffirmation of the mission—the saga—of colleges and universities. Institutional missions are normally grounded in high ideals, principles, and goals. A critical task for presidents is to enrich and enliven these fundamental values. They do so by maintaining institutional heritage and conveying a sense of tradition and purpose. This foundation is reaffirmed and enlarged as presidents advocate the value of education at their colleges and highlight their institution's expectations of its students.

This relationship of the moral leadership of presidents to saga is one of mutual reinforcement and benefit. Presidents can strongly influence the saga of their colleges and universities, but saga also furnishes high ideals for the platform and pulpit of the presidency. This is observable among the presidents of Michigan, with its particular but highly inclusive mission of education for the "common man" and of service to the public. On the other hand, the moral leadership of presidents bears an even deeper special relationship and responsibility to institutional saga at colleges with specialized missions, especially those serving particular constituencies. The experience of the presidents of schools such as Wellesley, Clark Atlanta, and Notre Dame leads to an interesting and likely more general conclusion: Presidents of these colleges and universities serving distinct populations feel greater incumbent responsibility than other presidents to invoke and to strengthen the special character of their institutions. They consequently refer with great frequency to institutional histories, founding principles, and mottoes in conveying the specialness of their colleges.

The presidents of these colleges and universities express their voice in contexts characterized by exclusivity, by a sense of specialness, and by the importance of the founding vision and purpose. A special passion accompanies the voice of presidents who are advocates for the education of women and black students who faced extraordinarily limited opportunities for much of the history of higher education in America. However, their institutions have historically been vulnerable and fragile. And this state of affairs is only exacerbated by recent claims that exclusive education for women and blacks is no longer needed in an era when these students have access to most other colleges and universities, including those of outstanding reputation. Similarly, against the growing secular influences of contemporary society, Notre Dame's presidents since the mid-twentieth century—Hesburgh and Malloy—battle the unique difficulties of maintaining the integrity of an education grounded in religious beliefs and values.

The responsibility of sustaining saga in the face of challenges by critics and by a changing social ethos contributes to the necessity that these presidents firmly rely on the distinctiveness of their institutions' founding missions and principles. One can readily conclude that the more particular the shape of institutional saga, the more specific and potentially ideological, if not also idiosyncratic, the exercise of the presidential voice. However, even in these instances in which particularity is necessary and expected, these presidents have also been able to craft rhetoric with a universal flavor and appeal. Their voices have not been limited by the distinction and particularity of their institutional sagas. On the contrary, they have been able to use the visionary ideals of their founders to enlarge society's thoughts about education and who should be educated.

A second important responsibility of the moral voice is its use by presidents in navigating the inherent tension between the egalitarian spirit of America and its sometimes contradictory, but essential and necessary, faith in meritocracy. This social and educational dilemma hinges on the conflict between two competing and often mutually exclusive aspirations. The first is a desire to make education available to all. The second is the reality that colleges and universities are selective and that they exist in large measure to produce an educated elite for society. Many presidents have expressed their thoughts about this problem in American higher education. The range of examples includes George Harris's notion that the college exists to develop an "aristocracy of merit, knowledge, character."[7] Nannerl Keohane's concern about elitism was that the world cannot be assumed to be "permanently divided into the strong and fortunate, who do the ministering, and the rest, who need our attention."[8] Nicholas Butler believed that an elite is necessary, that nature was inherently unequal, and that if "inequality of talent and capacity [is destroyed,] . . . life as we know it stops."[9] And finally, James Angell held the hope that the nation's educational opportunities would be accessible to the "humblest and poorest child upon its soil."[10]

Part of the inherent difficulty of the dilemma variously touched on by these presidents is that birthright, racial identity, gender, and similar factors over which individuals have no control can and do result in denial of access to education. And even with the requisite education, prejudice may prevent these students from attaining positions of leadership commensurate with their talent and merit. The black college presidents—Horace Bumstead, William Crogman, Elias Blake, and Thomas Cole—confirm the struggle of African Americans to reach their potential based on merit and to gain opportunity based on justice.

As an ideal, *noblesse oblige* has served to remind students of the world outside themselves—in George Rupp's words, "to understand [oneself] in a context wider than just very provincial interests."[11] Because of its heritage in another era, one predominated by white males, some allege that *noblesse oblige* is by definition and tradition elitist and exclusionary. This criticism, however well or ill founded, then creates a task for presidents to conceive more inclusive rhetoric to capture the *noblesse oblige* tradition. For example, in his response James Laney suggested substituting the notion of "leading out," drawing on the etymological meaning of "to educate," as a way of capturing the responsibility of the educated to serve others. If higher education is to ensure its special value to society, then the twin values of liberating education and of service to society must be maintained. It is the incumbent and important role of presidents to exert moral leadership in doing so. Regardless of the language used—be it *noblesse oblige*, leading out, or some variation—it is essential that students be challenged to reach beyond their own needs and to aspire to higher ideals. The matter finally is that from those to whom much is given, much is expected, and presidents must develop ways of conveying the spirit of that ideal.

The conflict, diversity of opinion, and debate among presidents about egalitarianism, meritocracy, and *noblesse oblige* indicate that there is no clear resolution of this dilemma for presidents and their moral voice. Their rhetoric reflects the hope that egalitarianism and meritocracy can coexist because both are in the final analysis based on principles of equity, fairness, and equality of opportunity. Since the initiation of universal public education in the eighteenth century, the needs of democracy and society have posed an interesting requirement of America's colleges and universities: to educate the entire citizenry as fully as possible *and* to identify and develop an elite from which to produce the very best trained leaders for society. There is no way to shirk that requirement. It is one deeply engrained in the American consciousness and in the founding of the nation's colleges and universities, both public and private. Presidents must continue to navigate moral positions simultaneously embracing the egalitarian and meritocratic hope about the education of the nation's citizens, while leading their institutions to provide the very best education to the elite who enter the gates of the academy.

A third important role of the moral voice is its authority in stimulating educational conversation on campus. Colleges and universities are in the "business" of education. But as truly academic and intellectual communities, it is also critical that students and faculty regularly engage in conversations about education itself. Robert Hutchins conceived the Great Conversation as one through which "higher education not only does its duty by morals and religion; it not only performs its proper intellectual task; it also supports and symbolizes the highest hopes and the highest aspirations of mankind."[12]

Tom Gerety elaborated Hutchins's notion. Gerety believed that a primary responsibility of his presidency was to maintain this campus conversation about education. To Gerety the conversation was moral at its core because education is likewise essentially moral.[13] Somewhat similarly, George Rupp assumed that the core curriculum at Columbia inspired the "moral imagination" and that education was at its heart a "moral enterprise."[14] But Gerety's "conversation" transpired not only in the curriculum and in the classroom, but in all aspects of campus life. He believed that students should be engaged in this educational conversation in their formal and informal discussions throughout the campus. His unique contention was that the voice of the president must directly encourage and sustain this great conversation about education. And this conversation is itself both educational and moral.

THE FUTURE OF THE MORAL PRESIDENCY

The conjectures of today's presidents about the future of the moral voice are of value in drawing conclusions about two important questions about the presidency and its ability to embrace a rich tradition of moral leadership in the present and the future. One is whether contemporary presidents view the articulation of a moral voice and vision as a critical part of their role. The second is to what degree today's presidents perceive themselves as being able to dedicate the time that they wish to their moral voice.

Two predictions emerge. One is that expression of moral leadership will continue to compete with other presidential responsibilities. In the foreseeable future these will likely remain as significant and consuming a feature of the president's job as in the present, if not more so. In this scenario, the moral voice will be limited and possibly reduced in importance by these other expectations vying for the attention of presidents. The other possibility is that the moral voice will be in greater demand because of an increasing need in society for discussion of ethics and values and moral leadership. The "pendulum" metaphor certainly applies to the history of the presidency. The era of academician-scholar presidents ended, depending on your opinion, somewhere between twenty-five and fifty years ago. This was followed by flirtation with presidents possessing expertise in business, management, finance, and fundraising. Now we are on the verge of returning to scholar presidents who are likely to be more attuned to the importance of moral leadership. In this scenario, the moral voice will become a more integral and visible aspect of the college presidency.

Historically, the moral leadership of presidents has remained influential in spite of significant changes in the American educational landscape. The German university model was transported to America in the form of the founding of Johns Hopkins. What followed was the flourishing of the research university, beginning in the latter nineteenth century and continuing to the present. This changed the nature of education, significantly enlarging its purpose and social expectations. But presidential moral leadership has remained despite this enormous increase in the emphasis on research and the rise of the multiversity. The moral voice of presidents also persists in the face of the increasing pluralism and secularity of a post-Protestant and some might argue post-Judeo-Christian era. Finally, the moral leadership of college and university presidents endures despite the widespread questioning of values and beliefs begun during the 1960s and 1970s and continuing to the present. In an ironic turn, society now longs for leaders who will speak precisely about values, ethics, civic responsibility, and morality in the public square.

A great threat challenging and possibly governing the future of the moral voice, however, may well be determined by the outcome of the battles currently underway—but as yet not fully resolved—over orthodoxy and ideology in the academy than on any changes in the nature of the presidency itself. Thus, this assessment of the past and the future returns us to the major problem raised previously by Harold Shapiro: moral discourse rests on common agreement that in the free interchange of ideas all sides of an argument are of value. Shapiro's fundamental question is whether the center can any longer hold. In raising the question, he highlights the basic conundrum of a democratic society: the social compact based on commonly agreed secular beliefs, a civil religion, is always at risk because of individualism.

But the most threatening potential difficulty for the moral voice of college presidents arises as a result of two problems that could occur concurrently. First is the concern about what happens if secular beliefs, what Shapiro calls "working hypotheses," are no longer commonly accepted. Second is the risk created by excessive emphasis on individualism, a possibility related to Shapiro's concern about the prevalence of "radical ideologies." Citing Alexis de Tocqueville's *Democracy in American*, Shapiro noted the danger that arises when "individual freedom weakens political ties and, therefore, increases the need for moral ties."[15] Douglas Sloan's assessment of the effect of these ideological battles on communities and societies is even more fearsome: "philosophers and theologians of postmodernism can maintain that different linguistic communities are incommensurable—there can be no movement and connection between them. The modernist irrationality of incommensurate, ultimate values has been expanded in the postmodernist irrationality of communities. When such communities disagree, they can only contend blindly with one another, or withdraw into sectarian isolation. It is not surprising that radical ethnocentrism finally becomes the ultimate basis for choosing and championing certain values rather than others. This is the logic of truth as convention, and it ends in a kind of communal positivism or emotivism."[16]

Colleges and universities are not immune from—in fact some argue that they are extremely fertile ground for promoting—a tendency to overemphasize individualism and ethnocentric identities of small groups at the expense of community coherence. Shapiro counseled that recognizing the importance and securing the foundation of these moral ties is a critical aspect of the moral leadership of college and university presidents. The ability of presidents to fulfill this responsibility will be instrumental in the creation, nature, and force of common principles and social bonds that provide coherence on campuses and in communities.

A crucial question, then, is to what extent the moral voice has been in the past and will need to be in the future reliant on a basic sense of these moral ties in society and in colleges and universities. According to Shapiro, these moral bonds are in jeopardy. Casual observation leads many to the same conclusion. Other commentators have described the prospect of what can be viewed as a battle for the heart and soul of the college and university.[17]

Though the challenge of politics and radical individualism has been interpreted in various ways by various commentators, they share a common concern about the impact of ideology in the academy. Kenneth Minogue views the problem as one of the university losing its singularity of purpose and uniqueness of mission as a vital institution in society by permitting contests of ideology within its gates.[18] Presidents have not been quiet about this danger. Citing the "new ideological edge . . . often called a 'search for values' . . . [but more likely] a longing for authority and discipline," Stephen Trachtenberg decried those critics of higher education who use the promotion of values to divert attention from their real goal of implanting a specific orthodoxy.[19] And well before the recent debates about political correctness (in fact even before the term was coined), A. Bartlett Giamatti, then president of Yale, expressed fear of the breakdown of consensus in the academy as the result of flawed assumptions about the desirability of eliminating tension and conflict and the methods becoming accepted for meeting that end.[20] Giamatti contended that in the university the pursuit of consensus, no matter how difficult or lengthy the process, was in danger of being replaced by codification as the method for resolving disputes and differences of opinion. His belief was that this movement toward legislation—codification—not only did not succeed in solving differences but actually exacerbated divisions and controversies. Giamatti was prescient about the rush to initiate various forms of speech and harassment codes on campuses during the 1980s and 1990s.

An unavoidable possibility for the future is that presidents will face significant difficulties in expressing the moral voice if coherence and acceptance of secular beliefs diminishes. Furthermore, these secular beliefs may not provide a suitably reliable foundation for moral discourse without more transcendent bases. Should that prospect be accompanied by a partial or full disintegration of moral ties in society and in the college and university, presidential moral leadership will be even more at risk. On the other hand, there is also the historically well documented possibility that a collapse of secular beliefs may create the context in which a resurgence of the moral voice could occur in a form recognizably similar, even if different in content, to that of a bygone era. In either case, presidential leadership will be crucial to the outcome.

What can be said about what is likely to occur? What, if anything, can college and university presidents do to maintain an ability to express the moral voice? Certainly it is unlikely that the contemporary moral voice will identically mirror that of previous eras. Whatever value may be attributed to existing orthodoxies, presidents will continue to search for idioms that may reflect earlier eras but that will also be expressive of themselves and their times. Shifts in belief and in the language for expressing ethics and values have taken place and will likely continue in the future. George Harris's assumptions in his inaugural address about the work of building the Kingdom of God do not possess anywhere near the same widespread acceptance today as they did at the beginning of the twentieth century. The audience of his time—Christian, or at least those steeped in a Judeo-Christian culture—no longer predominates the religious and cultural landscape. No matter how alluring the appeal for a return to an earlier, more orthodox and apparently simpler era, tomorrow's presidents will of necessity have to examine anew their social, cultural, educational, and religious foundations. From that assessment they will then develop the assumptions on which their distinctive moral voice will be grounded.

As presidents of today and in the future shape the moral voice, they will also benefit by drawing on its historical strengths and focal points. For example, we know that the moral voice has been consistently fundamental to issues such as character formation, the relationship of education to democracy, major generational issues, the moral nature of education, and an emphasis on social service. Presidents have also been able to bring crucial views to bear on issues such as academic freedom, freedom of speech, civil discourse, and human dignity. These matters are all basic to the vitality of education. Throughout history and to different generations of students, presidents then have shaped rhetoric that produced a voice of leadership on these important issues at the heart of the academy and society.

Contemporary presidents confirm the fundamental value of the moral voice. Their thoughts about moral leadership can also be an inspiration to the future leaders of America's colleges and universities. Thomas Cole's advocacy for educational opportunity for African Americans is critical not only to his university, but to all black colleges and to the future of the nation. James Duderstadt's challenge to bring moral purpose to the multiple facets and missions of a mega-university of the latter twentieth and early twenty-first centuries will influence the future of the large public research university. Edward Malloy's voice as a minister-president continues to show the validity of education at a religious university in the tradition of John Henry Newman and the earlier historical roots of the university. And finally, the statements made by Thomas Gerety, George Rupp, and Diana Chapman Walsh about the importance of free speech, about the role of academic freedom, and about the rationale for discussion of all ideas regardless of the threat they may pose, even to the fundamental assumptions of liberal learning itself, are examples of the existence and value of the moral voice.

The persistent exercise of the moral voice will be instrumental in maintaining and shaping the moral ties that Shapiro held as so critical to the functioning of society and of educational institutions. It is the voice of presidents that should determine the form and content of the social and political context for debate, for discussion, and for education at colleges and universities. It is the moral voice that will be fundamental to sustaining the discourse of liberal education. This will be especially true and essential as a response to the contemporary battleground of competing ideologies and of debate about what constitutes the heart and soul of the university.

In the final analysis, whenever and wherever presidents, regardless of the changing complexity of their responsibilities, affirm the core moral ideas and ideals of a liberal educational philosophy, the moral voice will be expressed and heard. Likewise, it is the presidential moral voice that will clarify the ideals for which students should strive and to which they should dedicate their education. And, as Thomas Gerety has so well stated, it should be our presidents who lead the educational conversation about the moral foundations of the college. The challenges of the future call for presidents to think thoroughly and to act wisely about the moral basis of their voice. For the sake of both their office and the academy, they need to embrace willingly and courageously the crucial role of presidential moral leadership in educational communities. And finally, they need to recognize that regardless of personal choice and style they will, as college and university presidents, be assumed to be and be perceived as moral leaders. They and we must not fail to understand these responsibilities—this moral leadership and voice—as integral to the college presidency and critical to the future of the academy.

NOTES

1. William H. Honan, "At the Top of the Ivory Tower the Watchword Is Silence," *New York Times*, July 24, 1994, Sec. E, p. 5.

2. Personal interview with President George Rupp of Columbia University, November 16, 1994.

3. Joseph Crowley, *No Equal in the World: An Interpretation of the Academic Presidency* (Reno: University of Nevada Press, 1994), pp. 3 and 35–36.

4. James McGregor Burns, *Leadership* (New York: Harper and Row, 1978), p. 4.

5. Ibid., p. 2.

6. James Laney, "The Moral Authority of the College or University President," *Educational Record* 65, no. 2 (Spring 1984), p. 17.

7. George Harris, "The Man of Letters in a Democracy," *Amherst Student* 33, no. 3 (October 11, 1899), p. 21.

8. Nannerl O. Keohane, "What Counts As a Life of Noblest Usefulness," Washington, D.C., Alumni Club, October 28, 1988, Keohane Speeches, 1986–1990, p. 8.

9. Nicholas Murray Butler, "The Education of Public Opinion," June 22, 1899, Butler Speeches, vol. 1, p. 10.

10. University of Michigan, *Exercises at the Inauguration of President Angell* (Ann Arbor: Courier Stearn, 1871), p. 6.

11. Personal interview with President George Rupp of Columbia University, November 16, 1994.

12. Robert Hutchins, *Freedom, Education and the Fund: Essays and Addresses, 1946–1956* (New York: Meridian Books, 1956), p. 100.

13. Personal interview with President Thomas Gerety of Amherst College, July 27, 1994.

14. Personal interview with George Rupp.

15. Harold T. Shapiro, "Ethics in America—Who Is Responsible?" *New York Times* Presidential Forum, December 1, 1987, Shapiro Collection, Box 178, p. 5.

16. Douglas Sloan, *Faith and Knowledge: Mainline Protestantism and American Higher Education* (Louisville, Ky.: Westminster John Knox Press, 1994), pp. 217–18.

17. Among those making this contention are Bill Readings, *The University in Ruins* (Cambridge, Mass.: Harvard University Press, 1996); and Bruce Wilshire, *The Moral Collapse of the University: Professionalism, Purity, and Alienation* (Albany, N.Y.: SUNY Press, 1990).

18. Kenneth Minogue, *The Concept of a University* (Berkley: University of California Press, 1973), pp. 111 and 113–14.

19. Stephen Joel Trachtenberg, "Presidents Can Establish a Moral Tone on Campus," *Educational Record* 70, no. 2 (Spring 1989), p. 9.

20. A. Bartlett Giamatti, *The University and the Public Interest* (Toronto, Ont.: McClelland and Stewart, 1976), pp. 181–82.

Bibliography

Adams, Myron W. *A History of Atlanta University*. Atlanta: Atlanta University Press, 1930.

Amherst Student 33, no. 3 (October 11, 1899), pp. 20–24.

Angell, James Burrill. "Ambitions and Ideals." *Michigan Alumnus* 3, no. 27 (July 1897), pp. 245–251.

————. *Commemorative Oration*. Ann Arbor: University of Michigan, 1888.

————. "The Debt of the University Graduate." *Michigan Alumnus* 5, no. 46 (July 1899), pp. 405–13.

————. *Environment and Selfhood*. Ann Arbor: University of Michigan, 1901.

————. "The Heroic Spirit of Life." *Unitarian*, 1890. pp. 5–6

————. *The Higher Education: A Plea for Making It Accessible to All*. Ann Arbor: University of Michigan Board of Regents, 1879.

————. "Knowledge and Wisdom." *University of Michigan Bulletin* 5, no. 20 (July 15, 1904), pp. 1–9.

————. "Lessons Suggested by Christ's Life to the Scholar." *University of Michigan Bulletin* 4, no. 13 (July 15, 1903), pp. 2–8.

————. "The Relation of the American Colleges to Christianity." *Quarterly Review of the Evangelical Lutheran Church* 7, no. 1 (January 1878), pp. 65–79.

————. "Shall the American Colleges Be Open to Both Sexes?" *Rhode Island Schoolmaster* 17, no. 8, pp. 265–269.

————. "The State and the Student." *Michigan Alumnus* 15, no. 146 (July 1909), pp. 433–38.

Atlanta University Bulletin no. 9 (April 1889).

Atlanta University Bulletin no. 11 (June 1889).

Atlanta University Bulletin no. 20 (June 1890).

Atlanta University Bulletin no. 21 (October 1890).

Atlanta University Bulletin no. 23 (December 1890).

Atlanta University Bulletin no. 31 (November 1891).

Atlanta University Bulletin no. 92 (May 1898).

Atlanta University Bulletin no. 113 (November 1900).

Averill, Lloyd J. "The Sectarian Nature of a Liberal Education." Pp. 73–84 in *Colleges and Commitments*, ed. Lloyd J. Averill and William W. Jellema. Philadelphia: Westminster Press, 1972.

Bellah, Robert N. "Civil Religion in America," *Religion in America*, Boston: Beacon Press, 1968, 3–23.

Birnbaum, Robert. *How Colleges Work: The Cybernetics of Academic Organization and Leadership*. San Francisco: Jossey-Bass, 1988.

Blake, Elias, Jr. Founder's Day address, Personal Papers, Elias Blake, Jr., February 19, 1980.

———. Inaugural address, Personal Papers, Elias Blake, Jr., October 27, 1978.

———. "Preventing a Backlash in Higher Education for Black Education." The Black Conference in Higher Education, Personal Papers, Elias Blake, Jr., February 1974.

———. Talk to graduates, Personal Papers, Elias Blake, Jr., undated.

Bloom, Alan. *Closing of the American Mind*. New York: Simon and Schuster, 1987.

Bornstein, Rita. "Back in the Spotlight: The College President as Public Intellectual." *Educational Record*, Fall 1995, pp. 56–62.

Bumstead, Horace. "Education in the South." *Bulletin of Atlanta University* no. 23 (December 1890), p. 7.

Burns, James McGregor. *Leadership*. New York: Harper and Row, 1978.

Butler, Louise Joyner. *The Distinctive Black College: Talladega, Tuskegee and Morehouse*. Metuchen, N.J.: Scarecrow Press, 1977.

Butler, Nicholas Murray. Address at the installation of President Swain, Swarthmore College, November 15, 1902. Columbia University, Rare Book and Manuscript Library, Miscellaneous Addresses and Articles by Nicholas Murray Butler, vol. 1, no. 45.

———. Anti–Ku Klux Klan plank for 1924 New York Republican State Convention. Columbia University, Rare Book and Manuscript Library, Nicholas Murray Butler Speeches, vol. 6, no. 91.

———. "Character Building," June 4, 1924. Columbia University, Rare Book and Manuscript Library, Nicholas Murray Butler Speeches, vol. 6, no. 79.

———. Christmas Eve letter to Columbia students. Columbia University, Rare Book and Manuscript Library, Nicholas Murray Butler Speeches, vol. 3, no. 1a.

———. Columbia Teachers College alumni address, Columbia University, Rare Book and Manuscript Library, Nicholas Murray Butler Speeches, vol. 6, no. 6.

———. "Education After the War." *Educational Review* 57, no. 1 (January 1919), pp. 67–68. Columbia University, Rare Book and Manuscript Library, Nicholas Murray Butler Speeches, vol. 3, no. 94.

———. "The Education of Public Opinion," June 22, 1899. Columbia University, Rare Book and Manuscript Library, Nicholas Murray Butler Speeches, vol. 1.

———. Essay in the *Churchman*, July 25, 1902. Columbia University, Rare Book and Manuscript Library, Miscellaneous Addresses and Articles by Nicholas Murray Butler, vol. 1, no. 41.

———. "Five Evidences of an Education." *Educational Review*, November 1901, p. 329.

Columbia University, Rare Book and Manuscript Library, Nicholas Murray Butler Speeches, vol. 1.

———. "The Kingdom of Light," June 7, 1916. Columbia University, Rare Book and Manuscript Library, Nicholas Murray Butler Speeches, vol. 3, no. 8.

———. Letter to J. Silas Harris, June 13, 1924. Columbia University, Rare Book and Manuscript Library, Nicholas Murray Butler Speeches, vol. 6, no. 82.

———. "Making Liberal Men and Women: Public Criticism of Present-Day Education, the New Paganism, and the University, Politics and Religion." Columbia University, Rare Book and Manuscript Library, Nicholas Murray Butler Speeches, vol. 5, no. 8.

———. "The Mission of the Modern University," November 10, 1923. Columbia University, Rare Book and Manuscript Library, Nicholas Murray Butler Speeches, vol. 6, no. 40.

———. "New Values," June 5, 1918. Columbia University, Rare Book and Manuscript Library, Nicholas Murray Butler Speeches, vol. 3, no. 69.

———. "Religious Instruction in Education." *Educational Review*, December 1899, pp. 427–436. Columbia University, Rare Book and Manuscript Library, Nicholas Murray Butler Speeches, vol. 1.

———. Remarks at the dedication of Earl Hall. March 8, 1902. Columbia University, Rare Book and Manuscript Library, Nicholas Murray Butler Speeches, vol. 3, no. 35.

———. "Scholarship and Service." *Educational Review*, June 1902, pp. 3–6. Columbia University, Rare Book and Manuscript Library, Nicholas Murray Butler Speeches, vol. 2.

———. "Some Fundamental Principles of American Education," university convocation, Albany, N.Y., June 30, 1902. Columbia University, Rare Book and Manuscript Library, Miscellaneous Addresses and Articles by Nicholas Murray Butler, vol. 1, no. 39.

———. "'Some Pressing Problems," July 1902. Columbia University, Rare Book and Manuscript Library, Nicholas Murray Butler Speeches, vol. 1, no. 38.

———. Thanksgiving Eve address, November 25, 1919. Columbia University, Rare Book and Manuscript Library, Nicholas Murray Butler Speeches, vol. 4, no. 48.

———. Untitled address, February 6, 1917. Columbia University, Rare Book and Manuscript Library, Nicholas Murray Butler Speeches, vol. 3, no. 18.

Cavanaugh, James W., C.S.C. "The Day of Visitation," September 20, 1908. University of Notre Dame Archives (UNDA), Notre Dame Early Presidents' Records (UPEL), Box 10.

———. "The Function of the Religious College." Pp. 72–83 in *The Conquest of Life*, ed. John A. O'Brien. Paterson, N.J.: St. Anthony Guild Press, 1952.

———. "Life and Duty." University of Notre Dame Archives (UNDA), Notre Dame Early Presidents' Records (UPEL), Box 10, undated.

———. "The Perfect Service." University of Notre Dame Archives (UNDA), Notre Dame Early Presidents' Records (UPEL), Box 10, undated.

———. "The Price of a Soul." Pp. 12–24 in *The Conquest of Life*, ed. John A. O'Brien. Paterson, N.J.: St. Anthony Guild Press, 1952.

———. "The Religious Life of the Student." University of Notre Dame Archives (UNDA), Notre Dame Early President's Records (UPEL), Box 10, undated.

————. "Saint Paul, Apostle of the World." Pp. 61–71 in *The Conquest of Life*, ed. John A. O'Brien. Paterson, N.J.: St. Anthony Guild Press, 1952.

————. "The Spirit of the Founders." University of Notre Dame Archives (UNDA), Notre Dame Early President's Records (UPEL), Box 10, undated.

————. "The Tests of a College." Pp. 133–134 in *The Conquest of Life*, ed. John A. O'Brien. Paterson, N.J.: St. Anthony Guild Press, 1952.

Clark, Burton R. *The Distinctive College: Antioch, Reed and Swarthmore*. Chicago: Aldine, 1970.

Clark, Tim. "All Things We Do, He Does Better." *Yankee Magazine*, March 1980, pp. 67–71, 120–36.

Cole, Thomas. Personal interview, February 16, 1995.

"The College: Former Columbia Dean to Be President." *Amherst Graduates Quarterly* 36, no. 1 (Summer 1983), pp. 5–8.

Commission of the Academic Presidency. *Renewing the Academic Presidency*. Washington, D.C.: Association of Governing Boards of Universities and Colleges, 1996.

Crogman, William H. "Life's Deeper Meanings." Pp. 17–24 in *Talks for the Times*, Cincinnati: Jennings and Pye, 1896.

————. "Negro Education: Its Helps and Hindrances," National Education Association, July 16, 1884.

————. "The Negroe's Claims," Plymouth, Mass., October 14, 1883. Pp. 172–198 in *Talks for the Times*, Cincinnati: Jennings and Pye, 1896.

Crowley, Joseph. *No Equal in the World: An Interpretation of the Academic Presidency*. Reno: University of Nevada Press, 1994.

Denby, David. *Great Books: My Adventures with Homer, Rousseau, Woolf, and Other Indestructible Writers of the Western World*. Boston: Simon and Schuster, 1996.

Duderstadt, James J. "Ethics in Higher Education." James J. Duderstadt Collection, Michigan Historical Collections, Bentley Historical Library, University of Michigan, unpaginated, Box 248.

————. Personal interview, March 6, 1995.

————. "State of the University Address," October 3, 1988. James J. Duderstadt Collection 1988–1989, Michigan Historical Collections, Bentley Historical Library, University of Michigan, unpaginated, Box 217.

————. Student inauguration luncheon address, October 4, 1988. JJD Speeches, James J. Duderstadt Collection 1988–1989, Michigan Historical Collections, Bentley Historical Library, University of Michigan, Box 217.

————. "The Thrill of Victory . . . the Agony of Defeat . . . and the Gnashing of Teeth . . . As College Presidents Attempt to Reform Intercollegiate Athletics." James J. Duderstadt Collection 1988–1989, Michigan Historical Collections, Bentley Historical Library, University of Michigan, Box 248, folder 1, unpaginated.

————. Untitled speech, senate assembly, March 19, 1990. James J. Duderstadt Collection, Michigan Historical Collections, Bentley Historical Library, University of Michigan, unpaginated, Box 235.

Ehrle, Elwood B., and John B. Bennett. *Managing the Academic Enterprise*. New York: Ace, 1988.

Enarson, Harold. "The Ethical Imperative of the College Presidency." *Educational Record* 65, no. 2 (Spring 1984), pp. 24–26.

Exercises at the Inauguration of President Angell. Ann Arbor: Courier Stearn, 1871.

Fanelli, A. Alexander. *John Kemeny Speaks*. Hanover, N.H.: Dartmouth College, 1999.

Freedman, James O. "Our Work Should Not Silence Our Wisdom." *Boston Globe*, January 19, 1997.

Gerety, Thomas. "The Freshman Who Hated Socrates: Freedom and Constraint in the Liberal Arts," Hartford, Conn., Trinity College, undated.

————. Personal interview, July 27, 1994.

————. "Speech to Hartford County Bar Association." *Amherst Graduates Quarterly* 46, no. 3 (Spring 1994), pp. 8–9.

————. Trinity College Convocation 1993, August 28, 1993.

————. "Work Hard, Play Hard: Rigor and Joy in the Liberal Arts," Hartford, Conn., Trinity College, undated.

Giamatti, A. Bartlett. *The University and the Public Interest*. Toronto, Ont.: McClelland and Stewart, 1976.

Harris George. "The Man of Letters in a Democracy." *Amherst Student* 33, no. 3 (October 11, 1899), pp. 21–24.

————. "The Ninety First Commencement." *Amherst Graduates Quarterly* 2 (November 1912), pp. 26–34.

————. "Values of Life." *Amherst Student* 45, no. 62 (June 10, 1912), pp. 1,7.

Hazard, Caroline. Address to the Congregational Conference in Rhode Island at Peacedale, May 23, 1905. Caroline Hazard, Personal Papers, Addresses, 1905–1916, Wellesley College Archives.

————. *A Brief Pilgrimmage in the Holy Land*. Boston: Houghton Mifflin, 1909.

————. *The College Year*. Boston and N.Y: Houghton Mifflin, 1910.

————. *From College Gates*. Boston: Houghton Mifflin, 1925.

————. *1910 Annual Report*. Wellesley College, *Annual Reports*, 1905–1913, Wellesley College Archives.

————. *Some Ideals in the Education of Women*. New York: Thomas Y. Crowell, 1900.

Hesburgh, Theodore. Address to the faculty, October 13, 1986. University of Notre Dame Archives, Theodore Hesburgh Speeches, 1968–1987, Box 142/23.

————. Address to the general faculty, October 4, 1983. University of Notre Dame Archives, Theodore Hesburgh Speeches, 1968–1987, Box 142/20.

————. "The Changing Face of Catholic Higher Education," April 8, 1969. University of Notre Dame Archives, Theodore Hesburgh Speeches, 1968–1987, Box 142/2.

————. Commencement address, Trinity College, Washington, D.C., May 31, 1954. University of Notre Dame Archives, Theodore Hesburgh Speeches, 1947–1967, Box 141/5.

————. Commencement address, University of Rhode Island, June 13, 1960. University of Notre Dame Archives, Theodore Hesburgh Speeches, 1947–1967, Box 141/15.

————. Convocation on apartheid, October 1985. University of Notre Dame Archives, Theodore Hesburgh Speeches, 1968–1987, Box 142/22.

————. Document addressed to the Religious Education Association of the United States and Canada, August 12, 1953. University of Notre Dame Archives, Theodore Hesburgh Speeches, 1947–1967, Box 141/4.

————. "The Examined Life," June 8, 1958. University of Notre Dame Archives, Theodore Hesburgh Speeches, 1947–1967, Box 141/12.

————. "The Future of Liberal Arts Education," February 9, 1980. University of Notre Dame Archives, Theodore Hesburgh Speeches, 1968–1987, Box 142/15.

————. "Liberal Education in the World Today," Association of American Colleges,

January 12, 1955. University of Notre Dame Archives, Theodore Hesburgh Speeches, 1947–1967, Box 141/71a.

———. "The Moral Dimensions of Higher Education," October 13, 1983. University of Notre Dame Archives, Theodore Hesburgh Speeches, 1968–1987, Box 142/20.

———. Opening Mass homily, September 11, 1977. University of Notre Dame Archives, Theodore Hesburgh Speeches, 1968–1987, Box 142/11.

———. "Reflections on a Church-Related University." June 21, 1979. University of Notre Dame Archives, Theodore Hesburgh Speeches, 1968–1987, Box 142/14.

———. "Science and Technology in Modern Perspective," June 8, 1962. University of Notre Dame Archives, Theodore Hesburgh Speeches, 1947–1967, Box 141/18.

———. Sermon opening the school year, September 25, 1955. University of Notre Dame Archives, Theodore Hesburgh Speeches, 1947–1967, Box 141/7.

———. "The Student Today," April 7, 1970. University of Notre Dame Archives, Theodore Hesburgh Speeches, 1968–1987, Box 142/3.

———. "The University in the World of Change," December 10, 1964. University of Notre Dame Archives, Theodore Hesburgh Speeches, 1947–1967, Box 141/21.

Honan, William H. "At the Top of the Ivory Tower the Watchword Is Silence." *New York Times*, July 24, 1994.

Hutchins, Robert. *Freedom, Education and the Fund: Essays and Addresses, 1946–1956.* New York: Meridian Books, 1956.

Katz, Michael B. *Reconstructing American Education.* Cambridge, Mass.: Harvard University Press, 1987.

Kemeny, Jean. *It's Different at Dartmouth.* Brattleboro, Vt.: Stephen Greene Press, 1979.

Keohane, Nannerl O. Alumni Association talk, June 7, 1981. Wellesley Archives, Keohane Speeches, 1981–1985, unpaginated.

———. Convocation address, September 5, 1985, Wellesley Archives, Keohane Speeches, 1981–1985.

———. "Educating Citizens for a Modern Democracy," February 26, 1987. Wellesley Archives, Keohane Speeches, 1986–1990.

———. "Educating Women for Leadership," City Club of Cleveland, April 26, 1991. Wellesley Archives, Keohane Speeches, 1991–1993.

———. "Educational Futures," September 25, 1986, Wellesley Archives, Keohane Speeches, 1986–1990.

———. "The Founding Enterprise," September 14, 1984, Wellesley Archives, Keohane Speeches, 1981–1985.

———. "The Liberal Arts Today," Rotary Club of Boston, March 2, 1983. Wellesley Archives, Keohane Speeches, 1981–1985.

———. U.N. Day celebration, Boston, Mass., October 24, 1983. Wellesley Archives, Keohane Speeches, 1981–1985.

———. "What Counts As a Life of Noblest Usefulness," Washington, D.C., Alumni Club, October 28, 1988. Wellesley Archives, Keohane Speeches, 1986–1990.

———. "Women, the Liberal Arts, and a Democratic Society," Duke University, March 4, 1989. Wellesley Archives, Keohane Speeches, 1986–1990.

———. "The Women of the 90s: How Should They Be Educated?" November 15, 1990, Wellesley Archives, Keohane Speeches, 1986–1990.

Kerr, Clark. *The Uses of the University.* Cambridge, Mass.: Harvard University Press, 1963.

Kerr, Clark, and Marian L. Gade. *The Many Lives of Academic Presidents: Time, Place and Character.* Washington, D.C.: Association of Governing Boards of Universities and Colleges, 1986.

Laney, James. "The Moral Authority of the College or University President." *Educational Record* 65, no. 2 (Spring 1984), pp. 17–19.

———. "Through Thick and Thin: Two Ways of Talking About the Academy and Moral Responsibility." Pp. 49–66 in *Ethics and Higher Education*, ed. William W. May. New York: Macmillan, 1990.

Malloy, Edward, C.S.C. Address to the faculty, President's Office, University of Notre Dame, October 2, 1989.

———. Address to the faculty, President's Office, University of Notre Dame, October 3, 1990.

———. Address to the faculty, President's Office, University of Notre Dame, October 1, 1991.

———. Address to the faculty, President's Office, University of Notre Dame, October 12, 1993.

———. Address to the trustees, President's Office, University of Notre Dame, Spring 1990.

———. Baccalaureate Mass homily, President's Office, University of Notre Dame, May 16, 1992.

———. Baccalaureate Mass homily, President's Office, University of Notre Dame, May 14, 1994.

———. Commencement address, Catholic University, Washington, D.C., President's Office, University of Notre Dame, May 9, 1992, unpaginated.

———. "The Control of Violence, Foreign and Domestic: Some Ethical Lessons from Law Enforcement," United States Air Force Academy, President's Office, University of Notre Dame, September 6, 1990.

———. *Final Report: Colloquy for the Year 2000.* May 7, 1993.

———. *Notre Dame: The Unfolding Vision.* New York: Newcomen Society of the United States, 1993.

———. Personal interview, September 20, 1994.

———. Sesquicentennial opening Mass homily, President's Office, University of Notre Dame, September 15, 1991.

Martin Warren, Bryan. "History, Morality, and the Modern University." Pp. 111–124 in *Moral Values and Higher Education: A Notion at Risk*, ed. Dennis L. Thompson. Provo, Utah: Brigham Young University, 1991.

McLoughlin, William G., and Robert Bellah, eds. *Religion in America.* Boston: Beacon Press, 1968.

Mead, Sidney. *The Nation with the Soul of a Church.* New York: Harper and Row, 1975.

Meras, Phyllis. "A Morning with a President." *Wellesley*, Fall 1993, pp. 4–7.

Minogue, Kenneth. *The Concept of a University.* Berkeley: University of California Press, 1973.

Morrill, Richard L. "Academic Planning: Values and Decision Making." Pp. 69–83 in *Ethics and Higher Education*, ed. William W. May. New York: Macmillan, 1990.

———. *Teaching Values in College.* San Francisco: Jossey-Bass, 1980.

Muller, Steven. "At 350, the U.S. University Is Vast but Unfocused." *New York Times*, September 7, 1986.

Neill, Herman Humphrey. "President George Harris." From the 1901 Olio, George Harris

Biographical File (AC 1866), Archives and Special Collections, Amherst College Library.

Nisbet, Robert, *The Degradation of the Academic Dogma*. London: Heinemann, 1971.

Pouncey, Peter R. "Abraham and Isaac." Amherst College Archives, Peter Pouncey General File. Archives and Special Collections, Amherst College Library.

———. "Ancient History and Ancient Morals." Pp. 85–103 in *Teaching What We Do: Essays by Amherst College Faculty*, ed. Peter R. Pouncey. Amherst, Mass.: Amherst College Press, 1991.

———. "Can Virtue Be Taught?" *Amherst* 36, no. 1 (Summer 1983), p. 8.

———. Convocation address, September 4, 1984. Amherst College Archives, Peter Pouncey General File, Archives and Special Collections, Amherst College Library.

———. Convocation address, September 5, 1985. Peter Pouncey Biographical File (N/A), Archives and Special Collections, Amherst College Library.

———. Convocation address, September 6, 1986. Peter Pouncey Biographical File (N/A), Archives and Special Collections, Amherst College Library.

———. Convocation address, September 4, 1989. Peter Pouncey Biographical File (N/A) Archives and Special Collections, Amherst College Library.

———. Convocation address, September 7, 1992. Peter Pouncey Biographical File (N/A), Archives and Special Collections, Amherst College Library.

———. "Dialectics and Dialectic." Peter Pouncey Biographical File (N/A), Archives and Special Collections, Amherst College Library.

———, ed. *Teaching What We Do: Essays by Amherst College Faculty*. Amherst, Mass.: Amherst College Press, 1991.

Readings, Bill. *The University in Ruins*. Cambridge, Mass.: Harvard University Press, 1996.

Reynolds, Noel B. "On the Moral Responsibilities of Universities." Pp. 91–110 in *Moral Values and Higher Education: A Notion at Risk*, ed. Dennis L. Thompson. Provo, Utah: Brigham Young University, 1991.

Ridgely, Torrence. *The Story of John Hope*. New York: Macmillan, 1948.

Rosovsky, Henry. *The University: An Owner's Manual*. New York: W. W. Norton, 1990.

Rupp, George. Inaugural address, October 4, 1993.

———. Personal interview, November 16, 1994.

———. Remarks for Pulitzer Prize jurors, President's Office, Columbia University, March 1, 1994.

———. "When the Cheering Stops," President's Office, Columbia University, May 19, 1994. [Handwritten insert to typed copy.]

Schwehn, Mark R. *Exiles from Eden: Religion and the Academic in America*. Oxford, Eng.: Oxford University Press, 1993.

Shapiro, Harold T. "American Higher Education: A Special Tradition Faces a Special Challenge," Academy for Educational Development, May 22, 1986. Harold T. Shapiro Collection, Ann Arbor Commencements, Michigan Historical Collections, Bentley Historical Library, University of Michigan, Box 178.

———. "Are Schools for Learning?" *Innovation* 15, no. 1 (August 1983), pp. 4–6.

———. Commencement address, December 20, 1987. Harold T. Shapiro Collection, Ann Arbor Commencements, Michigan Historical Collections, Bentley Historical Library, University of Michigan, Box 177.

―――. "The Culture of the Intellect and the Culture of the Heart," May 11, 1985. Harold T. Shapiro Collection, Commencement Addresses—External, Michigan Historical Collections, Bentley Historical Library, University of Michigan, Box 177.

―――. "Ethics in America—Who Is Responsible?" *New York Times* Presidential Forum, December 1, 1987. Harold T. Shapiro Collection, Ann Arbor Commencements, Michigan Historical Collections, Bentley Historical Library, University of Michigan, Box 178.

―――. Graduation address, May 3, 1980. Harold T. Shapiro Collection, Ann Arbor Commencements, Michigan Historical Collections, Bentley Historical Library, University of Michigan, Box 177.

―――. Inauguration address, April 4, 1980. Harold T. Shapiro Collection, Ann Arbor Commencements, Michigan Historical Collections, Bentley Historical Library, University of Michigan, Box 178.

―――. "A Personal Message." *University Record* 41, no. 15 (January 13, 1986), p. 1. Harold T. Shapiro Collection, Ann Arbor Commencements, Michigan Historical Collections, Bentley Historical Library, University of Michigan, Box 177.

―――. Racism draft. Harold T. Shapiro Collection, Ann Arbor Commencements, Michigan Historical Collections, Bentley Historical Library, University of Michigan, Box 206.

―――. "Tradition, Continuity, Discovery, and Change: A Conversation with Princeton's Past," Princeton University, President's Office, Princeton University, January 8, 1988.

―――. *Tradition and Change: Perspectives on Education and Public Policy.* Ann Arbor: University of Michigan Press, 1987.

―――. Untitled essay. *Science* 225, no. 4657 (July 6, 1984), p. 19.

Shapiro, James. "David Denby's Return to 'Great Books.' " *Chronicle of Higher Education* 18, no. 3 (September 13, 1996), p. A64.

Sloan, Douglas. *Faith and Knowledge: Mainline Protestantism and American Higher Education.* Louisville, Ky.: Westminster John Knox Press, 1994.

Sovern, Michael. Commencement address, May 19, 1982. The Addresses of Michael Sovern, Public Information Office, Columbia University.

―――. Commencement address, May 17, 1983. The Addresses of Michael Sovern, Public Information Office, Columbia University.

―――. Commencement address, May 16, 1984. The Addresses of Michael Sovern, Public Information Office, Columbia University.

―――. Commencement address, May 18, 1988. The Addresses of Michael Sovern, Public Information Office, Columbia University.

―――. Inaugural address, September 28, 1980. The Addresses of Michael Sovern, Public Information Office, Columbia University.

―――. Untitled address, Illinois Humanities Council, October 22, 1984. The Addresses of Michael Sovern, Public Information Office, Columbia University.

Stoke, Harold. *The American College President.* New York: Harper Brothers, 1959.

Sykes, Charles. *ProfScam: Professors and the Demise of Higher Education.* New York: St. Martin's Press, 1988.

Trachtenberg, Stephen Joel. "Presidents Can Establish a Moral Tone on Campus." *Educational Record* 70, no. 2 (Spring 1989), pp. 4–9.

Veblen, Thorstein B. *The Higher Learning in America*. New York: Hill and Wang, 1962.
Walsh, Diana Chapman. Friday All College Reception, August 6, 1993.
————. Inaugural panel at Simmons College, November 5, 1993.
————. Personal interview, November 28, 1994.
————. "Why Are We Here?" September 7, 1993.
Wellesley College. Louisville, Ky.: Harmony House, 1988.
Wilbee, Victor Roy. "The Religious Dimensions of Three Presidencies at University of Michigan." Ph.D. diss., University of Michigan, 1967.
Wilshire, Bruce. *The Moral Collapse of the University: Professionalism, Purity, and Alienation*. Albany, N.Y.: SUNY Press, 1990.

Index

About the Author

STEPHEN JAMES NELSON is Research Associate, Education Department, Brown University.